PETER MAGGS A

ELEMENTARY
OUTCOMES

Australia · Brazil · Mexico · Singapore · United Kingdom · United States

NATIONAL GEOGRAPHIC
LEARNING

Outcomes *Elementary Workbook*
Peter Maggs and Catherine Smith

Publisher: Gavin McLean

Publishing Consultant: Karen Spiller

Development Editor: Steve Longworth

Head of Strategic Marketing, ELT: Charlotte Ellis

Senior Content Project Manager: Nick Ventullo

Production Controller: Eyvett Davis

Cover Design: eMC Design

Text Design: Studio April

Compositor: Q2A Media Services Pvt. Ltd.

National Geographic Liaison: Leila Hishmeh

For product information and technology assistance, contact us at
Cengage Learning Customer & Sales Support, cengage.com/contact
For permission to use material from this text or product,
submit all requests online at **cengage.com/permissions**
Further permissions questions can be emailed to
permissionrequest@cengage.com

ISBN: 978-1-305-10225-5

National Geographic Learning
Cheriton House, North Way, Andover, Hampshire, SP10 5BE, United Kingdom

National Geographic Learning, a Cengage Learning Company, has a mission to bring the world to the classroom and the classroom to life. With our English language programs, students learn about their world by experiencing it. Through our partnerships with National Geographic and TED Talks, they develop the language and skills they need to be successful global citizens and leaders.

Locate your local office at **international.cengage.com/region**

Visit National Geographic Learning online at **NGL.Cengage.com/ELT**
Visit our corporate website at **www.cengage.com**

CREDITS

Although every effort has been made to contact copyright holders before publication, this has not always been possible. If notified, the publisher will undertake to rectify any errors or omissions at the earliest opportunity.

Photos

The publisher would like to thank the following sources for permission to use their copyright protected images:

4 (l) © PhotoAlto/Alamy Stock Photo; 4 (tr) © Westend61/Getty Images; 4 (mr) © PhotoAlto sas/Alamy Stock Photo; 4 (br) © StockLite/Shutterstock.com; 5 © Arie J. Jager/Getty Images; 6 (tl) © amana images inc./Alamy Stock Photo; 6 (tm) © image100/Alamy Stock Photo; 6 (tr) © OJO Images Ltd/Alamy Stock Photo; 6 (ml) © Fancy/Alamy Stock Photo; 6 (mr) © StockLite/Shutterstock.com; 6 (bl) © pcruciatti/Shutterstock.com; 6 (bm) © RonTech2000/iStockphoto; 6 (br) © Blend Images/Alamy Stock Photo; 7 (t) © PhotoDisc/Getty Images; 7 (m) © Tan Kian Khoon/Shutterstock.com; 7 (b) © picturepartners/Shutterstock.com; 10 © wundervisuals/iStockphoto; 11 (t) © Suzanne Tucker/Shutterstock.com; 11 (ml) © PhotoSlinger/Alamy Stock Photo; 11 (mr) © Rido/Shutterstock.com; 11 (b) © FrankRamspott/iStockphoto; 13 (l) © KeithBishop/iStockphoto; 13 (tm) © KSR/Shutterstock.com; 13 (tr) © D. Hurst/Alamy Stock Photo; 13 (mtm) © imageBROKER/Alamy Stock Photo; 13 (mtr) © JuliusKielaitis/Shutterstock.com; 13 (mmm) © R. Gino Santa Maria/Shutterstock.com; 13 (mmr) © Mikael Damkier/Shutterstock.com; 13 (mbm) © D. Hurst/Alamy Stock Photo; 13 (mbr) © Brand X Pictures/Getty Images; 13 (bm) © Craig Holmes/Alamy Stock Photo; 13 (br) © Zvyagintsev Sergey/Shutterstock.com; 14 (l) © SundayPhoto Europe a.s./Alamy Stock Photo; 14 (mr) © LuckyImages/Shutterstock.com; 14 (br) © PhotoDisc/Getty Images; 15 © Jaroslaw Wojcik/iStockphoto; 16 (tl) © filo/iStockphoto; 16 (tm) © Kayfish/iStockphoto; 16 (tr) © Skydive Erick/Shutterstock.com; 16 (ml) © imagestock/Getty Images; 16 (mm) © dumayne/iStockphoto; 16 (mr) © tiridifilm/iStockphoto; 16 (bl) © Lewis Wright/Getty Images; 16 (br) © Norma Cornes/Getty Images; 17 (t) © Ewen Cameron/Getty Images; 17 (b) © michaeljung/Shutterstock.com; 19 (t) © Phase4Photography/Shutterstock.com; 19 (m) © Alistair Scott/Shutterstock.com; 19 (b) © Steve Geer/Getty Images; 21 © Jorge Salcedo/Shutterstock.com; 22 (t) © Jose Luis Pelaez, Inc./Blend Images/Corbis; 22 (m) © Christopher Penler/Alamy Stock Photo; 22 (b) © Daisy Images/Alamy Stock Photo; 23 (t) © Eric Belisle/Getty Images; 23 (b) © Martin Valigursky/Shutterstock.com; 24 (t) © Creative Jen Designs/Shutterstock.com; 24 (ml) © Stewart Smith Photography/Shutterstock.com; 24 (mr) © Creative Travel Projects/Shutterstock.com; 24 (b) © Pixel Memoirs/Shutterstock.com; 25 (l) © gary yim/Shutterstock.com; 25 (tr) © Maxisport/Shutterstock.com; 25 (mr) © Fancy/Alamy Stock Photo; 25 (br) © Darko Novakovic/Getty Images; 26 (t) © abadesign/Shutterstock.com; 26 (b) © Chris Pritchard/Getty Images; 29 © Joe_Potato/iStockphoto; 31 (t) © Keith Homan/Shutterstock.com; 31 (b) © Tatiana Georgieva/iStockphoto; 32 (t) Courtesy of the United States Postal Service; 32 (m) © Mr Doomits/Shutterstock.com; 32 (b) Courtesy of the United States Postal Service; 35 (t) © Alberto Pomares/Getty Images; 35 (t) © Franck Camhi/Alamy Stock Photo; 35 (m) © qingqing/Shutterstock.com; 35 (b) © Monkey Business Images/Shutterstock.com; 36 (ml) © posztos/Shutterstock.com; 36 (mr) © robertharding/Alamy Stock Photo; 36 (b) © CO Leong/Getty Images; 37 © Lisa Klumpp/Getty Images; 41 (t) © RyanJLane/iStockphoto; 41 (b) © d13/Shutterstock.com; 43 (t) © daniel rodriguez/Getty Images; 43 (b) © Wilson Valentin/Getty Images; 45 © suedhang/Getty Images; 46 (tl) © Chagin/iStockphoto; 46 (tr) © Gene Chutka/Getty Images; 46 (ml) © IR Stone/Shutterstock.com; 46 (mr) © DIGIcal/Getty Images; 46 (bl) © sjlocke/iStockphoto; 46 (br) © Slawomir Fajer/iStockphoto; 47 (t) © digitalskillet/iStockphoto; 47 (bl) © Meeyoung Son/Alamy Stock Photo; 47 (br) © Johner Images/Alamy Stock Photo; 49 (Astrology Wheel) © Julie Ridge/Getty Images; 49 (Zodiac) © T-Immagini/iStockphoto; 50 (t) © 77DZIGN/Getty Images; 50 (b) © A-Digit/iStockphoto; 51 (t) © 77DZIGN/Getty Images; 51 (b) © A-Digit/iStockphoto; 53 (t) © Galyna Andrushko/Getty Images; 53 (ml) © Arkady Chubykin/Getty Images; 53 (mr) © Michael Chu/Getty Images; 53 (b) © Mark Goddard/Getty Images; 54 © JB Lacroix/WireImage/Getty Images; 55 (l) © kevinruss/iStockphoto; 55 (m) © Doug Sims/Getty Images; 55 (r) © Frans Dekkers/Getty Images; 56 © Art_man/Shutterstock.com; 58 © Gordon Shoosmith/Alamy Stock Photo; 59 (t) © egdigital/iStockphoto; 59 (b) © Syda Productions/Shutterstock.com; 60 © David Palmer/Getty Images; 61 (t) © anharris/iStockphoto; 61 (b) © by_nicholas/iStockphoto; 61 (b) © Daniel Padavona/Getty Images; 61 (background) © Diane Diederich/Getty Images; 62 © Khomulo Anna/Shutterstock.com; 65 (t) © shorrocks/iStockphoto; 65 (b) © doga yusuf dokdok/Getty Images; 66 (tl) © Jill Chen/iStockphoto; 66 (tr) © Jan Sandvik/Shutterstock.com; 66 (ml) © Fuat Kose/Getty Images; 66 (mr) © Elena Elisseeva/Getty Images; 66 (bl) © Andrejs Zemdega/Getty Images; 66 (bm) © Oleg Sarnavskyy/Shutterstock.com; 66 (br) © thumb/Getty Images; 67 (t) © doga yusuf dokdok/Getty Images; 67 (bl) © Renee Keith/Getty Images; 67 (br) © Plus/Getty Images; 68 © Peter Bernik/Shutterstock.com; 70 (left col) © Kristen Johansen/Getty Images; 70 (right col: tl) © Gang Liu/Shutterstock.com; 70 (right col: tr) © lisafx/iStockphoto; 70 (right col: ml) © Paul Hakimata/Alamy Stock Photo; 70 (right col: mr) © dstephens/iStockphoto; 70 (right col: bl) © Paul Hakimata Photography/Shutterstock.com; 70 (right col: br) © clearstockconcepts/iStockphoto; 71 © hidesy/iStockphoto; 72 (tl) © Tyler Stalman/iStockphoto; 72 (tml) © 2/Ocean/Corbis; 72 (tmr) © forestpath/Shutterstock.com; 72 (tr) © Yuri/iStockphoto; 72 (bl) © knape/iStockphoto; 72 (bml) © Daniel Laflor/Getty Images; 72 (bmr) © Denis Pepin/Shutterstock.com; 72 (br) © skynesher/iStockphoto; 73 © Mateusz Zagorski/Getty Images; 76 (l) © TheWhiteRabbit/Shutterstock.com; 76 (r) © TheWhiteRabbit/iStockphoto; 77 (t) © James Thew/Fotolia.com; 77 (mt) © da-kuk/iStockphoto; 77 (mm) © Tropinina Olga/Shutterstock.com; 77 (mb) © Steve Cole/Getty Images; 77 (b) © Olga Lipatova/Shutterstock.com; 78 (tl) © Anastasija Popova/Shutterstock.com; 78 (tm) © Tom Bean/Alamy Stock Photo; 78 (tr) © Gigra/Shutterstock.com; 78 (mr) © MoreISO/iStockphoto; 78 (mr) © Volodymyr Kyrylyuk/Shutterstock.com; 78 (b) © Colleen E. Scott/Scott Designs/Shutterstock.com; 79 (t) © BananaStock/Jupiterimages; 79 (bl) © IVY PHOTOS/Shutterstock.com; 79 (br) © edge69/iStockphoto; 83 (t) © pink_cotton_candy/iStockphoto; 83 (b) © bikeriderlondon/Shutterstock.com; 84 © NASA; 85 © Lenscap Photography/Shutterstock.com; 86 © Dave Long/Getty Images; 88 (tll) © Ingvar Bjork/Shutterstock.com; 88 (tm) © Creative Crop/Getty Images; 88 (tr) © angelo gilardelli/Shutterstock.com; 88 (bl) © luckypic/Shutterstock.com; 88 (bm) © Umberto Shtanzman/Shutterstock.com; 88 (br) © Luis Louro/Shutterstock.com; 89 (t) © dem10/iStockphoto; 89 (mtl) © Victor Maffe/Getty Images; 89 (mtr) © Alexander Raths/Getty Images; 89 (ml) © WendellandCarolyn/iStockphoto; 89 (mr) © Paul Malyugin/Getty Images; 89 (r) © pearley/iStockphoto; 90 (l) © Image Source/Getty Images; 90 (r) © Julien Grondin/Getty Images; 91 (tl) © Okea/Getty Images; 91 (tr) © scyther5/Shutterstock.com; 91 (bl) © Ayaaz Rattansi/Getty Images; 91 (br) © Colonel/Getty Images; 94 © Karen Grigoryan/Shutterstock.com; 95 (t) © Peter Zelei/iStockphoto; 95 (mtl) © Steve Debenport/iStockphoto; 95 (mtm) © EdBockStock/Shutterstock.com; 95 (mtr) © GWImages/Shutterstock.com; 95 (mb) © Image Source Plus/Alamy Stock Photo; 95 (b) © Image Source Plus/Alamy Stock Photo.

Cover: © Dheny Patungka.

Printed in Greece by Bakis SA
Print Number: 08   Print Year: 2021

CONTENTS

GRAMMAR *be*

1 Complete the conversation using the words in the box.

Hi	'm	's	meet

A: ¹ *Hi.* I ² .... Richard. What ³ .... your name?
B: Jodi. Nice to ⁴ .... you.

2 Complete the sentences with the correct full form of the verb *be*.
1 He *is* a student.
2 You .... from Spain.
3 She .... from Mexico.
4 They .... students, too.
5 We .... teachers here.
6 It .... my surname.

3 Write the contracted forms of the verbs in exercise 2.
1 ......*'s*......   4 ....
2 ....   5 ....
3 ....   6 ....

4 Write the words in the correct order to make questions.
1 first / What's / name? / your
What's your first name?
2 surname? / What's / your
....
3 from? / Where / are / you
....
4 part? / Which
....

5 ❂ 1.1 Listen and check your answers.

6 Match the questions in exercise 4 to the answers below.
a Brown.   [2]
b England.   [   ]
c Keira.   [   ]
d Manchester. It's in the north. [   ]

LISTENING

7 ❂ 1.2 Listen to the conversations (1–3) and match them to the photos (a–c).

a

b

c

8 Listen again and circle the correct answer.
Conversation 1
1 Brad is from the (USA) / UK.

Conversation 2
2 His first name is *Julio* / *da Silva*.
3 His surname is *Julio* / *da Silva*.

Conversation 3
4 Ken is a *student* / *teacher*.
5 Yolanda is from *Argentina* / *Spain*.
6 Posadas is in *the south* / *the north*.

Learner tip

Try to listen to English every day. Listen to the radio, listen to music and watch TV.

VOCABULARY Countries

9 Look at the pictures. Unscramble the letters and write the names of the countries. Start each country with a capital letter.

1 zbaril *Brazil*   2 apnaj ....

3 tlyia ....   4 nicha ....

5 yakne ....

10 Complete the names of the countries with the vowels (*a, e, i, o, u*).

1 P o l a n d
2 M __ x __ c __
3 C __ n __ d __

4 S __ __ d __ __ r __ b __ __
5 S p __ __ n

11 Write the name of each country in exercises 9 and 10 in the correct part of the world.

Africa	....		
Asia	....	....	
Europe	....	....	....
the Middle East	....		
North America	....		
Central America	....		
South America	*Brazil*		

PRONUNCIATION Syllable stress

Language note

A syllable is a part of a word that has a vowel sound.
The word *name* has one syllable.
The word *surname* has two syllables.
The word *Italy* has three syllables.

12 🔊 1.3 Listen to the words and tick (✓) the number of syllables in each word.

Japan	1 syllable [ ]	2 syllables [ ]
Kenya	1 syllable [ ]	2 syllables [ ]
Italy	2 syllables [ ]	3 syllables [ ]

13 Listen again. Underline the stressed syllable.

o◯	◯o	◯oo
Ja<u>pan</u>	Kenya	Italy
....	....	....

14 🔊 1.4 Listen and write the words in the correct group in exercise 13.

China   Mexico   Brazil

DEVELOPING CONVERSATIONS
Which part?

15 Complete the conversations with the phrases below.

| are you | the capital | I'm from |
| It's in | your mum | Which part |

1 A: ¹ *I'm from* Brazil.
   B: Oh, which part?
   A: Recife. Do you know it?
   B: No.
   A: ² .... the north.

2 A: Where ³ .... from?
   B: Italy.
   A: Which part?
   B: Rome. It's ⁴ ....

3 A: Is ⁵ .... English?
   B: No. She's from Poland.
   A: Oh! I'm from Poland. ⁶ .... is your mum from?
   B: Gdansk.
   A: Oh, me too!

16 Look at the map of Poland. Read the text and choose the correct words.

Hi, I'm Dagmara. I'm from Poland. Warsaw is the ¹ *city* / *capital*. It's in the ² *west* / *east*. It's a great place. But I'm not from Warsaw. I'm from Gdansk. Do you know it? It's in the ³ *north* / *south*. My mum's from Krakow in the ⁴ *north* / *south*, and my dad's from Lodz in the ⁵ *middle* / *east*. My grandparents are from Poznan in the ⁶ *east* / *west*.

VOCABULARY Jobs and workplaces

1 Complete the descriptions with the words in the box.

civil servant	designer	nurse	police officer
receptionist	shop assistant	teacher	waiter

1 I'm a .... I work in a large hospital here in Warsaw.
2 Elena is a .... in a secondary school in Valencia.
3 I answer the phone in a language school in Rome. I'm a
   ....
4 Suki works as a .... in a department store in Osaka.
5 I work in a government office in Stuttgart. I'm a ....
6 Ana works in a small studio in New York as a ....
7 Michel is a .... He works in a famous restaurant in Paris.
8 I'm a .... I work on the street and protect people.

2 Match the sentences (1–8) in exercise 1 to photos (a–h).

a

f

d

b

g

e

c

h

3 Cross out the incorrect words in the dialogues.

1 A: What *are / do* you do?
   B: I *do / 'm* a teacher.
   A: What *are / do* you teach?
   B: *I'm / teach* English.

2 C: What *is / do* your job?
   D: I *'m / work* a designer.
   C: Where *are / do* you work?
   D: I *'m / work* in a studio in Tokyo.
   C: *Are / Do* you enjoy your work?
   D: *I / I'd* love it.

GRAMMAR Present simple

4 Correct the sentences.

1 Where he live?
   Where does he live?
2 Who does you live with?
   ....
3 What time are they get up?
   ....
4 What you do in your free time?
   ....
5 How does they travel here?
   ....
6 How many languages are you speak?
   ....

5 Match the answers below with the questions in exercise 4.

a Around six. *3*
b Near the city centre. ....
c They walk. ....
d One. English! ....
e My parents. ....
f I go running. ....

6 Write questions from the prompts.

1 you work / in an office
   Do you work in an office?
2 they work / in a secondary school
   ....
   ....
3 she speak / Italian
   ....
   ....
4 he / play football
   ....
   ....
5 you and your family live / in Scotland
   ....
   ....

7 Write negative answers to the questions in exercise 6.

1 *No, I don't.*
2 ....
3 ....
4 ....
5 ....

DEVELOPING WRITING
An application form

8 Is this an application form for
1 a job?   3 a college course?
2 a place at a university?

9 Complete the description. Use the information in the application form.
Carlo [1] .... is a [2] .... He works in a [3] .... in [4] .... , in the north of [5] .... He wants to work in [6] .... He wants to study ....

JOB APPLICATION

First name:	*Carlo*
Surname:	*Mancini*
Address:	*24101 Via Berbera, Verona, 37191, Italy*
Telephone:	*041 450216*
Current occupation:	*Waiter*
Email address:	*cmancini@ciaomail.com*
Country of origin:	*Italy*
Position applied for:	Waiter

Describe yourself in 20–30 words.
I'm a waiter. I work in a small restaurant in Verona, a beautiful city in the north of Italy. I want to work in London and study English.

HAWTHORN ART COLLEGE, OXFORD
Ben Herman
Art teacher
24 Lime Street, Oxford, OX12 1LS
Tel: 01842 71204
email: hermanb@art.com

University of Blackpool Students' Union
Designer
Salary £25,000
UBSU
We are looking for a designer to join a small friendly team in a busy studio in Cape Town.
www.ubsu.co.uk

10 Look at the documents and complete the job application form. Use capital letters where necessary.

JOB APPLICATION

First name:	....
Surname:	....
Address:	....
Telephone:	....
Current occupation:	....
Email address:	....
Country of origin:	....
Position applied for:	....

Describe yourself in 20–30 words.
I'm an art teacher. I work in a .... in .... , a beautiful city in the centre of .... I want to work as a .... in ....

READING

11 Read the three texts. Do they come from
1 a newspaper?   2 a website?   3 a school notice board?

Name: Angelika   **Occupation:** Teacher   **Country:** Germany

Hi. I'm Angelika. I'm from Hamburg, in Germany. Hamburg's in the north.
I'm a teacher. I work in a big secondary school in the centre of the **city**.
I really enjoy my job. It's great!

Name: Jianyu   **Occupation:** Civil Servant   **Country:** China

I'm Jianyu. I'm from Guangzhou. It's a big city in the south of China – it has a **population** of 14 million people. There are a lot of people! I'm a civil servant. I work in a government office. It's boring. I want a different job. I want to become a police officer.

Name: Salima   **Occupation:** Nurse   **Country:** Morocco

Hello. I'm Salima. I'm from Morocco. I live in a small **town** called Rommani. 15,000 people live there. I work in a hospital. I'm a nurse. It's difficult because I work very long hours, but I like my job.

Glossary

city: a very big, important town where people live and work.
population: the number of people that live in a town or city.
town: a smaller place than a city, where people live and work.

12 For each person, answer the following questions.
1 What's his / her name?
a ....   b..................................
c ....
2 Where's he / she from?
a..................................   b..................................
c ....
3 Where does he / she work?
a..................................   b..................................
c ....

13 Who is each sentence about? Write *A* for Angelika, *J* for Jianyu and *S* for Salima.
1 He / She works long hours.
2 He / She wants to be a police officer.
3 He / She works in a secondary school.
4 He / She works for the government.

VOCABULARY Describing places

1 Find ten words for things in a city in the wordsnake.
   Now write the words next to the correct number in the
   list below.

Language note

Look at the spelling of plurals.
river – river**s**
church – church**es**
universit**y** – universit**ies**

rivertrafficpalacechurchfactoryuniversitycathedralrestaurantparkbeach

1 .... *river* ....
2 ....
3 ....
4 ....
5 ....
6 ....
7 ....
8 ....
9 ....
10 ....

2 Write the plurals of the words. Which word has
   no plural?
   1 river   ....
   2 beach   ....
   3 park   ....
   4 factory   ....
   5 traffic   ....
   6 palace   ....

GRAMMAR *there is / there are*

3 Cross out the incorrect phrases to complete the sentences.

1 *There's / There are* a few cafés in the High Street.
2 *There's / There are* a lot of traffic in the city.
3 *There isn't / There aren't* any good restaurants.
4 *There isn't / There aren't* much crime near the station.
5 *There's / There are* too many people at the beach.

4 Look at the picture. Complete the sentences with *There's, There isn't, There are* or *There aren't*.

1 .... a river in the city.
2 .... some restaurants.
3 .... any people on the beach.
4 .... a beach near the city.
5 .... much traffic.
6 .... two churches.
7 .... many trees in the park.
8 .... two cinemas in town.

Vocabulary Builder Quiz 1

Download the Vocabulary Builder for Unit 1 and try the quiz below. Write your answers in your notebook. Then check them and record your score.

1 Complete the sentences with nouns formed from the verbs in brackets.

1 She's a .... in that new restaurant. (wait)
2 Do you know that Kevin's a civil .... now? (serve)
3 She wants to be a fashion .... (design)
4 I'm a .... at Sheffield University. (study)
5 Caleb works as a shop .... here. (assist)

2 Complete the collocations with the correct preposition.

1 The other people .... my class are really nice.
2 The building is in the middle .... the city.
3 She works .... the north of the city.
4 My brother works .... the government.
5 I often go swimming .... my free time.

3 Cross out the word in each group which doesn't collocate.

1 I work *a job / in a city / at home / every day.*
2 She likes *her job / the area / there / this city.*
3 Do you live *on your own / in a house / long hours / in an old building?*
4 Do you want *to become a teacher / to sleep / a different job / at night?*
5 You can walk *everywhere / at the police station / to work / to the river.*

4 Match the words (1–5) to their opposites (a–e).

1 cheap   a late
2 boring   b expensive
3 long   c interesting
4 early   d big
5 small   e short

5 Complete the sentences with the words in the box.

beach   cathedral   factory   museum   university

1 There's a service in the .... every Sunday.
2 My brother is a student at the ....
3 Do you want to spend a day at the .... next weekend?
4 They're opening a new car .... in my town.
5 You can see some amazing old things in the ....

Score ___ /25

Wait a couple of weeks and try the quiz again.
Compare your scores.

VOCABULARY Free time activities

1 Look at the pictures and complete the crossword with the activities.

Across
4
5

Down

1   3

2   4

2 Match a verb in column A with a noun in column B.

A		B	
1	watching	a	guitar
2	meeting	b	computer games
3	playing the	c	TV
4	doing	d	the cinema
5	playing	e	new people
6	going out	f	to music
7	listening	g	sport
8	going to	h	to dinner

3 Complete the sentences with the activities in exercise 2.

1 I like *watching TV* in the evenings. I like quiz shows but the news is boring.

2 They love .... Yuri likes European films but Asako prefers Hollywood movies.

3 Mariella and Julietta spend over two hours a day .... Their favourites are swimming and aerobics.

4 Asha never hears us when we call her. She's always .... on her mp3 player.

5 I spend a lot of time .... I love it! Sometimes, I perform in public.

6 We like .... , but we don't have a lot of money, so we usually eat at home – it's cheaper!

7 I like going to clubs to dance but I'm not interested in ....

8 My little sister loves .... Her favourite is Nintendo Wii.

GRAMMAR Verb patterns

4 Complete the sentences with *like* or *want*.

1 I don't .... to speak to you today.
2 We don't think you .... meeting new people.
3 Does Alison .... to come shopping with us?
4 Do they .... playing computer games?
5 Oliver! We don't .... to listen to your music all evening, thank you.
6 You don't really .... to go out for dinner tonight, do you?

5 Complete the sentences with the correct form of the verbs in brackets.

1 I like .... new people. It's interesting. (meet)
2 Shona .... to go out this weekend. (want)
3 The kids love .... In fact they're at the pool now. (swim)
4 .... you .... doing sport? (like)
5 Everybody has got tickets for the film, but I don't want .... (go)
6 Ben .... really .... dancing. He likes watching TV. (not like)

DEVELOPING CONVERSATIONS
Arrangements

> **Language note**
> -
> You usually arrange to meet *at* a place *at* a time. *Let's meet **at** the station **at** 8 o'clock.*

6 Choose the correct words to complete the conversation.

A: Do you ¹ *want / like* to go to dinner?
B: That ² *listens / sounds* nice. ³ *Where / What* do you want to go?
A: I like Thai food. ⁴ *Where / What* about you?
B: Yeah, great. ⁵ *What / When* time do you want to meet?
A: ⁶ *Is / Are* 7.30 OK?
B: Good. See you later then.
A: See you. Oh, ⁷ *when / where* do you want to meet?
B: ⁸ *At / On* the bus stop.
A: OK. See you there ⁹ *at / on* 7.30.

7 ⏺ 2.1 Listen and check your answers.

LISTENING

8 ⏺ 2.2 Listen to Joshua talking to Ana about his friends. Which activity does each friend like?

Friends		Activities	
Jack	*d*	a	shopping
Will		b	studying
Emily		c	doing sport
Grace		d	listening to music
Daniel		e	dancing
Chloe		f	watching TV

9 Listen again. Are the statements true or false? Circle T or F.

1 Jack likes doing sports. T F
2 Emily is Will's sister. T F
3 Emily and Will like the same things. T F
4 Grace has got brown hair. T F
5 Daniel is Chloe's brother. T F
6 Joshua likes doing sport. T F

VOCABULARY Daily life

1 Write the words and phrases in the box in the correct column.

out for dinner	breakfast	out dancing
up	a shower	to a concert
a coffee	home from work	lunch
to bed		

have	go	get
	out for dinner	

2 Complete the story with *have*, *get* and *go*.

I ¹ .... up at seven o'clock and
² .... a shower. I don't have time to
³ .... breakfast. Instead, I ⁴ ....
a coffee and then leave for work. We stop at one to
⁵ .... lunch. At one-thirty it's back to work.
I ⁶ .... home from work around nine. On
Mondays my wife and I ⁷ .... out for
dinner and on Fridays we ⁸ .... out
dancing or even ⁹ .... to a concert. But on
the other days of the week we ¹⁰ .... to
bed at eleven.

3 Correct the words in bold.

1 I **go** up at 6 o'clock.

   ....

2 I **drinks** coffee at breakfast.

   ....

3 We **has** lunch at 2 o'clock.

   ....

4 On Friday evenings I **get** out dancing.

   ....

5 On Saturday night I **am** to bed at 11.30.

   ....

GRAMMAR Adverbs of frequency

4 Complete the list with the words in the box.

usually	hardly ever	occasionally

100%	always
	....
	sometimes
	....
	....
0%	never

5 Choose the correct adverb of frequency to complete the sentences.

1 We don't like late nights, so we *always / never* go to bed at 9pm.
2 They don't have a TV, so they *usually / hardly ever* watch the news.
3 Jess *usually / always* finishes work at 6pm. She sometimes finishes later on Fridays.
4 I *never / occasionally* drink alcohol. I hate it.
5 She *hardly ever / occasionally* does her homework on the bus. She sometimes finishes it before she gets home.

6 Write the words in the correct order to make sentences.

1 my homework / before dinner / usually / I / do

   ....

2 on Saturdays / She / dancing / always / goes out

   ....

3 have / at home / lunch / sometimes / They

   ....

4 at weekends / watch TV / We / never

   ....

5 hardly ever / before 9pm / from work / He / gets home

   ....

READING

7 Quickly read the notices on the school noticeboard. Match the three headings below with the messages.

1 Do you like going to the cinema?   [ ]
2 Men and women wanted!   [ ]
3 Looking for friends   [ ]

8 Read the notices again. Are the sentences true or false? Circle T or F.

1 Josie doesn't like James Bond films.   T   F
2 The film starts at 6.30.   T   F
3 Patricia doesn't know a lot of people here.   T   F
4 She often goes swimming after her English class.   T   F
5 She's in English class every afternoon.   T   F
6 Dejan and Ken always play football at the weekend.   T   F
7 They are really good at football.   T   F

Rose College Message Board

A Hi! I'm Patricia. I'm from Argentina and I'm new here. I'm studying English for six weeks and I want to meet new friends to spend our free time together. What activities do you enjoy? I like listening to music and dancing. Maybe we could go to a club together at the weekend? I also like swimming. And I love shopping! I usually go shopping after my English class. I'm in Ms Sharp's class every morning from 9.30 to 12.30. After that, I'm free every afternoon, so please leave a message on this board, or see me at break.

B I love the cinema and films! What about you? I want to start a cinema club for people who love films. I've got four tickets for the fantastic new James Bond film premiere at the Regal cinema, in Leicester Square. It's at 6.30 on Friday 22nd. Do you want to come with me? Email me on josie@gomail.com.
Josie

C Do you want to get fit, or do you like playing football? Don't just sit on the sofa all weekend watching TV! We play football every weekend in the park. We're very bad at it, but we love it. We need people — men and women — to play with us. It's fun! Meet outside the park at 11.00 this Sunday. Dejan and Ken.

9 Find these words in the text and match them to their meanings (1–4).

club	message	premiere	sofa

1 the first time a film is shown ....
2 a place where you can dance and meet people ....
3 a note or words that you send to another person ....
4 a long soft chair for two or more people ....

Learner tip

When you find a word you don't know in a text, you can sometimes guess the meaning of the word. First, ask if the word is a noun, an adjective or a verb. Then look at the words next to the word you don't know. They can give you clues about its meaning.

VOCABULARY
In an English class

10 Match the words in the box (1–10) to the pictures (a–j).

1 dictionary	2 money	3 paper	4 pencil	5 rubber
6 scissors	7 tissues	8 video	9 water	10 window

 a
 b 1
 c
 d
 e
 f
 g
 h
 i
 j

11 Complete the sentences using words in exercise 10.

1 Watch the *video* and remember what you see.
2 If you don't have a pen, you can write in ....
3 It's cold in here. Maria, can you close the ...., please?
4 If you don't know the word, check the meaning in a ....
5 Write your answers on the ....
6 Check your answers. If you make a mistake, use your .... and then write the correct answer.
7 Read the questions and then write the answers on a piece of ....

12 Match the two halves of the sentences.

1 Listen to	a your homework.
2 OK, take	b what you think.
3 Can you read	c their conversation.
4 Remember to do	d a break for five minutes.
5 Just say	e the light, please?
6 Can you turn off	f the text and answer the questions?

PRONUNCIATION

1 ♪ **2.3 Listen to the words and underline the stressed syllable.**

1 scissors	3 relax	5 cathedral
2 window	4 manager	6 dictionary

2 ♪ **2.4 Listen and circle the word in each group which doesn't go.**

1 ●●•   homework   relax   money

2 •●•   early   tonight   arrange

3 ●••   exercise   cinema   computer

3 Listen again and repeat the words.

GRAMMAR
Countable and uncountable nouns

4 Are the words countable or uncountable? Circle C or U.

1 pen	Ⓒ	U	5 traffic	C	U
2 car	C	U	6 food	C	U
3 time	C	U	7 tissue	C	U
4 rubber	C	U	8 water	C	U

> **Language note**
> --
> We use *a* for words which start with a consonant.
> *a table, a phone*
> We use *an* for words which start with a vowel.
> *an office, an English class*

5 Choose the correct word.

1 Do you have *a* / *an* / *some* / *a lot* new student in your class?
2 Do you have a cold? I've got *a* / *an* / *some* / *a lot* tissues.
3 There is *a* / *an* / *some* / *a lot* of traffic on the roads today.
4 Do you have *a* / *an* / *some* / *a lot* English class today?
5 Do you want *a* / *an* / *some* / *a lot* water?
6 Bill Gates has *a* / *an* / *some* / *a lot* of money.

6 Complete the text with the words in the box. You can use some words more than once.

a	a lot	an	any	many	much	some

 Hi. I'm Helen Fox. I live with my husband, Jeff, in Plymouth. I'm ¹*a* teacher and Jeff's ² .... engineer. We don't have ³ .... children but we've got ⁴ .... pets. We've got ⁵ .... dog called Lucky and two cats, Minnie and Max. We don't have ⁶ .... money, but we have ⁷ .... of friends, and we have good lives. There aren't ⁸ .... shops near our house. There's only ⁹ .... small supermarket and ¹⁰ .... old newsagent's.

DEVELOPING WRITING
Writing a description of yourself

7 Complete the questions with the words and phrases in the box.

do you like	you do	do at the weekend
live with	name	live

1 What's your *name*?
2 Where do you .... ?
3 Who do you .... ?
4 What do .... ?
5 What .... doing in your free time?
6 What do you usually .... ?

8 Read Jack's profile on his blog and match the information to the questions (1–6) in exercise 7.

Jack's blogspot

Profile

[*1*] Jack Jenkins

[   ] **Occupation:** Student

[   ] **Location:** Sheffield, UK

[   ] **Favourite weekend activities:** going to the cinema, watching football on TV, playing football with friends.

[   ] with my flatmates, Dave and Andy

[   ] **Hobbies:** swimming, playing computer games, chatting with friends on the internet

9 Complete the blog with the phrases in the box.

At the weekend, I usually	I'm a / an	I live with
In my free time, I like	~~I live in~~	

Jack's blogspot

Hi, I'm Jack Jenkins. ¹ *I live in* Sheffield, in the UK. ² ....
.... my two friends, Dave and Andy,
in a small flat.

³ .... student at the university
here. I'm studying Spanish. I want to be a teacher.

⁴ .... swimming,
playing computer games and chatting with my friends
on the internet. But I don't have a lot of free time
because I study in the evenings. ⁵ ....
.... go to the cinema or
watch football on TV. I sometimes play football with
friends.

10 You are going to write a paragraph about yourself. First,
answer the questions in exercise 7. Write notes.

11 Write a web profile of yourself using the notes you
made in exercise 10. Use the model text in exercise 9.

Vocabulary Builder Quiz 2

Download the Vocabulary Builder for Unit 2 and try the quiz
below. Write your answers in your notebook. Then check them
and record your score.

1 Cross out the word in each group that doesn't collocate.
1 read   *a novel / in English / your mobile phone / a book*
2 play   *the piano / football / a computer game / TV*
3 say   *a word / a conversation / what you think / no*
4 leave   *work / the house / homework / for school*

2 Match the verbs (1–6) to the nouns (a–f).
1	listen to	a	the window
2	take	b	lunch
3	do	c	music
4	have	d	sport
5	close	e	a football match
6	watch	f	a break

3 Complete the compound nouns in the sentences.
1 Please write the words in your note....................
2 Femi has a great social .... He's out every night!
3 Charlie loves computer .... He plays them all day.
4 I can take you to the train ....
5 You need to buy your train .... before you get on the
train.

4 Choose the correct words.
1 I need to *learn / go* to drive.
2 Try to use *computer games / new words* in class.
3 The *film / work* starts at seven.
4 That *sounds / listens* nice.
5 You can use *a rubber / scissors* to cut that paper.

5 Complete the sentences with the words in the box.

a coffee   lunch   any kids   go to the theatre   a short sleep

1 A: Do you have ....?
   B: Yes, two girls.
2 I have a busy social life. I .... every week.
3 We usually have .... at around twelve thirty.
4 I'm tired. I want .... before we go out.
5 I usually have .... with my breakfast.

Score ___ /25

Wait a couple of weeks and try the quiz again.
Compare your scores.

VOCABULARY Local facilities

1 Find eight words in the wordsnake for places in a city.

1 *bank*
2 ....
3 ....
4 ....
5 ....
6 ....
7 ....
8 ....

bankcafébookshopsportscentreclothesshopchemistpostofficeshoeshop

2 Match the places (1–8) in exercise 1 with (a–h).

a □ b □ c □

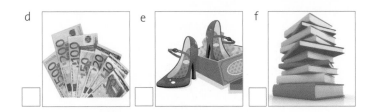

d □ e □ f □

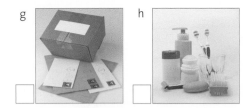

g □ h □

3 Write the names of the places where:

1 you can have lunch ....*café*............
2 you can buy stamps ....
3 you go to buy something to read ....
4 you can put money in or take money out ....
5 they sell toothpaste and shampoo ....
6 you can buy a jacket ....

GRAMMAR Prepositions of place

4 Where's the ball? Complete the descriptions for each small picture below with the words in the box.

on	opposite	next to	between	at

1 .... the end of the street
2 .... the right
3 .... the left
4 .... the box
5 .... the boxes
6 .... the box
7 .... the box

5 Look at the street plan and cross out the incorrect description.

1 The hotel is *on the left* / ~~on the right~~.
2 The hotel is *between* / *opposite* the cinema and the department store.
3 The university is *at* / *on* the end of this street.
4 The chocolate factory is *at* / *on* the right.
5 The church is *opposite* / *between* the cinema.
6 The museum is *next to* / *opposite* the internet café.

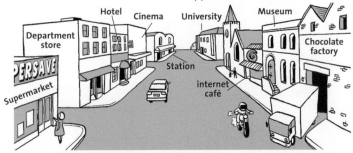

6 Look at the street plan and complete the sentences.

1 The station is *on* the left, ... the university.
2 The university is .... the end of this street.
3 The supermarket is .... the left.
4 The hotel is .... the department store.
5 The internet café is .... the church and the museum.
6 The chocolate factory is .... the supermarket.

DEVELOPING CONVERSATIONS
Asking for information

7 **Make phrases using the nouns in the box and verbs 1–4. You can use the verbs more than once.**

1 send   2 get   3 change   4 have

| lunch | a package | some stamps | a jacket |
| a coffee | some money | some aspirins | |

Example: **send** a package; **send** some money

8 🔊 **3.1 Listen to the dialogue. Then replace the verbs in italics with verbs from exercise 7 which have the same meaning.**

Sue: I need to get some stamps from the post office.

Meena: I want to go to the post office, too. I need to ¹ (*mail*) .... a package to my sister. It's her birthday next week.

Sue: Ah, that's nice. Oh, yes and I want to ² (*exchange*) .... some money for our skiing holiday, too.

Meena: OK. And then we can ³ (*eat*) .... lunch. I'm hungry!

Sue: I don't want to eat but I'm cold. I want to ⁴ (*drink*) .... a coffee.

Meena: OK! Then I'd like to go to the chemist. I want to ⁵ (*buy*) .... some aspirins for Anil. And is there a clothes shop near here?

Sue: Yes, there's one opposite the cinema. Why?

Meena: I need to ⁶ (*purchase*) .... a jacket for our holiday. It's cold in the mountains!

Language note

We often use **get** instead of *buy*, and **have** instead of *drink* or *eat*.
I need to **get** some toothpaste.
I usually **have** a coffee after I **have** lunch.

LISTENING

9 🔊 **3.2 Why is Jane calling? Listen and tick (✓) the correct answer.**

1 To buy a house. ☐
2 To buy a flat. ☐
3 To rent a flat. ☐

10 **Listen again and complete the form.**

Property in Selfield

Name of agency:	¹ *Gibbs* Properties
Property available from:	² Beginning of ....
Address of property:	³ 12 .... Drive
Total cost of flat:	⁴ £.. per month
Landlord's telephone number:	⁵ ....
Local facilities:	⁶ Supermarket and ....

Glossary

property: a house or a flat
rent: to pay money regularly to stay in a house or flat
landlord/landlady: the owner of a house or flat that someone rents
tenant: a person who stays in a house or flat and pays rent

VOCABULARY In the house

1 Complete the crossword.

Across
1.
2.
4.
7.
9.

Down
1.
3.
5.
6.
8.

2 Read the descriptions and write the names of four rooms in the house.
1 You watch TV in the evening here. ....
2 You make your breakfast here. ....
3 You sleep here. ....
4 You wash yourself here. ....

3 Complete the text using words from exercises 1 and 2.
When Sam gets home he goes into the [1] *kitchen* and gets a cold drink, usually beer, out of the [2] .... Then we get dinner ready and then sit down and eat. After dinner we clear the [3] .... and do the washing up in the [4] .... Then we go into the [5] .... We sit on the [6] .... and Sam watches [7] .... and I read my book. Then I go to the [8] .... to have a shower. I go to [9] .... around 10. Sam usually comes into the [10] .... about an hour later. I don't usually wake up.

GRAMMAR
Pronouns, possessive adjectives and *'s*

4 Complete the table.

Subject	Object	Adjective	Pronoun
I			mine
	you	your	
he		his	
	her		hers
	us	our	
they			theirs

5 Complete the sentences in the speech bubbles with a possessive adjective.

[1] .... *name is Jelena Potje and I live in Belgrade with my daughter Dunja.* [2] .... *live in a small flat by the river.*

My wife and I don't really want to sell [3] .... *house, but she wants to find a place near* [4] .... *parents.*

This is [5] .... *new flat – we love it!* [6] .... *son, Carl, loves* [7] .... *room and our daughters think* [8] .... *room is great too!*

6 Replace the words in bold with a possessive pronoun or *'s*.
1 It's not his house, it's **my house**!
  It's not his house, it's mine!
2 Our car is smaller than **their car**.
  ....
3 I like my jacket but I love **the jacket of Bella**.
  ....
4 Is their fridge the same model as **her fridge**?
  ....
5 Does this toothbrush belong to Dave?
  Is it **the toothbrush of Dave**?
  ....
6 Your car is the same as **our car**.
  ....

7 Correct the words in bold.
1 This DVD is **me**.
  ....
2 **John** house is beautiful.
  ....
3 This isn't my pencil. It's **she**.
  ....
4 No, it isn't Bob and Martha's. It's **us**!
  ....
5 **I** parents live here.
  ....
6 He loves **he** car.
  ....

READING

8 Read the texts. Who is the website for?

1 people who want to buy a house ☐

2 people who want to go on holiday abroad ☐

3 people who want to swap their home for a short time ☐

HOMESTAY

You want to go on holiday, but don't have any money? Now you can go on holiday free, with HOMESTAY. Just swap your own home for one of these. You can swap for a weekend, a week, or even a month or more!

Here are our favourite properties this week.

Garden Flat, Jenkins Road, Brighton

This beautiful flat is in a great **location**, in the centre of town in Brighton, on the south coast. There are lots of things to do here. You can **explore** the town and the beach, or even go to London on the train. There are lots of good places to eat in Brighton, with many of them very near. Right next to the flat, there's Café Coco, a popular café where you can have lunch or a coffee.

Inside, the flat is modern and comfortable. There's a **spacious** living room, with a TV and two large sofas. The kitchen is small, but there's a fridge and a table and chairs. You can see the sea from the one large bedroom. You share a garden with the friendly neighbours.

No pets.

Rose Cottage, Tretower

This lovely cottage is in the small, quiet village of Tretower in Wales. This is a great place to relax, go walking and explore the mountains, or do whatever you want. There's a post office and a bookshop in the village, and there's a pub down the road, which does great sandwiches and salads. The town of Brecon is 9 miles away, where you can find a few supermarkets and a good choice of restaurants. There's also a great museum.

The cottage is small and **traditional**. It has a cosy living room, two sunny bedrooms – each with its own bathroom – and a large family kitchen. The garden is large and sunny.

Children and pets welcome.

9 Read the texts again and write *G* for Garden Flat and *R* for Rose Cottage.

1 There's a lot to do there. ......*G*......

2 It's very near the sea. ....

3 It's a quiet place. ....

4 There are two bedrooms. ....

5 You can't take your dog. ....

6 There's a pub near the property. ....

Glossary

swap: change one thing for another
location: place or area
explore: travel around a new place to find out about it
spacious: with a lot of space inside
traditional: in a style that has existed for a long time

10 Choose the correct words in the summary.

Garden Flat is a good place for a person who likes
¹ *relaxing /* (*going out*). It's right in the centre of the town,
² *next / near* a lot of restaurants and cafés. The flat has
a large ³ *living room / kitchen* and a bedroom with a
view of the sea.

Rose Cottage is in a ⁴ *small / large* village in Wales. It's
a good place for someone who likes ⁵ *the countryside /
shopping*. The ⁶ *old / modern* cottage is small, but it has
a large garden.

VOCABULARY Collocations

1 Match the verbs to the nouns. Some verbs can be used more than once.

1 put on
2 cut
3 brush
4 turn up
5 share
6 wash

a your teeth
b the TV
c your hands
d a flat
e your shoes
f some vegetables

> **Learner tip**
>
> Some verbs in English are very common, like *get*, *put*, *turn*.
> When you learn these verbs, try to learn some of the nouns that go with them, too.

2 Complete the sentences with the nouns in the box.

| dog | hair | make up | music | plates | sandwich |

1 He needs to wash the *plates*.
2 She always cuts their .... herself.
3 He doesn't want to share his ....
4 He hardly ever brushes the ....
5 She loves putting on ....
6 I love this song. Turn up the ....

3 Choose the correct word.

1 I need to dry my hair. Is there a *new / clean* towel?
2 Please *put / set* those plates in the cupboard.
3 Dinner's ready! It's on the kitchen *table / cupboard*.
4 I always *put / set* my alarm clock for seven o'clock.
5 It's hot in here! Turn the air conditioning *on / down*.
6 The *cupboard / sink* is a mess. Look at all these dirty plates!

GRAMMAR can / can't

4 Complete the sentences with *can* or *can't*.

1 This room is a mess! I *can't* find my glasses.
2 He .... drive there. It's not for cars.
3 The café's open. We .... have a cup of tea here.
4 The writing is too small.
   I .... read it.
5 You .... see the sea from here.
   Look at that boat.
6 The computer's broken.
   She .... check her emails.

5 Complete with *Can I* or *Can you*.

1 The music is very loud. *Can you* hear me?
2 I'm thirsty. .... get a drink from the fridge?
3 .... set the table for me, please?
4 When you go to the shop, ... get some milk?
5 .... buy some stamps? Do you sell them here?
6 .... help me with this homework?

6 Correct the sentences. There is one mistake in each sentence.

1 He cans come to the meeting tomorrow.
   He can come to the meeting tomorrow.
2 You can help me with this homework, please?
   ....
3 You can't smoked in here.
   ....
4 Can I to use this towel?
   ....
5 We cant' use this room today.
   ....
6 I can't finding my keys.
   ....

PRONUNCIATION can / can't

7 ◓ 3.3 Listen and tick (✓) the sentence you hear, *a* or *b*.

1 a I can come next week. [✓]
  b I can't come next week. [ ]
2 a He can help us. [ ]
  b He can't help us. [ ]
3 a They can see the film. [ ]
  b They can't see the film. [ ]
4 a We can drive there. [ ]
  b We can't drive there. [ ]
5 a She can watch TV in here. [ ]
  b She can't watch TV in here. [ ]
6 a I can make you a sandwich. [ ]
  b I can't make you a sandwich. [ ]

8 Listen again and repeat the sentences.

DEVELOPING WRITING
A note to a friend describing where you live

9 **Read the note quickly and tick (✓) the correct answer.**

1 Kelly's note is for:
  a a tourist
  b a friend
  c her mother

2 The note gives information about:
  a Kelly's job
  b the inside of Kelly's home
  c things to do in the town

> Hi, Sarah
> Welcome to Number 78, Juniper Street!
> This is a great area and there are lots of things to do here. There's a pub on the corner and a restaurant opposite the house. There aren't any cinemas here, but you can take the bus into town and there are two there. There is a bookshop along the road, but I like shopping in town. I hope you have a great time!
> Cheers, Kelly

10 **Read the note again and write answers to the questions.**

1 Where's the pub? *On the corner.*
2 Where's the restaurant? ....
3 How can Kelly get to town? ....
4 How many cinemas are there in town?
  ....
5 Where's the bookshop? ....

11 **Look at the map and write a note to your friend, Ben, who is staying in your flat.**

> [1] *Hi* Ben
> Welcome to Number [2] ...., [3] .... Road!
> This is a great area and there are lots of things to do here. There's a [4] .... on the corner and a [5] .... opposite the flat. There aren't any [6] ...., but you can take a [7] .... into town and there are lots there. There is a [8] .... along the road, but I like shopping in town.
> I hope you have a great time!
> Cheers, [9] ....

restaurants in town — | café | pub |
← Lime Road
| clothes shop | ⊠ bus stop to town | No. 33 |
my flat

Vocabulary Builder Quiz 3

Download the Vocabulary Builder for Unit 3 and try the quiz below. Write your answers in your notebook. Then check them and record your score.

1 Complete the verbs in the sentences.

1 I need to b.................. some new clothes. I haven't got a thing to wear.
2 How much will it cost to s.................. this package to the USA?
3 The children always b.................. their teeth before bed.
4 Is there a bank near here? I need to c.................. some money.
5 We s.................. a flat with two friends.
6 Please w.................. your hands before dinner.

2 Choose the correct words.

1 Put *on / off* your coat. It's cold outside.
2 It's very hot in here. Can I turn the air-conditioning *up / off*?
3 Please turn the music *up / down*. It's too loud!
4 You can hang *up / off* the washing in the bathroom.
5 My alarm clock always goes *out / off* at seven thirty.

3 Cross out the word in each group that doesn't collocate.

1 put on *dinner / your jacket / your shoes / make up*
2 a *warm / tidy / clean / expensive* jacket
3 wash *your hands / your room / some clothes / the dishes*
4 a tidy *room / cupboard / bread / person*
5 clean *your bedroom / the car / the sea / your shoes*

4 Match the beginnings (1–5) to the endings (a–e).

1 I'm hungry. Can we get
2 Before we leave the house, I need to find
3 It's your turn to
4 I always have a shower before I get
5 The milk is on the table. Could you put

a wash the dishes.
b something to eat here?
c it back in the fridge for me?
d dressed in the morning.
e my keys.

5 Complete the sentences with the words in the box.

apartment	study	balcony	sink

1 He has a .... because he works from home.
2 I like to sit on my .... and have a coffee in the morning sun.
3 Could you put the dirty dishes in the .... please.
4 My sister shares an .... with three other women.

Score ___/25

Wait a couple of weeks and try the quiz again. Compare your scores.

GRAMMAR Past simple

1 Complete the table with the correct verb forms.

Infinitive	Past simple
be	¹ *was / were*
have	² ....
do	³ ....
⁴	went
come	⁵ ....
⁶	saw
⁷	showed
⁸	played
read	⁹ ....
need	¹⁰ ....

2 Tick (✓) the irregular verbs in the table in exercise 1.

3 Complete the sentences using the past simple forms of the verbs in exercise 1.
1 I *had* a good weekend.
2 They .... The Killers on Saturday night.
3 He .... *War and Peace*.
4 My parents .... to my house for lunch.
5 She .... her homework.
6 We .... football in the park.

4 Complete the text with the past simple form of the verbs in brackets.

We ¹ *spent* (spend) the weekend in York with some friends in their new house. It ² .... (be) really fun. Their house is in a great area, and there ³ .... (be) lots of things to do. On Friday night, we ⁴ .... (stay) in and ⁵ .... (watch) a film on TV. On Saturday, we ⁶ .... (go) to a market near their house, and I ⁷ .... (buy) a new jacket. On Saturday night, they ⁸ .... (take) us to their favourite Chinese restaurant. On Sunday, our friends ⁹ .... (cook) lunch for us. It was a perfect weekend!

DEVELOPING CONVERSATIONS *That sounds ...*

5 Read the conversations and match each one to a photo.

1 Lee: So, how was New York?
  Aisyha: Great! We stayed in the Waverley Hotel.
  Lee: That sounds *nice / bad*.
  Aisyha: Yes, it was very comfortable.

2 Ben: Do you want to come to the park with me tomorrow? There's a free concert with Kasabian.
  Hassan: That sounds *interesting / bad*. I really like them. What time is it?
  Ben: I think it starts at two o'clock.

3 Phil: How was your weekend?
  Gudrun: Andreas was ill. He stayed in bed all weekend.
  Phil: That sounds *great / bad*. Is he OK now?
  Gudrun: He's fine. It was only a cold.

a
b
c

Conversation 1   photo [   ]
Conversation 2   photo [   ]
Conversation 3   photo [   ]

6 Read the conversations again and choose the correct adjective.

7 🔊 4.1 Listen and check your answers.

PRONUNCIATION Past simple forms

8 🔊 4.2 Listen to the pronunciation of the past tense *-ed* ending of regular verbs.

/t/ walked   /d/ played   /ɪd/ visited

9 🔊 4.3 Listen to the past tense verbs and put them in the correct column in the table.

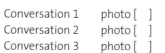

cooked	wanted	chatted	showed	liked
rained	needed	tried	relaxed	

/t/	/d/	/ɪd/
....	....	....
....	....	....
....	....	....

READING

10 Where would you see this text?

1 On a website.
2 In a newspaper.
3 In a magazine.

Travel Advisor Hotel Reviews

| ACCOMMODATION | FLIGHTS | REVIEWS | ACTIVITIES |

1 Not for everyone
I just got back from the Aloha Hula hotel with my wife and grand-children. It's a nice place and the weather was good, but it wasn't a very good hotel for families. The food was nice and the rooms were clean, but some **guests** were too **noisy**. We told the staff, but they weren't very interested or friendly. Bad staff and bad **service**. Don't go there! *Hiro Tanaka, Nagoya, Japan*.

STAR RATING ✱

2 Two weeks wasn't enough
We spent two weeks at the Aloha Hula hotel. We had a great time and the hotel was fantastic. It was cheap and clean with really nice **staff**. Two weeks wasn't enough – we wanted to stay longer. The Hawaiian people were really friendly and the food was **delicious**. It rained for one week, but we still enjoyed a relaxing holiday. *Elisa T, Bari, Italy*.

STAR RATING ✱ ✱ ✱ ✱

3 Surfing USA!
I spent four weeks in Maui and loved it. The beaches were clean, the sea was warm, the surfing was so good and … it was very sunny! Our hotel (the Aloha Hula) wasn't fantastic, but it was OK. The staff were friendly, but the rooms were dirty and the food wasn't great. I had lunch in the restaurant and was ill. I spent the day in bed. *Manny W, Hamburg, Germany*.

STAR RATING ✱ ✱

Glossary

guest: someone staying in a hotel
noisy: making a lot of noise, loud, not quiet
staff: the people who work in a place (for example, in a hotel)
service: the help guests in a hotel get from the staff
delicious: that tastes really good

11 Read the reviews again and put a ✓ or a ✗ under each holiday.

	Review 1	Review 2	Review 3
The weather was good	✓	✗	✓
Maui was nice			
The food was good			
The rooms were clean			
The staff were friendly			

12 Cross out the incorrect information.

1 Hiro went to Hawaii *alone / with his family*.
2 Hiro thought his hotel was *good / bad* for families.
3 Elisa had a *good / bad* holiday.
4 Elisa was *happy / unhappy* when her holiday ended.
5 Manny *liked / didn't like* the sea and the beaches in Maui.
6 Manny spent a *day / week* in bed.

VOCABULARY Months, seasons and dates

1 Find the words for the months in the wordsquare.
Look →, ↓ and ↘.Write them in order.

T	J	A	N	U	A	R	Y	N	E
E	A	P	I	O	Y	O	H	O	K
A	S	R	M	B	R	C	L	V	T
J	E	I	M	A	E	T	A	E	E
J	U	L	Y	O	P	O	I	M	S
N	F	N	P	G	E	B	E	B	E
D	E	C	E	M	B	E	R	E	P
E	B	T	P	W	A	R	E	R	T
P	R	A	L	F	R	R	S	A	E
A	U	G	U	S	T	D	C	S	M
M	A	Y	C	N	R	N	G	H	B
S	R	V	A	E	P	B	O	Y	E
O	Y	E	L	I	C	T	B	E	R

2 Write one word from the box next to each sentence.

autumn	spring	summer	winter

1 The weather becomes warmer. The trees
are green and flowers come out. ....*spring*....

2 It's hot and the days are long. People go
on holiday and go to the beach. ....

3 The weather becomes colder. The
leaves on the trees are yellow and orange. ....

4 It's cold and the days are short. There
are no leaves or flowers. ....

Language note
- -

In British English, we write dates like this:
10th March 1966 = 10/03/66
In American English the day and the month are the
other way round:
10th March 1966 = 3/10/66.

3 Match the dates in column A to the words in column B.

	A		B
1	13/08	a	January the thirty-first
2	09/05	b	August the thirteenth
3	26/12	c	October the twenty-second
4	31/01	d	June the twelfth
5	22/10	e	May the ninth
6	12/06	f	December the twenty-sixth

4 Write the dates in full.
1 Independence Day, USA – 4/7
   The fourth of July
2 Liberation Day, Italy – 25/4
   ....
3 Culture Day, Japan – 3/11
   ....
4 Children's Day, Brazil – 12/10
   ....
5 Workers' Day, Malaysia – 1/5
   ....

5 🔊 **4.4 Listen and check your answers.**

GRAMMAR Past simple negatives

6 Rewrite the sentences in the negative form.

1 I got up early.
I didn't get up early.

2 She had a great holiday.
....

3 They took me out for dinner.
....

4 There was a large dog on the table.
....

5 We went to the cinema last Friday.
....

6 You did your homework at the weekend.
....

7 Write the words in the correct order to make sentences.

1 very / wasn't / That / long. / film
That film wasn't very long.

2 do. / wasn't / There / to / anything
....

3 wasn't / There / anyone / party. / knew / at the / I
....

4 buy / I / didn't / shops. / anything / at the
....

5 didn't / weekend. / go / last / We / anywhere
....

6 wanted / money. / but she / She / it / any / didn't have
....

8 Complete the text with the past simple form of the verbs in brackets.

We ¹ ***didn't go*** (not go) anywhere on vacation last year, so in January my wife and I ² ***went*** (go) to Cancun, in Mexico, for a weekend. We ³................. (not take) our children. They ⁴................. (stay) with their grandparents. Cancun is really beautiful. Every day it ⁵................. (be) sunny and warm. It ⁶................. (not rain) at all! We ⁷................. (not do) any work at all! My wife ⁸................. (buy) some beautiful shoes but we ⁹................. (not get) anything for the children.
When we got back home, the children ¹⁰................. (not be very happy). They ¹¹................. (have) a great time with their grandparents and they ¹²................. (not want) to come home!

LISTENING

9 🔊 **4.5 Listen to three conversations about what people did at the weekend. Match the photos to the conversations.**

Conversation 1   photo [   ]
Conversation 2   photo [   ]
Conversation 3   photo [   ]

a

b

c

10 Listen again and circle the things each person did.

Conversation 1
Bella: had fish for dinner   got presents
         bought a new jacket   saw a film
Conversation 2
Claire: went to a museum   visited her sister
         saw her parents   went to a rock festival
Conversation 3
Rob: stayed in bed   left home at one
         took some photos   saw some of the match on TV

11 Listen again. Are the statements true or false? Circle T or F.

1 Bella's birthday was on Sunday.   T Ⓕ
2 Mark had pizza at the restaurant.   T F
3 Claire had a good time in Dublin.   T F
4 Claire saw Julie with a man.   T F
5 Rob left home at twelve.   T F
6 The ticket was expensive.   T F

VOCABULARY Going on holiday

1 Match the pictures to the words in the box.

boat	money	taxi	car
sightseeing	train	hotel	swimming

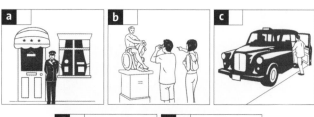
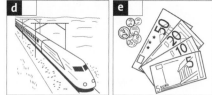

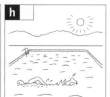

2 Cross out the word in each group which doesn't go with the verb.

1 fly   *Continental Airlines / to New York / sightseeing*
2 go   *out for dinner / a day in Rome / swimming*
3 rent   *a taxi / a flat / a boat*
4 stay   *with my parents / in a flat / to Tokyo*
5 spend   *the night in Paris / a hotel / all my money*
6 take   *with friends / the bus / a taxi*

3 Complete the sentences with the verbs in exercise 2.

1 I can't *fly* first class because it's too expensive!
2 Do you want to .... a day in Hong Kong?
3 We want to .... in this bed and breakfast. The owners are very friendly.
4 They love to .... sightseeing when they visit Rome.
5 We always .... a car when we go to Spain.
6 You can .... the train from London to Paris now.

Learner tip

When you learn new words, write them down with words they often go with. For example:

go shopping   *go to work*   *have a shower*

GO   HAVE

go to school   *have dinner*   *have a meeting*

DEVELOPING WRITING

Describing a holiday

4 Read the email quickly. Why is Ben writing to Laura?

1 To invite her to lunch.
2 To tell her about his holiday.
3 To invite her to go on holiday.

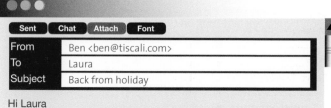

From   Ben <ben@tiscali.com>
To   Laura
Subject Back from holiday

Hi Laura

We got back from Rome this afternoon. We all had a great time. On Friday we went sightseeing. We saw the Spanish Steps and the Villa Borghese. It was really interesting.

The next day, we spent three hours walking around the Coliseum and the Forum. Then we went shopping in Via Condotti. In the evening, we had pizza in a little restaurant in Trastevere.

On Sunday we rented a car and we went along the Appian Way – the world's oldest motorway! I loved it, but Chloe didn't like it. It rained on the first day, but after that the weather was great.

I hope you and the family are well.

See you soon.

Love Ben

5 Read the email again. Match the two halves of the sentences.

1 We had   a three hours walking around
2 We went   b a great time
3 We saw   c a car
4 We spent   d was great
5 The weather   e sightseeing
6 We rented   f the Spanish Steps

6 Look at the postcard and the diary page and complete the email about a holiday.

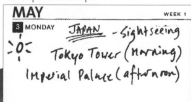

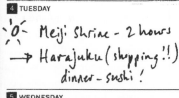

MAY   WEEK 1

3 MONDAY   JAPAN – Sightseeing
                Tokyo Tower (morning)
                Imperial Palace (afternoon)

4 TUESDAY   Meiji Shrine – 2 hours
                → Harajuku (shopping!!)
                dinner – sushi!

5 WEDNESDAY Tokyo Disneyland –
                by car!
                Sophie: ☺
                James: ☺

¹ *Hi* Evie

We got back from ² .... this morning. We ³ .... a great time! On Monday we went ⁴ .... We ⁵ .... Tokyo Tower (it's like the Eiffel Tower, but it's red!) and the Imperial Palace. It was really interesting.

The next day we spent ⁶ .... walking around the Meiji Shrine. Then we went shopping in Harajuku. We loved it! In the evening we ⁷ .... to a restaurant. We had ⁸ .... It was delicious!

On ⁹ .... we rented a ¹⁰ .... and went to Tokyo Disneyland. I enjoyed it but James didn't ¹¹ .... it. The weather was ¹² .... all the time – it was sunny every day!

I hope ¹³ .... and the family are well.

See you soon,

¹⁴ .... Sophie

GRAMMAR Past simple questions

7 Complete the questions.
1 Sean cooked lunch. Did Sean *cook lunch?*
2 We went to a concert. Did you .... ?
3 Paul was ill. Was .... ?
4 They watched TV. Did .... ?
5 Her earrings were expensive.
   Were .... ?
6 Brenda stayed in bed yesterday.
   Did .... ?

8 Change the words in bold to make correct questions.
1 **Are** you go on holiday anywhere?
   Did you go on holiday anywhere?
2 **Were** the food good?
   ....
3 How **did** your summer?
   ....
4 **Did** it very expensive?
   ....
5 Where **was** you stay?
   ....

9 Look at the answers and complete the questions.
1 Where .... ?   To Spain.
2 Who .... with?   Julian and Emma.
3 Was .... ?   Yes, it was sunny every day.
4 Were .... ?   Yes, they were all really friendly.
5 Did .... ?   Yes, we had a great time.
6 How long .... for?   For two weeks.

Vocabulary Builder Quiz 4

Download the Vocabulary Builder for Unit 4 and try the quiz below. Write your answers in your notebook. Then check them and record your score.

1 Complete the sentences with the words in the box.

clear	sunny	rainy	free	fun	warm

1 I've got some .... tickets for the music festival. Do you want to come?
2 Look at that .... sky! There isn't a single cloud.
3 It's a really .... day today. There isn't a cloud in the sky!
4 On a .... day I usually stay inside.
5 Wash your hands with soap and .... water.
6 London is a really .... city. There's so much to do.

2 Cross out the word in each group that doesn't collocate.
1 miss *a train / the bus / the start of the film / a taxi*
2 have *a picnic / fire / a cold / lunch*
3 rent *a bed and breakfast / a boat / a car / a flat*
4 go *sightseeing / to a festival / a taxi / on holiday*
5 stay *in a hotel / to Rome / in bed / at home*

3 Find words that are both verbs and nouns to complete the sentences.
1 In the mountains we get a lot of deep .... in the winter.
   When it started to .... , the children ran outside to play.
2 Did you enjoy your .... in Rome?
   They always .... at the same bed and breakfast.
3 We can .... about it now, but it wasn't very funny at the time.
   Did you have a good.................... last night?
4 Today there will be heavy .... in the north.
   I was at the beach when it started to .... heavily.

4 Complete the sentences with *a* or *the*.
1 Do you want to meet in .... usual place?
2 Greg's off work this week with .... bad cold.
3 It's a lovely day. Let's have .... picnic.
4 .... weather here is warm in July.
5 A rabbit makes .... nice pet.

5 Match the beginnings (1–5) to the endings (a–e).
1 We went   a about Ireland.
2 I celebrated   b to New York on Saturday.
3 They watched an   c fruit and vegetables every day.
   interesting documentary
4 It's important to eat   d my birthday with a big party.
5 We flew   e sightseeing every day on our holiday.

Score ____/25

Wait a couple of weeks and try the quiz again.
Compare your scores.

05 SHOPS

VOCABULARY
Describing what you want to buy

1.

green	yellow	short	square	wood	shirt
cake	jeans	round	cheese	plastic	fish
dress	leather	cotton	brown		

colour	material	clothes	food	shape
red	wool	jacket	fruit	long
white		shoes	meat	small

2. **Look at the pictures and complete the crossword.**

Across

3.   5.

4. 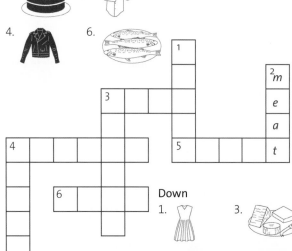   6.

Down
1.
2.
3.
4.

3. **Choose the correct words.**
   1 I wear blue *jeans* / *cake* and a T-shirt at work.
   2 Mozzarella is a soft Italian *fish* / *cheese*.
   3 She wears her black leather *jacket* / *meat* when she's on her motorcycle.
   4 Japanese 'sushi' is rice and *cheese* / *fish*.
   5 I don't eat *cake* / *meat* – I'm a vegetarian.
   6 For his birthday party we got him a chocolate *cake* / *dress*.

4. **Cross out the word that doesn't go with the others.**
   1 red   ~~meat~~   green
   2 short   shirt   shoes
   3 white   wool   wood
   4 cake   cotton   fruit
   5 yellow   square   round

GRAMMAR *this / that / these / those*

5. **Circle the correct word.**
   1 *This* / *These* dress is very comfortable.
   2 *This* / *These* jackets over here are from Poland.
   3 *This* / *These* was my grandfather's house.
   4 *This* / *These* shoes were very cheap.
   5 *This* / *These* shop sells fantastic clothes.
   6 *This* / *These* shirt is from Thailand.

6. **Complete the sentences with *that* or *those*.**
   1 I love .... shoes!
   2 Did you buy .... jacket today?
   3 I think .... jeans are too small for him.
   4 .... bananas are ready to eat now.
   5 Did you hear what .... man just said?
   6 Where did you get .... hat?

7. **Look at the pictures. Complete the sentences with *this*, *that*, *these* or *those*.**

   1 I paid €10 for .... shirt.
   2 Are .... shoes plastic?
   3 Excuse me. How much are .... ?
   4 Don't take .... bag – it's mine!
   5 Come and take a look at ....
   6 Is .... your bag?

LISTENING

8 🔊 **5.1 Listen to three conversations of people shopping. Match the pictures to the conversations.**

9 Listen again and tick (✓) the items they bought.

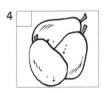

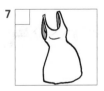

10 Listen again. Are the statements true or false? Circle T or F.

Conversation 1
1 The shoppers are American.   T   F
2 They spend €30.   T   F

Conversation 2
3 The man buys about eight bananas.   T   F
4 The mangos are 20 baht each.   T   F

Conversation 3
5 The woman pays the shopkeeper 3,200 rupees.   T   F
6 The woman is British.   T   F

DEVELOPING CONVERSATIONS
Questions in shops

> **Language note**
> --
> In informal spoken English, British pounds are often called *quid* (no *s*). American dollars are called *bucks*.
> *£20 = twenty quid*   *$20 = twenty bucks*

11 Read the conversation. Put the phrases in the box into the correct place.

Can I have some …	Anything else?
How much …	What are they made of?
How much are the …	How many …

Woman: Excuse me. [1] *How much are the* cakes?
Shopkeeper: These white ones?
Woman: No, those yellow ones.
Shopkeeper: These? Three for a quid.
Woman: [2] ....
Shopkeeper: Eggs, sugar and flour, of course.
Woman: Oh, OK.
Shopkeeper: [3] .... would you like?
Woman: Three, please.
Shopkeeper: [4] ....
Woman: [5] .... bread, please?
Shopkeeper: [6] .... would you like?
Woman: One loaf is fine.
Shopkeeper: That's two quid. Thanks, love.

12 🔊 **5.2 Listen and check your answers.**

PRONUNCIATION Numbers

13 🔊 **5.3 Listen to the numbers and circle the number you hear.**

1	13	30	3	316	360	5	2014	2040
2	115	150	4	590	519	6	14,000	40,000

> **Language note**
> --
> In American English, we say 150 like this: *one hundred fifty*. In British English, we say 150 like this: *one hundred and fifty*.

14 🔊 **5.4 Listen to the numbers and write *AE* or *BE* for the variation of English you hear.**

1	120	*AE*	3	214	....	5	1030	....
2	318	....	4	3060	....	6	9040	....

15 Listen again. Repeat the numbers.

GRAMMAR Present continuous

> **Learner tip**
>
> Use short forms (*I'm, you're, she's, it's, we're, they're*) as much as possible in conversation as this sounds much more natural. In written English, use short forms in emails or any other informal writing, but avoid using them in formal letters.

1 **Write the words in the correct order to make sentences. Then add the short form.**

1 are / sleeping / They
They are sleeping. They're sleeping.

2 is / shopping / the / He / doing
....

3 are / university / We / at / studying
....

4 watching / I / TV / am
....

5 working / are / You / hard
....

6 growing / She / fast / is
....

2 **Rewrite the sentences in exercise 1 as negative short forms.**

1 *They aren't sleeping.*

2 ....

3 ....

4 ....

5 ....

6 ....

3 **Complete the sentences using the verbs in brackets. Use short forms when appropriate.**

1 *We're having* a sale this week. (have)

2 Just a moment, please. I ....
to someone on the phone. (talk)

3 My sister and her boyfriend ....
with me at the moment. (stay)

4 Those shirts .... very well. (not sell)

5 He's in the living room. I think he
.... a film. (watch)

6 Your daughter .... very well
in English and Art. (do)

7 Ruby is happy because she ....
today. (not work)

8 Where .... you .... ? (go)

4 **Correct the sentences. There is one mistake in each sentence.**

1 We having a sale this week.
We're having a sale this week.

2 They's watching TV.
....

3 We're do well.
....

4 Are you studing at university?
....

5 How is you feeling today?
....

6 I working hard.
....

LISTENING

5 🔊 **5.5 Steve is following a customer. Why? Listen and tick (✓) the correct answer.**

1 He wants to sell him a shirt. [ ]

2 He thinks he's stealing from the shop. [ ]

3 He wants to show him to the fourth floor. [ ]

6 **Listen again. Which picture shows the man that Steve is describing?**

READING

7 **Read the magazine article and choose the best title.**

1 Department stores are too expensive   ....

2 Department stores – old and new   ....

3 The worst department store in the world   ....

Where can you buy anything, from cakes to coats? The answer, of course, is a department store.

The first department store was probably the Bon Marché in Paris. 'Bon Marché' means 'bargain' in French. It started in 1838 as a small shop where you could buy lots of different things in one place. This was **unusual** at that time. By 1852 it was a **successful** business and moved to a beautiful building which was designed by Gustave Eiffel. The store is still there today, and is doing very well.

One of the most famous department stores in the world is Harrods in London, which opened nearly 150 years ago. You can buy anything there, from dogs and cats to **gold bars**. Some people say it is expensive, but twice a year it has a sale when you can find some fantastic bargains. For many people, the food hall is the best department. It sells 300 cheeses and 50 different kinds of fresh fish. You can even buy a **wedding cake** for £2,000!

Online shopping is becoming more and more popular, and some people say that department stores are losing customers. But people in the city of Busan, South Korea, still like shopping in **real** shops, too. In 2009 the biggest department store in the world opened in Busan. It's called Shinsegae Centum City, and it has 14 floors and more than 6,000 people work there. There's a cinema, some restaurants, a gym, and even a garden. It really is a department store for the 21st century!

Glossary

unusual: something that does not happen often

successful: something that does well

gold bar: a heavy piece of precious yellow metal

wedding cake: a special cake that you eat when you get married

real: something that exists

8 **Try to complete the sentences with the numbers in the box. Don't look back at the article!**

300	2009	1852	14
nineteenth	1838		

1 The Bon Marché opened in *1838*.

2 In ...., Gustave Eiffel designed a new store for the Bon Marché.

3 Harrods opened in the .... century.

4 Harrods sells .... different cheeses.

5 Shinsegae Centum City opened in ....

6 The store at Shinsegae Centum City has .... floors.

9 **Now read the article again and check.**

10 **Choose the correct information.**

1 The original Bon Marché shop was in *Paris / London*.

2 When it opened, the Bon Marché sold *good value / expensive* things.

3 Harrods *sells / doesn't sell* animals.

4 The food hall in Harrods has a *small / large* choice of things to buy.

5 Shopping is *popular / unpopular* in South Korea.

6 6,000 people *visit Shinsegae Centum City every day / work at Shinsegae Centum City*.

DEVELOPING WRITING
Writing a postcard

1 Read the postcard quickly. Answer the questions.
1 Who is it to? Where is he/she?
2 Who is it from? Where is he/she?

Dear Brad

¹ We're having a great time here in New York. I'm writing this postcard from the Rainbow Room at the top of one of the city's tallest buildings. We're having a drink here in the café and looking at the Empire State Building. The view is amazing.

² There's a lot to do here. We're staying in a hotel near Central Park and can walk to most of the interesting places. Yesterday we visited the Museum of Modern Art. It was fun.

³ But the best thing about New York is the shopping. We went shopping yesterday in Barney's – it's a famous department store. I bought a T-shirt there. It was quite expensive, but I love it. Ann bought a bag. We got something for you too!

Love,
Suchart

⁴ 201-8 Udagawa Cho
Shibuya-ku
Tokyo 150-0042
Japan

2 Match the parts of the postcard (1–4) to the descriptions below.
a What they did yesterday and where they're staying ....2.........
b What shops they visited and what they bought ....
c The name and address of the person the postcard is for ....
d Where they are and what they're doing right now ....

3 Imagine you are on holiday. You are going to write a postcard. Circle the answers to the questions.
1 What sort of time are you having?
   great   good   not great   terrible
2 Where are you?
   Paris   Italy   Buenos Aires   Thailand
3 Where are you writing the postcard from?
   a café   the beach   the hotel   a restaurant
4 What are you doing right now?
   lying on the beach   eating dinner
   listening to music   having a drink
5 What are you looking at?
   the city   the sea   the mountains   the cathedral
6 Where are you staying?
   in a hotel   at a B&B   in a hostel   at a campsite
7 What did you visit yesterday?
   a museum   a castle
   an island   the beach
8 What did you buy?
   some souvenirs   a T-shirt
   some food   a bag

4 Use your answers to the questions in exercise 3 to complete your postcard. Don't forget to write the name of the person you're writing to, their address and your name in the correct places.

Dear ....

We're having a ¹ .... time here in
² .... I'm writing this postcard from
³ .... We're
⁴ .... and looking at
⁵ .... The view is amazing.

There's a lot to do here. We're staying ⁶ ....
and can walk to most of the interesting places. Yesterday
we visited ⁷ .... It was fun.

But the best thing about this place is the shopping! We
went shopping yesterday afternoon. I bought
⁸ .... We got something for you too!

Love

....

VOCABULARY Department stores

5 Choose the correct words.

1 You can buy a sweater for your father in the *sports /* (*menswear*) department.
2 A *shop assistant / security guard* stops people stealing things.
3 To get some perfume, visit the *womenswear section / beauty department*.
4 A *shop assistant / security guard* helps you find what you want in the shop.
5 The *sports / menswear* section is the place to go to buy football boots.
6 The *womenswear / menswear* section has some great new designer dresses.
7 You try on clothes before you buy them in the *changing rooms / beauty department*.

6 Match the letters from the store plan (a–h) with the words (1–8).

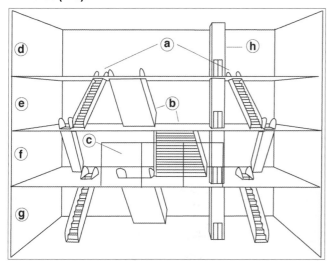

1	*stairs*	[*b*]	5	first floor	[ ]
2	lift	[ ]	6	main entrance	[ ]
3	escalator	[ ]	7	ground floor	[ ]
4	second floor	[ ]	8	basement	[ ]

7 Match the questions (1–6) to the answers (a–f).

1 Can I try these on? [*b*]
2 Can I pay here? [ ]
3 How do I get to the second floor? [ ]
4 Where's womenswear, please? [ ]
5 Do you sell books for children? [ ]
6 When does the sale end? [ ]

a It's on the fourth floor.
b Of course. The changing rooms are over there.
c Yes, there are some down there, on the bottom shelf.
d There's an escalator just here.
e Sorry, this till's closed. Could you use that one?
f On Saturday. There are some great bargains.

8 🔊 **5.6 Listen and check your answers.**

Vocabulary Builder Quiz 5

Download the Vocabulary Builder for Unit 5 and try the quiz below. Write your answers in your notebook. Then check them and record your score.

1 Find and complete the opposites of the words.

1 happy   un_____
2 bottom   t_____
3 up   d_____
4 go out   go _____

2 Cross out the word in each group that doesn't collocate.

1 a cup of *tea / coffee / cheese / milk*
2 a piece of *cheese / customer / cake / clothing*
3 a litre of *petrol / bananas / milk / water*
4 the top *floor / shelf / of the stairs / department*

3 Choose the correct word.

1 Jake always wears a smart wool *jumper / T-shirt*.
2 Those plates go on the *medium / bottom* shelf.
3 That's *an unusual / a main* dress! It's beautiful.
4 Lula always wears a black *leather / bottom* jacket.
5 They need to move offices because the business is *growing / going* fast.
6 My brother works in the *toy / escalator* section of the store.

4 Complete with the prepositions in the box.

for	in	of	on	up	by

1 I love this dress. I'm going to try it ....
2 This bag is made .... Italian leather.
3 Go .... the escalator to get to the shoe department. It's on the third floor.
4 Can we go .... through the main entrance?
5 We booked a meal .... two in a restaurant.
6 These shoes are reduced .... 50%.

5 Match the beginnings (1–5) to the endings (a–e).

1 I'll get in the queue   a opportunities for people who work hard.
2 The man stole   b of clothing into the changing rooms.
3 There are lots of   c the shop with her husband.
4 She manages   d some shoes from the shop.
5 You can take four items   e to pay for these jeans.

Score ___ /25

Wait a couple of weeks and try the quiz again. Compare your scores.

06 EDUCATION

VOCABULARY School and university

1 Unscramble the letters to find eight adjectives.

1 flirdeyn .... *friendly* ....
2 bogirn ....
3 pulapor ....
4 sagtren ....
5 lyaz ....
6 neci ....
7 hufpell ....
8 dcuffiilt ....

2 Put the words in exercise 1 in two columns: *positive* and *negative*.

positive	negative
............*friendly*............	....
....	....
....	....
....	....

> **Learner tip**
>
> When you learn new adjectives, write them with their opposites, or write whether they're positive or negative.

3 Choose the correct word.

1 All the teachers here are nice and (friendly)/ *lazy*.
2 I'm not enjoying my course. The work is really *nice / difficult*.
3 Mr King is very *popular / boring*. We all like him.
4 Tim didn't do very well in his exams because he was *lazy / nice*.
5 One student in my class is *helpful / strange*. He never speaks.

4 Cross out the word in each group which doesn't go.

1 a building can be: strange expensive helpful
2 a person can be: expensive popular patient
3 a course can be: difficult varied friendly
4 a teacher can be: varied helpful nice
5 work can be: boring lazy difficult

5 Complete the sentences with the words in the box.

expensive friendly modern patient popular varied

1 The course is very .... It's different every day.
2 My teacher is so .... She never gets angry.
3 They built the hospital in 2010. It's very....................
4 I can't study there because it's .... I don't have the money.
5 My classmates are all really nice. They're very ....
6 The university is very .... Everyone wants to come here.

6 Look at the pictures and complete the subjects with vowels (*a, e, i, o, u*).

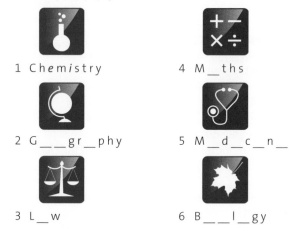

1 C h e m i s t r y
2 G _ _ _ g r _ _ p h y
3 L _ w
4 M _ _ t h s
5 M _ d _ _ c _ n _
6 B _ _ _ l _ g y

7 Match the subjects in the box with the definitions.

Engineering	History	IT
Literature	~~Marketing~~	PE

1 You study how to sell things. *Marketing*
2 You read books and talk about them. ....
3 You learn about computers. ....
4 You do sports. ....
5 You learn about making machines, roads and bridges. ....
6 You study about life in the past. ....

8 Cross out the word which doesn't belong in each group.

1 **Arts:** Literature History IT
2 **School subjects:** Maths Geography Medicine
3 **Sciences:** Literature Chemistry Biology

PRONUNCIATION *are*

9 🔊 6.1 Listen to the sentences. Write the missing words.

1 *How are* you?
2 .... working?
3 .... you studying?
4 What .... they in?
5 .... hungry?
6 .... you staying?

10 Listen again and repeat the sentences. In which of the sentences is *are* pronounced in weak form, with the schwa sound, /ə/?

DEVELOPING CONVERSATIONS

How's the course going?

11 Match the words in the box to their opposites. Which two words don't have opposites?

bad	boring	difficult	easy
friendly	good	interesting	nice

........*bad*............ ....

....

....

12 Rewrite the sentences with the words in brackets in the correct place.

1 It's interesting. (very)
   It's very interesting.
2 I like the teacher. (don't)
   ....
3 It's difficult. (quite)
   ....
4 She's very well. (not)
   ....
5 The other students are friendly. (really)
   ....
6 I did well in my exams. (very)
   ....

13 Choose the correct words to complete the dialogues.

Hassan: How's the course [1] *being / (going)*?
Brendan: Really well. I'm really [2] *like / enjoying* it.
Hassan: What's good about it?
Brendan: Well, the teacher is very [3] *good / well*. I really like her. And the other students are very friendly.
Hassan: Wow. It sounds great! Is there anything you don't [4] *like / liking*?
Brendan: No. I'm really happy!

Lucy: How's the course going?
Ahmed: Not [5] *really / very* well. It's really boring. And it's a lot of work.
Lucy: Oh, dear.
Ahmed: I think I chose the wrong [6] *subject / work*.
Lucy: Oh, no.
Ahmed: Yes. I don't really like chemistry. I'm not [7] *sure / interesting* it's what I want to do.

14 🔊 6.2 Listen and check your answers.

LISTENING

15 Match the questions (1–5) to the answers (a–e).

1 What do you do?   a My third.
2 What are you studying?   b Very well.
3 What year are you in?   c I'm a doctor.
4 How's the course going? d Yes, it's great.
5 Are you enjoying it?   e History.

16 🔊 6.3 Listen to Felix, Keiko and Luis talking about what they're studying. Circle the subject each person is studying.

1 **Felix**
English
Law
Engineering

2 **Keiko**
English
Law
Engineering

3 **Luis**
English
Law
Engineering

17 Listen again. Are the sentences true or false? Circle T or F.

1 Felix's course is going well.   T F
2 Felix's exams weren't difficult.   T F
3 The other students on Keiko's course are nice.   T F
4 Keiko's teachers are helpful.   T F
5 Luis's course is interesting.   (T) F
6 Luis is in the first year of the course.   T F

READING

1 Read the magazine article and tick (✓) the best title.

1 The oldest universities in the world   [   ]
2 Universities around the world   [   ]
3 The top five universities in the world   [   ]

University of Bologna, *Bologna, Italy*

The University of Bologna is older than Oxford, Cambridge or the Sorbonne in Paris. It first offered degree courses in 1088 and was the first place to be called a 'university'. Every year around 100,000 students pay €1,500 to study here.

Indira Gandhi National Open University, *Delhi, India*

The Indira Gandhi University is nearly thirty years old. It is bigger than any other university in the world. Every year it takes two and a half million **undergraduates** on courses from engineering and languages to law and art.

Harvard College, *Massachusetts, USA*

In 1636 nine undergraduates started their courses at Harvard. Today, it takes 18,000 undergraduates every year and many people think it's the best university in the world. It is older and richer – it is **worth** $22 billion – than any other university in the United States.

The University of the Faroe Islands, *Tórshavn, Faroe Islands*

With just 142 students, the university of this small group of islands between Scotland and Iceland is the smallest in the world. It opened in 1965 and now offers literature, science and technology classes, all in Faroese, the language of the islands

George Washington University, *Washington D.C., USA*

Private universities all over the world are more expensive than national universities. Aoyama Gakuin University in Japan **charges** some students $16,000 a year. But the most expensive universities in the world are American. Students at George Washington University, in the US capital, pay more than $40,000 a year..

Glossary

undergraduate: someone studying for a degree
worth: the value of something (in money)
charge: to ask someone to pay money for something you are selling

2 Match each university to its description.

1 The University of Bologna   a   is worth $22 billion.
2 Indira Gandhi University   b   has under 150 students.
3 Harvard College   c   charges around $40,000 a year.
4 The University of the Faroe Islands   d   opened in 1088.
5 George Washington University   e   is in India.

3 Read the article again and choose the correct answer.

1 The word *study / degree / university* originated at the university of Bologna.
2 Indira Gandhi University is almost *25 / 30 / 35* years old.
3 *1.5 / 2 / 2.5* million students enter Indira Gandhi University every year.
4 Harvard College opened its doors for the first time in *1965 / 1088 / 1636*.
5 Harvard takes *sixteen / eighteen / twenty-two* thousand undergraduates every year.
6 The Faroe Islands are between Scotland and *Ireland / Iceland / Greenland*.
7 The University of the Faroe Islands opened in *1965 / 1088 / 1636*.
8 The more expensive courses all over the world are in *national / foreign / private* universities.

VOCABULARY Courses

4 Match the verb groups (1–6) with nouns (a–f) to make phrases.

1 do / pay for / enjoy   a   help / advice / information
2 borrow / pay / cost   b   at six o'clock / in May
3 fail / have / pass   c   a course / a class
4 start / finish   d   2 hours / days / years
5 last   e   £10
6 give   f   an exam

5 Complete the text with the correct form of verbs from exercise 4. Verbs can be used more than once.

Last year I ¹*did* a Spanish class. The class ².................... at 6 and ³.................... at 8. It ⁴.................... 2 hours. The course ⁵.................... in May and ⁶.................... in October. It ⁷.................... six months The course ⁸.................... £1,000. I didn't have all the money, so I ⁹.................... £500 and I ¹⁰.................... the other £500 from my parents. I really ¹¹.................... the course but, at the end, we ¹².................... an exam. I didn't study much so I ¹³.................... it. My friend Daisy worked very hard and she ¹⁴.................... her exam.

6 Look at the text in exercise 5. Write questions.

1 *When did you do your Spanish course?*
   Last year.
2 ....
   In May.
3 ....
   In October.
4 ....
   Six months.
5 ....
   £1,000.
6 ....
   Yes, I did. At the end of the course.
7 ....
   No, I failed it.
8 ....
   Yes, I did. It was great!

GRAMMAR Modifiers

7 Put the modifiers in the box in the correct place in the chart.

not	really	quite	not very	very

✓✓	✓	✗	✗✗
very /	....	....	....

8 Write the words in the correct order to make sentences.

1 is / James / lazy. / quite
   James is quite lazy.
2 are / nice. / The / very / students / other
   ....
3 books / interesting. / really / These / are
   ....
4 friendly. / classmates / quite / are / My
   ....
5 very / My / expensive. / is / university
   ....
6 new / really / is / My / teacher / good.
   ....

9 Complete the sentences with the correct form of *be + not + very* + the adjective in brackets.

1 They *aren't very friendly*. They didn't say a word.   (friendly)
2 It .... Not many people like it.   (popular)
3 These shoes .... Buy them!   (expensive)
4 This party... We're leaving.   (good)
5 Those books .... Don't read them.   (interesting)
6 This exercise .... I can do it!   (difficult)

10 Replace the words in bold with a different word from the box.

quite	really	great	very

1 Lucia is **very** nice and friendly.   ....
2 The course isn't very varied. It's **a little** boring.   ....
3 This book is quite good, but it's not **fantastic**.   ....
4 Ms Blake is a **really** good teacher.   ....

GRAMMAR Comparatives

1 Complete the table.

	Adjective	Comparative
One syllable	.... tall	older .... bigger
-y → -ier	.... funny lazy	easier ....
more + adj	expensive .... creative	.... more interesting ....
irregular forms	.... bad	further better ....

2 Look at the information. Complete the sentences with comparatives from exercise 1.

		José	Pepe
1	Born	14/7/90	24/7/90
2	Height	1m 80cm	1m 85cm
3	Car value	€12,000	€11,000
4	English ability	***	*****
5	Distance from Madrid	140km	118km
6	Difficulty of job	*****	***

1 José is *older* than Pepe.
2 Pepe is .... than José.
3 José's car is .... than Pepe's.
4 Pepe's level of English is .... than José's.
5 José lives .... from Madrid than Pepe.
6 Pepe's job is .... than José's.

3 Look at the information in exercise 2 again. Complete the sentences. Use the comparatives in the box.

cheap	~~young~~	bad	difficult	short	near

1 Pepe is *younger* than José.
2 José is .... than Pepe.
3 Pepe's car is .... than José's.
4 José's level of English is .... than Pepe's.
5 Pepe lives .... to Madrid than José.
6 José's job is .... than Pepe's.

4 Complete the text using the comparative form of the adjectives in brackets.

> I am [1] .... (tall) than my sister and I am [2] .... (intelligent), too. The funny thing is that she is [3] .... (old) than me. But I have to say she is much [4] .... (good) at sports than me. She's a [5] .... (fast) runner and a [6] .... (high) jumper. I prefer studying to sports. I may be [7] .... (slow) than her and [8] .... (bad) at sport, but I think overall I'm [9] .... (creative) and [10] .... (interesting).

VOCABULARY Languages

Language note

The names of countries (*England*), the adjectives describing the people (*English*) and the language (*English*) always start with a capital letter.

5 Look at the countries and write the words for the languages people speak there.

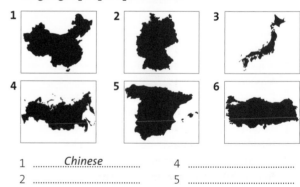

1 ....*Chinese*........   4 ....
2 ....   5 ....
3 ....   6 ....

6 Complete the sentences using some of the languages in exercise 5.

1 People in many South American countries speak *Spanish.*
2 Over one billion people speak ....
3 Many languages across Central Asia are very similar to ....
4 Many people in Ukraine and the Baltic States speak ....
5 .... writing uses many Chinese characters.
6 Mozart and Beethoven both spoke ....

DEVELOPING WRITING
Describing your favourite teacher

7 Read the text quickly. What did the writer think of:
1 the teacher?   2 the teacher's lessons?

Win a Holiday!

**Describe your favourite teacher
in no more than 80 words.**

The competition winner can choose one week in
TOKYO, NEW YORK OR PARIS!

1 My favourite teacher was Charlie Parker, my maths
teacher. I liked the subject but I was a lazy student.

2 He was a short man with brown hair and glasses.
He was very patient, which is why I liked him.

3 What made him a good teacher was that his
lessons were interesting and he was very creative.
The time always went by quickly in his classes.
I'll never forget Charlie Parker!

**8 You are going to write a short essay about your favourite
teacher. Underline or write the answers to the questions.**

1 What was the name of your favourite teacher?
   ....

2 What subject did he / she teach?
   ....

3 How did you feel about the subject?
   (I **loved   liked   didn't like   hated** it)

4 What sort of a student were you?
   good   average   bad   lazy

5 Describe your teacher's size:
   tall   short   big   small   medium-built

6 Describe your teacher's hair:
   brown   black   blond   fair   grey   no hair

7 Describe his / her personality:
   funny   friendly   sensitive   positive

8 Describe his / her lessons: **funny   interesting**

9 Describe him / her as a teacher: **funny   sensitive
   positive   fair   patient   creative   flexible**

**9 Use your answers from exercise 8 above to complete
your essay.**

My favourite teacher was called [1] .... He / She was
my [2] .... teacher. I [3] .... the subject and/but
I was a [4] .... student.

She / He was a [5] .... woman / man with [6] ....
hair. She / He was [7] ...., which is why I liked her/him.

What made her / him a good teacher was that her / his
lessons were [8] .... and she / he was very [9] ....
The time always went by quickly in her / his classes. I'll never
forget .... !

Vocabulary Builder Quiz 6

Download the Vocabulary Builder for Unit 6 and try the quiz
below. Write your answers in your notebook. Then check them
and record your score.

**1 Write the opposites of the adjectives, using the prefixes *im*
or *un*.**
1 patient   ....
2 popular   ....
3 important   ....
4 helpful   ....
5 friendly   ....

2 Cross out the word in each group which doesn't collocate.
1 modern   *university / fashion / decision*
2 helpful   *woman / advice / break / teacher*
3 popular   *teacher / problem / student / restaurant*
4 friendly   *man / skill / boss / teacher*
5 difficult   *subject / exam / decision / grade*
6 experienced   *person / teacher / half / artist*
7 patient   *trainer / boss / person / idea*
8 slow   *car / computer / grade / horse*

**3 Complete with the correct preposition or put – if no
preposition is needed.**
1 Good luck .... the exam!
2 I don't like speaking .... public.
3 We can prepare .... the talk at the weekend.
4 She is an inspiration .... many young women.
5 There have been a lot of changes .... my office.
6 I love riding .... my bike.

4 Match the beginnings (1–6) to the endings (a–f).
1 Your advice   a students are getting
                               higher grades.
2 She didn't prepare for   b about how to solve the
                               problem.
3 Much of the world's   c the exam.
4 New research shows that d problems with the
                               teacher.
5 One student experienced e population lives in
   a lot of   poverty.
6 He had some great ideas f was very useful.

Score ____ /25

**Wait a couple of weeks and try the quiz again.
Compare your scores.**

VOCABULARY Relationships

1 Complete the words for family names with *a, e, i, o* or *u*.

1 grandfather
2 gr__ndm__th__r
3 h__sb__nd
4 w__f__
5 s__n
6 d__ __ght__r
7 __ncl__
8 __ __nt
9 br__th__r
10 s__st__r
11 c__ __s__n

2 Look at the family tree. Complete the sentences with words from exercise 1.

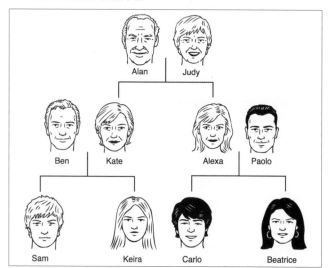

Alan Judy

Ben Kate Alexa Paolo

Sam Keira Carlo Beatrice

1 Alan is Keira's *grandfather*.
2 Alexa is Judy's ....
3 Ben is Carlo's ....
4 Paolo is Alexa's ....
5 Kate is Ben's... .
6 Alexa is Kate's ....
7 Beatrice is Sam's ....
8 Judy is Carlo's ....

3 Look at the family tree in exercise 2. Who is saying each of the sentences?

1 Sam is my brother. *Keira*
2 Carlo is my son and Alan is my dad. ....
3 Kate is our aunt. .... and ....
4 Keira is my daughter and Kate is my wife. ....
5 Paolo is our daughter's husband.
.... and ....
6 Keira is my sister. ....
7 Paolo is my sister's husband. ....
8 Beatrice is my daughter and Alexa is my wife. ....

GRAMMAR Auxiliary verbs

4 Write the words in the correct order to make questions.

1 you / swim? / Can
   Can you swim?
2 go / Did / yesterday? / you / out
   ....
3 married? / they / Are
   ....
4 you / me? / Can / hear
   ....
5 speak / Does / English? / she
   ....
6 Sue's / he / brother? / Is
   ....
7 a / Are / student? / you
   ....

5 Complete the answers to the questions in exercise 4.

1 Yes, I *can*.
2 No, we ....
3 Yes, they ....
4 No, I ....
5 Yes, she ....
6 No, he ....
7 Yes, I ....

6 Complete with the correct form of *do* or *be*.

1 *Do* you like classical music?
2 A: Are you from Japan?
   B: Yes, I ....
3 .... your parents visit you last weekend?
4 A: Your favourite subject is English. Right?
   B: Yes, it ....
5 .... it raining?
6 Where .... you born?
7 .... your brother speak English?

7 Look at the sentences. Are the bold words auxiliaries or main verbs?

	Main verb	Auxiliary verb
1 She **is** a nice woman.	✓	
2 What **do** you do?		
3 Do you **have** any brothers and sisters?		
4 I **do** my homework at the same time every day.		
5 **Are** you watching TV?		
6 What **did** he say to you?		

LISTENING

8 🔊 **7.1 Listen to two people having a conversation. What is the relationship between them?**
1 They are old friends.
2 They are classmates.
3 They are husband and wife.

9 Listen again. Choose the correct information.
1 Marco has two brothers and *a sister / two sisters / no sisters*.
2 Marco's *father / mother / brother* is a school teacher.
3 Marco can speak *three / four / five* languages.
4 Inge's father is *forty / forty-eight / fifty* years old.
5 Marco *lives / doesn't live / wants to live* with his parents.
6 Marco has a wife *and son / and daughter / but no children*.

10 Look at the answers and complete the questions from Marco and Inge's conversation. Listen again and check.
1 Do you have any brothers *or sisters*?
  Yes, I do.
2 Are .... in Italy?
  Yes, they are.
3 .... do you speak?
  Five.
4 What .... teach?
  Skiing.
5 .... are they?
  They're both forty.
6 .... with them?
  No, but we live in the same city.
7 .... OK?
  Oh, yes. Sure.

Learner tip

If you want to express surprise at what someone says, you can use auxiliary verb + pronoun (*Is it? / Are you?*) with rising intonation.

PRONUNCIATION Showing surprise

11 🔊 **7.2 Match a response to each statement. Listen and check.**
1 Sean and Caitlin can speak Mandarin Chinese.   a Are we?
2 We only paid €2 for this.   b Can they?
3 Look. It's snowing.   c Did you?
4 We are about thirty minutes late.   d Was she?
5 Fiona was off work all last week.   e Does he?
6 James has a Porsche and a Ferrari.   f Is it?

12 Listen again and repeat the responses.

DEVELOPING CONVERSATIONS
Adding information

Language note

- -

In the U.S. it's common for younger people to address older people as 'sir' or 'ma'am'.
Dormitory: (American English) a large building near a college or university where students live.
In British English people say a *hall of residence*.

13 Complete the conversation with the additional information in the box.

I want to work here in New York City.
It's our graduation party.
They live in Ohio.
I share an apartment with two other students.
I have a job at the Bank of America.
There's a party at our college.

Karl: So, Luke. Do your parents live here in New York?
Luke: No, sir. [1] ....
Karl: I see. So do you live in a college dormitory?
Luke: No, sir. [2] ....
Karl: Is that right? And tonight you want to take Britney there?
Luke: No, sir. [3] ....
Karl: Is there? And will there be any teachers at this party?
Luke: Oh, yes, sir. [4] ....
Karl: Is it? Good. And ... do you have plans to return to Ohio?
Luke: No, sir. [5] ....
Karl: Do you? And do you know exactly what you want to do?
Luke: Oh, yes, sir. [6] ....
Karl: Really? Son, I think it's time you started calling me Karl ...

14 🔊 **7.3 Listen and check your answers.**

VOCABULARY
Jobs and activities in the home

1 Cross out the noun or phrase in each group that doesn't collocate.

1	tell	*games* / jokes
2	do	the washing / a story at bedtime
3	pick up	the dishwasher / my son from school
4	feed	the dog / the light switch
5	read	games / a story at bedtime
6	empty	the dog / the dishwasher
7	repair	the light switch / the cat
8	sing	jokes / songs
9	look after	a story / my grandmother
10	play	games / my baby brother

2 Look at the pictures. Write an activity from exercise 1 under each picture.

....

....

....

....

....

3 Complete the text with verbs from exercise 1.

My little sister and I are very close. I usually ¹ *look after* her when our parents go out. She thinks I am the best. I make her laugh when I ² .... her jokes, and when it's time for bed I ³ .... her a story and sometimes I even ⁴ .... her a song. She is easy to please. At weekends we ⁵ .... games or go to a local farm and ⁶ .... the animals.

GRAMMAR *have to / don't have to*

4 Complete the table with *has to / have to / doesn't have to / don't have to*.

	necessary	not necessary
I You We They	*have to*	....
He She It	....	....

5 Complete the sentences with the phrases in exercise 4.
1 I work from Monday to Friday. I **don't have to** work at weekends.
2 Tell Molly she can go out but she .... be home by ten.
3 Aylin .... come with us, but she can if she wants.
4 You .... pay – it's free!
5 They .... work very hard. They don't have any free time.
6 A doctor .... study for many years before he or she can qualify.
7 Police and military officers .... wear a uniform.
8 Mark .... drive to work – he lives next door to his office.

6 Complete the second sentence so it means the same as the first.
1 It isn't necessary for you to go to school tomorrow.
   You don't have to go to school tomorrow.
2 It isn't necessary for me to get up early next week.
   .... get up early next week.
3 It is necessary for us to keep our room clean.
   .... keep our room clean.
4 It is necessary for Tim take his exam again.
   .... take his exam again.
5 It isn't necessary for Daisy to feed the dog today.
   .... feed the dog today.
6 It is necessary for Mia and Betty to look after Luisa this morning.
   .... look after Luisa this morning.

7 Correct the mistake in each sentence.
1 They haves to go to school on Saturdays.
   They have to go to school on Saturdays.
2 We doesn't have to do any homework tonight.
   ....
3 I has to see the doctor today.
   ....
4 I emptied the dishwasher, so John doesn't has to.
   ....
5 Toby don't have to go to work today.
   ....
6 A teacher have to work very hard.
   ....

READING

8 You are going to read an article that Paul and Martina wrote about two special people. Use the words in the box to write the name of the people they wrote about.

Paul ....

Martina ....

| best friend | grandfather | grandmother |
| oldest friend | sister | |

Special People

Paul

I met Liam at school. We were eleven, and we're 36 now, so that's twenty-five years ago. He really is my oldest friend. We didn't really know each other very well at first, but then when we were in our third year, we were both in the school football team, and we became friendly. Liam is a nice guy. He's very funny – he's always telling jokes – but he has a sensitive **side** too. And he's really reliable. When I got **divorced**, he phoned me every day for three months. But nowadays we don't see each other very much. We talk on the phone maybe once or twice a year, but we're both busy now, with work. And he got married a year ago. We don't see each other very often, maybe once a year. To tell the truth, I don't really like his wife, and I don't think she likes me.

He's always been a special person in my life. Well, not always, because he's not my **real** grandfather. He was my grandmother's second husband. He married her when I was ten years old. But when I was a child, when I was growing up, he was a very positive person, very strong. He was strict, too. When I was a teenager, he got angry with me when I stayed out late or was **rude** to my parents. My grandmother died a few years ago, and my grandfather was **lonely**, so he moved so he could be nearer to us. He lives just round the corner, but we speak most days on the phone. I like to check he's OK. I usually see him once or twice week. We go out to the park. He often looks after my daughter in the evening or at the weekend, too. He's very good with kids. He sings songs with her, and reads her bedtime stories, just like he did with me when I was young. I feel very happy that he lives so near and I can see him so often.

Martina

9 Read the texts again and write notes for each person.

	Paul	Martina
1 How did they meet?	....	....
2 What kind of person is he / she?	....	....
3 How often do they talk?	....	....
4 How often do they see each other?	....	....

Glossary

side: part
divorced: no longer married because your marriage has been legally ended
real: true, natural
rude: not polite
lonely: unhappy because you are not with other people

10 Are the sentences true or false? Circle T or F.

1	Paul and Liam met a long time ago.	Ⓣ F
2	Liam helped Paul when he had problems.	T F
3	Paul is good friends with Liam's wife.	T F
4	Martina's grandmother married twice.	T F
5	Martina's grandfather doesn't live very near.	T F
6	Martina gets on well with her grandfather.	T F

VOCABULARY Describing people

1 Find eight words in the wordsquare to describe people's characters. Look →, ↓ and ↘.

E	F	I	T	A	N	T	W	Q	H
U	T	D	K	S	A	O	T	U	W
O	C	N	O	T	Q	E	X	I	N
L	A	G	Y	R	M	R	R	E	I
C	O	N	F	I	D	E	N	T	J
L	P	U	L	C	B	L	R	L	R
E	U	L	D	T	R	H	N	I	G
V	O	F	U	N	N	Y	W	M	A
E	S	B	T	M	S	O	B	T	M
R	E	L	I	A	B	L	E	F	V

2 Match the adjectives in exercise 1 to the people they describe.

1 someone who has strong rules ..... *strict* .....
2 someone who makes you laugh or smile ....
3 someone who learns things quickly and well ....
4 someone who is sure they can do something well ....
5 someone who is healthy and strong ....
6 someone who talks a lot ....
7 someone who doesn't talk a lot ....
8 someone you can trust ....

3 Complete the sentences using the words in exercise 1.

1 Kevin really makes me laugh. He's very *funny*.
2 My parents are so .... They never let me stay out after 10 o'clock at night.
3 That woman didn't say a word at dinner. She's very ....
4 Jim will arrive on time. He's always ....
5 You did that crossword quickly. You're really ....
6 Louisa goes running every day. She's quite ....

LISTENING

4 🌀 **7.4** Listen to two people talking. They are discussing Jason, Luis and Kerry, who all had an interview for a job in an office. Underline the correct two adjectives or phrases about each person.

Jason: Spanish   confident   serious   funny
Luis: nice   loud   good experience
        speaks three languages
Kerry: clever   loud   no experience   quiet

5 Listen again. Who are the sentences about? Write *J* for Jason, *L* for Luis, and *K* for Kerry.

1 He / She studied IT. ..... *Luis* .....
2 He / She answered the questions well. ....
3 He / She told a joke in the interview. ....
4 He / She left university six months ago. ....
5 He / She didn't go to university. ....
6 He / She worked at Miller's. ....

6 Complete the summary with the words in the box.

confident	loud	nice
quiet	reliable	young

The woman liked Jason because he was
¹ *confident*. She thought Luis was nice, but maybe a bit
² .... She also liked Kerry and thought
she had a lot of good experience and would be
³ ....

The man thought Jason was too ⁴ ....
He liked Luis and thought he was a really
⁵ .... guy. He thought Kerry was clever,
but a bit too ⁶ ....

DEVELOPING WRITING
Describing a special person

Language note

We use *and* to join two pieces of information.
She's funny *and* confident.
We use *but* to contrast two different things.
She's quiet *but* confident.

7 Complete the sentences with *and* or *but*.

1 She likes coffee *and* tea.
2 I speak Spanish .... I don't speak French.
3 Jake is confident .... friendly.
4 The children can be difficult .... I love them.
5 Kathy's a quiet person .... she's really funny.
6 I have a job .... I go to work every day.

8 Look at the photo and text on Laura's blog. Answer the questions about the person Laura is describing.

1 Who is she?   *Amalia, Laura's sister*
2 Where does she live? ....
3 What does she do? ....
4 What adjectives describe her character? ....
5 What does Laura like about her? ....
6 How often does Laura see her? ....
7 What do they do together? ....

Blogspot

This is a photo of me with my sister, Amalia. She's a year older than me and she's at Copenhagen University now.

She's very clever and she's studying Medicine. Amalia's very confident and friendly. She's sometimes a bit loud but she really understands me too. She's really funny and she always makes me laugh.

We see each other once a month. She visits me at home. We like to go shopping and go to the cinema. We talk about our lives and our friends. I tell her everything! Amalia is my sister but she's also my best friend.

9 You are going to write about a special person. First answer the questions. Use the words in the box or your own ideas.

best friend	cousin	brother	sister
funny	confident	loud	quiet
reliable	every day	once a week	clever
go swimming	go for a drink	watch TV	talk

1 Who is he / she? ....
2 Where does he / she live? ....
3 What does he / she do? ....
4 What adjectives describe his / her character? ....
5 What do you like about him / her? ....
6 How often do you see him / her? ....
7 What do you do together? ....

10 Write about your special person. Use your answers to the questions in exercise 9 and the model text in exercise 8 to help you.

Vocabulary Builder Quiz 7

Download the Vocabulary Builder for Unit 7 and try the quiz below. Write your answers in your notebook. Then check them and record your score.

1 Complete the compound nouns.
1 My best.................. lives in the USA.
2 His grand.................. is a famous painter. She is still working now.
3 James met his new girl.................. at work.
4 I spent the whole weekend doing house.................. , but now it looks awful again.

2 Choose the correct word.
1 Do you get *in / on* well with your brothers?
2 We usually wake *up / after* at seven o'clock in the morning.
3 I can pick you *on / up* after work, if you like.
4 Could you look *on / after* the children on Tuesday evening?

3 Complete the sentences with words formed from the words in brackets.
1 He spoke .... in the interview.   (confident)
2 ...., we arrived at the station before the train left.   (luck)
3 Despite the .... weather, we had a great day at the beach.   (cloud)
4 I worked as a .... in a hotel last summer.   (clean)
5 He's very .... He never misses a single lesson.   (rely)
6 You don't need to pay to get a good ....   (educate)

4 Complete the sentences with the verbs in the box.

affect	feed	trust	make	repair	set

1 Do you think it's important to .... rules for children?
2 I don't .... you to drive my car.
3 Many people think that stress can .... your health.
4 Did you remember to .... the cats?
5 Do you think you can .... the car yourself?
6 Pete's really funny. He can always .... me laugh.

5 Match the beginnings (1–5) to the endings (a–e).
1 Can you help me empty   a to private school.
2 I stayed   b the kids to school?
3 What time do you take   c the dishwasher, please?
4 Do you want me to read   d in touch with Sandy after she moved.
5 They sent their kids   e a story?

Score ____ /25

Wait a couple of weeks and try the quiz again.
Compare your scores.

08 PLANS

VOCABULARY Common activities

1 Match the verbs (1–6) to the activities (a–f).

1 do
2 write
3 go
4 go for
5 have
6 play

a a walk
b home
c the shopping
d a meeting
e tennis
f an email

2 Write the activities in exercise 1 under the correct picture.

1 *have a meeting*

2 ....

3 ....

4 ....

5 ....

6 ....

3 Complete the sentences with the correct form of the verbs in the box.

do	get	go for	go to	~~have~~	play

1 What time do you want to *have* dinner?
2 We always .... baseball on Saturdays.
3 Did you .... your homework last night?
4 I don't want to drive. Can we .... a taxi?
5 I usually .... to the library on Friday evenings.
6 Did you .... a run at the weekend?

GRAMMAR *going to*

4 Choose the correct words.

1 I *going to* / *I'm going to* look for a bookshop in town.
2 We *'re going* / *'re going to* leave at 10 o'clock.
3 He *'s going to* / *going to* show me his new camera.
4 They *'re going to* / *'s going to* visit the cathedral.
5 Hurry up! You *'re going to be* / *'re going to* late.
6 Jen *'s going to* / *are going to* tell me about her new boyfriend.

5 Write sentences with the correct form of *be going to* and the prompts. Use contractions where appropriate.

1 I / write / a letter / to my sister
I'm going to write a letter to my sister.
2 we / go home / early / because we're tired
....
3 Tom / study / for the test / in his bedroom
....
4 you / meet / my new friends / at the party tonight
....
5 my parents / drive / to my house
....

6 Complete with the correct negative form of *be + going to* and the verbs in brackets. Use contractions.

1 Kerry *isn't going to come* to the party. (come)
2 I'm .... at home tonight. (stay)
3 They .... dinner there again. (have)
4 We .... out in the rain. (go)
5 It .... fun. (be)
6 You .... your work. (finish)

7 Complete the dialogue with the correct form of *be + going to* and the verbs in the box.

bring	be	have	need	see

Richard: Is it [1] *going to be* sunny at the weekend?
Jan: Yes, I think so. That's what I heard on the radio.
Richard: Good! Then we're [2] .... the party outside.
Jan: OK. But we're [3] .... some more chairs.
Richard: I'm [4] .... John later. I can ask him to bring some.
Jan: Good idea. [5] .... he .... some extra plates and glasses, too?
Richard: Yes, he is.

8 🔊 **8.1 Listen and check your answers.**

LISTENING

9 🔊 **8.2 Listen to the conversation. What are Katrina and Julia going to do on Saturday?**

> **Learner tip**
>
> People usually prefer to say, *I'm going* ... rather than *I'm going to go* ....
> Not repeating the verb *to go* is shorter and easier to say.
> For example: *I'm going to the shops* rather than *I'm going to go to the shops*.

10 Who said what? Write *K* for Katrina and *J* for Julia.

1 What are you doing tomorrow night? [*K*]
2 I can't. I'm going to meet some friends for dinner. [ ]
3 How about another time? [ ]
4 But I'm free on Saturday. [ ]
5 Do you want to meet at the station? [ ]
6 Oh, yes, please. [ ]

11 Listen again. Are the sentences true or false? Circle T or F.

1 Katrina is going to the cinema tomorrow night. T F
2 Katrina's going to the cinema alone. T F
3 Julia's going to have dinner with friends on Saturday night. T F
4 Julia's going to visit her parents on Sunday. T F
5 Katrina's going to get the nine thirty-seven train. T F
6 Katrina and Julia are going to drive to London. T F

PRONUNCIATION *going to*

> **Learner tip**
>
> We can say *gonna*. It isn't correct English to write *gonna* but some people do. Lots of pop songs use *gonna*. It's used in conversation with people we know well. With people we don't know well, we say *going to*.

12 🔊 **8.3 Listen and circle the word you hear: *gonna* or *going to*.**

1 So, are you going to cook dinner for me tonight? gonna going to
2 It's going to be so romantic! gonna going to
3 I'm not going to go to bed early! gonna going to
4 Are you going to do your homework now? gonna going to
5 Tonight we're going to watch football on TV. gonna going to
6 Is he going to clean his room? gonna going to

13 🔊 **8.4 Listen and repeat the sentences. Say *gonna*.**

1 It's gonna be great!
2 I'm gonna go now.
3 Are you gonna eat that?
4 We're gonna leave at eight.
5 They're gonna lose the match!

DEVELOPING CONVERSATIONS
Making suggestions

14 Write the words in the correct order to make questions.

1 see? / do / you / What / want / to
   What do you want to see?
2 o'clock? / seven / Michel's Café / at / How / about
   ....
3 tonight? / you / What / are / doing
   ....
4 for / to / Do / want / first? / go / a coffee / you
   ....
5 go / you / somewhere? / want / to / out / Do
   ....

15 Complete the conversation with the questions in exercise 14.

Lee: ᵃ*3*
Dagmara: Nothing. Why?
Lee: ᵇ...................
Dagmara: Yeah. We can go to the cinema in town.
Lee: Good idea. ᶜ...................
Dagmara: There's a new film with George Clooney. I love him. I think it starts at eight.
Lee: OK. ᵈ...................
Dagmara: That sounds great. Do you know a good place to meet?
Lee: ᵉ...................
Dagmara: Perfect. See you there!

16 🔊 **8.5 Listen and check your answers.**

VOCABULARY Life events and plans

1 Look at the pictures and complete the sentences using a verb from box A and a word from box B.

A	get (x2)	have	leave	move	start	stop	win

B	a baby	a business	divorced	home
	house	the lottery	married	working

1 Martha is going to .... very soon.

2 My friend Tina .... last year.

3 Sue and Phil are going to ....

4 Dan .... when he was eighteen.

5 We're going to .... next year.

6 Gina finally .... at the age of 80.

7 Ann and Ben .... recently.

8 I want to .... my own ....

1

2

3

4

5

6

7

8

2 Complete the text with phrases from exercise 1.

Troy Palmer ¹*left home* at sixteen. He was working as a mechanic when he met pet shop assistant Lou-Ann Campbell when he was seventeen. A year later Lou-Ann told Troy that she was going to ²............................. They weren't happy but decided to ³............................. anyway. Lou-Ann ⁴............................. at the pet shop, while Troy continued fixing cars. One day, Troy bought a ticket and ⁵............................. Their lives changed forever. They bought a bigger house and then an even bigger one. They ⁶............................. five or six times before they found a place they were happy in. Troy ⁷............................. his own car sales .... Everyone expected them to ⁸............................., but they didn't. Instead, they had five more children and lived happily together.

GRAMMAR *would like to* + verb

3 Complete the sentences with the correct form of *would like to* and the verb in brackets.

1	We*'d like to visit* Australia.	(visit)
2	I .... Russian.	(learn)
3	They .... money.	(save)
4	You .... own business.	(start)
5	I .... rich.	(be)
6	She .... a dog.	(have)

4 Rewrite the sentences in exercise 3 in the negative form.

1 *We wouldn't like to visit Australia.*

2 ....

3 ....

4 ....

5 ....

6 ....

5 Complete the sentences with the words in the box.

'd like	Do you like	doesn't like
like	Would you like	wouldn't like

1 I *like* swimming. I go every week.

2 They .... to start their own business, but it's difficult.

3 He .... his flat. He wants to move somewhere different.

4 .... football?

5 We .... to leave this city. We're really happy here.

6 .... to come with us next Saturday?

READING

6 Read the text. Where could you see this type of text? Tick (✓) the places.

1 On the internet   [   ]
2 In an email from a friend   [   ]
3 In a magazine   [   ]
4 In a novel   [   ]
5 In a newspaper   [   ]

7 Tick (✓) the correct answer.

According to the text ...	Aries	Taurus	Gemini	Cancer	Leo
1 ... whose week is going to start badly but end well?	....	....	....	....	....
2 ... whose week is going to start well but end badly?	....	....	....	....	....
3 ... who's going to start something new?	....	....	....	....	....
4 ... who isn't going to do much this week?	....	....	....	....	....
5 ... whose week is going to be successful?	....	....	....	....	....
6 ... which two signs may experience life changes this week?	....	....	....	....	....

8 Cover the text. Match the two halves of the extracts.

1 You don't want to see anyone this week,
2 But don't worry – everything's
3 Before then get out of the house, go for
4 And you can expect a friend to give you
5 Everything is fine at the start of the week
6 Take the right path and the events of

a but it isn't going to stay that way.
b this week could change your life.
c or do your homework, or feed the dog.
d going to be better by Friday.
e a walk in the park and stay positive!
f some good advice this week.

9 Read the text again and check your answers.

WEEKLY HOROSCOPES

 ARIES (March 21 – April 19)
You don't want to see anyone this week, or do your homework, or feed the dog. You don't want to do anything. Just stay in and watch an old film with just a big box of chocolates as company. So why don't you?

 TAURUS (April 20 – May 20)
You're up and down right now. One moment you're happy and the next you're sad. But don't worry – everything's going to be better by Friday. Some big changes are coming in your life. Before then, maybe you can get out of the house, go for a walk in the park and **stay** positive!

 GEMINI (May 21 – June 21)
This is going to be a great week for health, romance and business. Go for a run, do some shopping or have a romantic dinner with someone you like. You can't lose this week! A friend is going to give you some good advice this week – you need to listen carefully and take it.

 CANCER (June 22 – July 22)
Everything is fine at the start of the week but it isn't going to stay that way. Maybe you're going to have a fight with a close friend, or your partner. Do what you need to do before Wednesday because after then things are going to get difficult and stay that way until next week.

 LEO (July 23 – August 22)
Do you need to get fit? Or learn a language? This is a good time to start something new. You never know where it may take you or who you might meet. Take the right path and the **events** of this week could change your life.

> **Glossary**
>
> **stay:** not change, remain the same
> **events:** things that happen

VOCABULARY For and against

1 Cross out the word that doesn't collocate.

1 provide *help / crime / a service*
2 create *traffic problems / tax / jobs*
3 *save / lose / improve* money
4 cause *problems / crime / tourists*
5 make people *safety / richer / poorer*
6 *save / lose / attract* tourists
7 *cause / increase / reduce* tax
8 *be good / be nice / be bad* for the environment
9 cut *jobs / tax / help*

2 Complete the table with the phrases in exercise 1.

Positive actions	Negative actions
provide help	create traffic problems
provide a service	lose money
....	....
....	....
make people richer	....
....	lose tourists
....	be bad for the environment
cut / reduce tax	....

3 Complete the text with the words in the box.

lose	jobs	money	tax
cause	make	tourists	

Increase in tax for shops and hotels

The government is going to increase ¹ *tax* for shops and hotels. This is going to ² .... problems for people in this country and visitors to it. Businesses are going to cut ³ ...., which is going to ⁴ .... a lot of people poorer. We live in a beautiful, historic city which usually attracts ⁵ ...., but they aren't coming now, so we are all going to ⁶ .... money. Why didn't the government save ⁷ .... during the good times?

DEVELOPING WRITING
Giving opinions with reasons for and against

Language note

- -

We use *because* to answer the question *Why?*
She called the police **because** she heard a noise.
We use *so* to describe a result.
She heard a noise, **so** she called the police.

4 Complete the sentences with *because* or *so*.

1 I had a sandwich *because* I was hungry.
2 It's my birthday, ... we're going out for dinner.
3 I'm at work now, ... I can't speak to you.
4 I love her .... she's my sister.
5 It's going to save money, ... I'm for it.
6 I'm against it .... it's going to cause problems.

5 Read the text. Tick (✓) the items which they are going to build.

Swimming pool	....	Cinema	....
Department store	....	Shops	....
Car park	....	Community centre	....

LAMARSH COUNCIL AND McKINNON CONSTRUCTION

Lamarsh Council has approved a plan to build a shopping mall in the town centre.

In the mall there are going to be fifty shops, five restaurants, one large department store and a cinema. What do you think?

We would like to hear your opinions.

Please complete the form below.

✂- -

Reasons for a new shopping centre	It's going to create jobs. It's going to attract people to the area. It's going to make local people richer. It's going to be good for the environment.
Reasons against a new shopping centre	

Please return to Lamarsh Council, Town Hall, Main Street, Lamarsh

6 Read the reply above from one person. Is she for or against the shopping mall?

7 Here are some reasons for and against the shopping mall in exercise 5. Put them in the appropriate column.

> increase noise   make shopping easier
> reduce parking spaces in town   provide a service
> ~~increase crime~~   increase pollution
> attract people to the town   ~~create jobs~~
> increase business for local shops   it's bad for the environment

FOR	AGAINST
create jobs	*increase crime*
....	....
....	....
....	....
....	....
....	....
....	....

8 You are going to complete the form about the shopping mall. Give reasons why you are <u>for</u> or <u>against</u> it. Use the text in exercise 5 and the ideas in exercise 7, or your own ideas.

LAMARSH COUNCIL AND McKINNON CONSTRUCTION

Lamarsh Council has approved a plan to build a shopping mall in the town centre.

In the mall there are going to be fifty shops, five restaurants, one large department store and a cinema. What do you think?

We would like to hear your opinions.

Please complete the form below.

✂ -

Reasons for a new shopping centre	I think it's a good / bad idea because
	I also think ,
	so .
Reasons against a new shopping centre	Finally, I think ,
	so I am for / against this development.

Please return to Lamarsh Council, Town Hall, Main Street, Lamarsh

Vocabulary Builder Quiz 8

Download the Vocabulary Builder for Unit 8 and try the quiz below. Write your answers in your notebook. Then check them and record your score.

1 Match 1–6 with a–f to make compound nouns.
1 check-   a instrument
2 metro   b bike
3 motor   c mall
4 street   d line
5 musical   e light
6 shopping   f up

2 Cross out the word in each group that doesn't collocate.
1 romantic   *dinner / film / music / plan*
2 rich   *woman / competition / doctor / city*
3 serious   *problem / accident / man / date*
4 extra   *class / noise / money / care*
5 improved   *roads / airport / pollution / school*

3 Find words that are both verbs and nouns to complete the sentences.
1 I .... to live abroad after university.
   I'm not sure your .... will work.
2 The government's spending ....s will be serious.
   Shops usually .... their prices after Christmas.
3 We went for a long .... on Sunday morning.
   She wants to .... her own restaurant in the future.
4 I read about your amazing trip on your ....
   She'd like to .... about her experiences one day.

4 Match the verbs (1–6) to the nouns (a–f).
1 build   a round the world
2 grow   b your job
3 lose   c new roads
4 keep   f fit
5 run   d your own business
6 travel   e fruit

5 Complete the sentences with the words in the box.

abroad	divorced	library	lottery

1 Is there a .... in your town where you can borrow books?
2 They won a lot of money on the ....
3 My parents got .... last year.
4 My plan is to study ....

Wait a couple of weeks and try the quiz again. Compare your scores.

Score ___/25

09 EXPERIENCES

GRAMMAR Present perfect

1 Complete the table with the words in the box.

Have	Has	~~have~~	has	haven't	hasn't

	+	−	?
You We They	1 _have_ .... seen	2 .... seen	3 .... seen ?
He She It	4 .... seen	5 .... seen	6 .... seen ?

2 Write the words in the correct order to make two conversations.

Dialogue 1

1 A: been / Prague? / you / to / Have

....

2 B: haven't. / you? / No, / Have / I

....

3 A: but / go. / like / No, / to / I'd

....

Dialogue 2

4 C: seen / *Room*? / you / Have

....

5 D: have. / you? / Yes, / Have / we

....

6 C: it / No. / good? / Is

....

7 D: it's / amazing. / Yes,

....

Learner tip

We ask *Have you ever **been to** (New York)?* to find out about general experience, but when we want to know more details, we ask *When / Where did you **go**?*, not *When / Where did you **be**?*
I've been to (Rome) means *I went (to Rome at some point in my life)* and then I came back (home).

3 Complete the conversation with the words in the box.

go	been	went	see	seen	have	haven't

A: Have you ever [1] .... to Brazil?
B: Yes, I [2] .... And you?
A: No, I [3] ...., but I'd love to. Where did you [4] ....?
B: To Rio de Janeiro. We [5] .... there for the carnival.
A: How was it?
B: Fantastic. I've never [6] .... anything like it in my life!
A: And did you [7] .... the statue of Christ?
B: Yes, we did. And Sugarloaf Mountain. We loved Brazil!

4 Choose the correct words.

1 I *have / has* seen this film three times.
2 Eve and Oliver *have been / they been* to Mexico.
3 *Have / Has* Rafael seen *Ave Maria*?
4 Have *ever you / you ever* been to Berlin?
5 We *hasn't / haven't* been to Vietnam but we'd love to go.
6 Carla knows Italy very well but *she haven't / she hasn't* been to Croatia.

5 Look at the information and complete the sentences.

	Countries		Films	
	South Africa	Mexico	*Theeb*	*The Revenant*
John	✓	✗	✓	✗
Chloe	✓	✓	✗	✗
Sonia	✗	✗	✓	✓

1 John and Chloe *have been* to South Africa.
2 John and Sonia .... *Theeb*.
3 Sonia .... to South Africa.
4 John and Chloe .... *The Revenant*.
5 Chloe .... *Theeb*.
6 John and Sonia .... to Mexico.
7 Chloe .... to Mexico.
8 Sonia .... *The Revenant*.

6 Correct the mistake in each sentence.

1 I has been to Paris more than ten times.

....

2 You have ever been to New York?

....

3 Ella has seen never *Star Wars*.

....

4 When have you been to Poland?

....

5 Paul haven't been to Spain.

....

DEVELOPING CONVERSATIONS
Recommending

7 Which adjectives are positive and which are negative? Write + or –.
1 It's great! +
2 It was really embarrassing! ....
3 It's too expensive! ....
4 It was very exciting! ....
5 It's awful! ....
6 It's so relaxing! ....
7 It's amazing! ....
8 It's really boring! ....
9 It's beautiful! ....

8 Choose the correct words to complete the rules.
When you want to recommend something to someone, use ¹ *You should! / Don't!* and when you don't recommend it, use ² *You should! / Don't!*

9 Complete the conversation with *You should!* or *Don't!*
Didi: Do you know where you're going on holiday this summer?
Maya: I can't decide. I'm thinking of going to France.
Didi: ¹*You should!* It's a beautiful place. We're thinking of going to Venice.
Maya: ².. It's a beautiful place but there are too many people there in summer!
Didi: OK, we're also thinking of going to Miami.
Maya: ³.. We've been there lots of times. It's great! The weather is fantastic!
Didi: Have you? Oh yes, I thought we could go shopping there.
Maya: ⁴.. It's boring. The European styles are more interesting.
Didi: Oh, OK. So where do you want to go in France?
Maya: I thought I'd go to Paris.
Didi: ⁵.. It's full of tourists! Why don't you go south?
Maya: Yes, maybe. A friend of mine, Tina, told me I should go to Bordeaux.
Didi: ⁶.. It's so relaxing and the food is amazing! My friend, Carla, told me we should go to *Le Petit Chat* for a good meal in Miami.
Maya: ⁷..
Didi: Why this time?
Maya: It's awful! If you want a really good meal in Miami, go to *Gianni's*. It's a wonderful Italian restaurant.
Didi: Why don't I just go to Italy?
Maya: Oh, ⁸.. The Italians are so stylish and the shops are full of beautiful clothes!
Didi: But you just told me not to. Oh, forget it!

10 ⏺ 9.1 Listen and check your answers.

LISTENING

11 ⏺ 9.2 Listen and tick (✓) the places Veronica has been to.

St Catherine's Monastery

The Sphinx

The Valley of the Kings

12 Put a tick (✓) or a cross (✗) in each column. Then listen again and check your answers.

Who has ...	Veronica	Veronica's husband
1 been to Egypt before?	✗	....
2 been to Luxor?	....	....
3 seen the Sphinx?	....	....
4 been to St Catherine's?	....	....
5 been to the Red Sea?	....	....

13 Are the sentences true or false? Circle T or F.
1 When he was in Egypt before, Veronica's husband was in the south.   T   F
2 Veronica thought Luxor was romantic.   T   F
3 Veronica's husband was ill.   T   F
4 The trip to St Catherine's monastery was quick.   T   F
5 Veronica likes swimming but her husband doesn't.   T   F
6 Veronica's husband has a friend in Jordan.   T   F

VOCABULARY Problems

1 Match the verbs (1–7) to the phrases (a–g).

1	forget	a	your flight
2	make	b	your passport
3	miss	c	to lock the door
4	lose	d	ill
5	hurt	e	a mess
6	feel	f	the wrong turn
7	take	g	yourself

2 Cross out the word or phrase in each group that doesn't collocate.

1 It was very embarrassing. I forgot to *call him* / *his name* / *tell him you called*.
2 Mum was surprised that I didn't make *a noise* / *my homework* / *a mess* last night.
3 It took a long time to get home because I missed my *car* / *bus* / *train*.
4 Have you ever lost *your wallet* / *your sleep* / *your temper*?
5 Andy told me that you hurt *your hand* / *yourself* / *you*.
6 I didn't sleep very well and today I feel *worst* / *sick* / *ill*.
7 I knew I was in trouble when I took the wrong *road* / *idea* / *turn*.

3 Complete the sentences with phrases from exercise 1. Use the correct tense and change the person (*me/you/she*, etc.) where appropriate.

1 I *lost my passport* so I couldn't go travelling.
2 I drove past the station. I ....
   and ended up at the museum.
3 Harrison Ford crashed his plane and
   .... badly.
4 Someone stole my car because I
   ....
5 There was a delay on the road to the airport, so I
   ....
6 On the first day I ate something bad and I
   .... for the rest of the holiday.
7 I like everything neat and tidy so please don't
   ....

GRAMMAR Past participles

4 Complete the crossword with the verb in brackets in each sentence in the correct tense.

Across

1 When ***did*** you get here?   (do)
3 I .... my arm two years ago in a game
   of rugby.   (break)
4 She's never .... any James Bond films.   (see)
6 Has anyone ever .... anything from you?   (steal)
8 Have you ever .... down the stairs?   (fall)
9 My sister .... off her bicycle yesterday.   (fall)
11 I .... you in the library but I couldn't call
   out to you.   (see)

Down

1 Have you ever .... anything bad?   (do)
2 When I got married I was so happy I ....   (cry)
4 The police found the person who ....
   my bicycle.   (steal)
5 Have you ever .... a bone?   (break)
7 I .... a mistake in my homework.   (make)
10 Our team .... 1–0. We were all really sad. (lose)
12 My dad .... €100 on the lottery last
   Saturday.   (win)

READING

5 Read the text and match the photos (1–3) to the paragraphs (a–c) below.

 1    2    3

> **Learner tip**
>
> When you read and you see words you don't know, ask yourself if the word is a verb, noun or adjective. You can then try to work out its meaning by thinking about how it is used, and the context it is used in.

● ● ●

Special Days   'Special experiences for special people'

SPECIAL OFFERS
GIFT VOUCHERS

SPORT
ADVENTURE
FOOD
ART

Do you need an idea for a special present? What do you buy the person who's got everything? And what about you? Is there something you've always wanted to do? Why not **treat** a special person or yourself to a Special Days experience? We offer a number of different experiences, from sport to art, food and adventure. There's something for everyone. It's an experience you are never going to forget.

OUR MOST POPULAR EXPERIENCES

[a]   Have you ever dreamt of **floating** quietly in the air, looking up at the **clouds**? A flight in a hot-air balloon is relaxing and peaceful, and you get a great view of the beautiful countryside on this two-hour flight. Please note that balloon flights can only happen when the weather is good.

£180 for two people

[b]   Have you ever tried this? It's amazing! You jump off a crane 160 feet in the air. It's like falling, but you are **attached** to a strong **rope**. It's a bit scary, but very exciting! Please note that people with heart problems can't do bungee-jumping.

£45 per person

[c]   Have you ever eaten sushi and wanted to know how to make it yourself? Well, it looks difficult, but it's easier than you think. In this special four-hour class, you can learn how to make delicious, **healthy** sushi and take it home to enjoy. The course is run by a chef from *Hello Sushi* restaurant in London.

£79 per person

6 Match these statements from people (1–3) to the correct experience (a–c).

1 'Lovely. So relaxing. I'd like to do it again really soon.'
Mr Porter, Glasgow

2 'I learnt and took some home with me. A great day!'
Mary F, Windsor

3 'I did it with my friends. It was amazing watching them!'
Hannah, Cardiff

7 How much do you remember about the experiences? Answer the questions, then read about the experiences again and check your answers.

1 How long is the balloon flight?   ....*two hours*.........

2 What kind of weather do you need for the balloon flight?   ....

3 How high is the crane for the bungee-jump?   ....

4 How much does it cost for two people to do a bungee-jump?   ....

5 How long is the sushi-making class?   ....

6 Who runs the sushi-making course?   ....

8 Look back at these highlighted words in the text and try to work out what they mean. Answer the questions. Don't use a dictionary.

1 *treat* (verb)   Is this something you do every day, or just for special days?

2 *float* (verb)   Is this a slow, peaceful way of moving, or fast and loud?

3 *cloud* (noun)   Where can you usually see this? Above or below you?

4 *rope* (noun)   What is this used for?

5 *attached* (verb)   Give an example of two things that can be *attached* to each other.

6 *healthy* (adjective)   Is this something which makes you strong and well or weak and not well?

9 Match the words (1–6) in exercise 8 to these definitions.

a   move slowly in the air.   [   ]

b   do something special to make someone happy   [   ]

c   joined or fixed to something   [   ]

d   a white or grey shape in the sky which is made of drops of water   [   ]

e   describes something that keeps you well and not sick   [   ]

f   very strong, thick string   [   ]

VOCABULARY Describing experiences

1 **Find eight words in the wordsnake for describing experiences.**

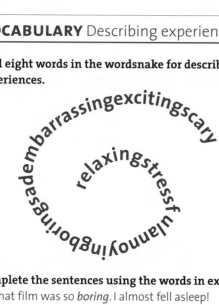

barrassingexcitingscary
relaxingstressf
embarrassingscary
boringannoyingful

2 **Complete the sentences using the words in exercise 1.**

1 That film was so *boring*. I almost fell asleep!
2 It was very .... when I dropped my coffee. I felt really stupid.
3 Work was really .... this week. I had a lot to do and no time.
4 Their holiday was very .... They came back feeling really calm.
5 That big dog looks .... I don't want to go near it.
6 Our plane was late and we waited in the airport for two hours. It was really ....
7 I was really .... when my friends left after their trip. I cried.
8 It was very .... to see George Clooney in the street.

PRONUNCIATION Joining words together

3 🔊 **9.3 Listen and mark the words which are joined together.**

1 The train is cheaper.
2 We love it!
3 She arrived two weeks ago.
4 We slept in a tent.
5 It was a great experience.
6 He fell and broke his arm.

4 **Listen and repeat the sentences. Join the words together.**

DEVELOPING WRITING
Describing an experience

> **Language note**
> --
> We can use a variety of adjectives in our writing to make it more interesting.

5 **Replace the word *nice* in the sentences with adjectives in the box.**

beautiful	~~delicious~~	interesting
relaxing	friendly	

1 This food is nice. Can I have some more, please?   *delicious*
2 This book is nice. I wanted to read it all night.   ....
3 My holiday was nice. I feel very calm.   ....
4 Your brother is nice. He talked to me a lot.   ....
5 Your shoes are nice. Were they very expensive?   ....

6 **Read the text and answer the questions.**
1 Who did the writer see?
....
2 What was the weather like?
....
3 How did the writer feel when the band came on stage?
....

> **The best day of my life**
> 1 Have you ever seen Coldplay? Last year I saw them for the first time. I went with my friend, Adriana. We paid over $300 for our tickets.
>
> 2 The concert was in a big park outside the city. It was a hot, sunny day and there were a lot of people there. They played all my favourite songs and I danced all evening.
>
> 3 The concert was fantastic! It was a dream come true because I've always wanted to see Coldplay. When the band came out on to the stage, I was so happy I couldn't speak. It was one of the best experiences of my life!

7 **Read the text again and number the paragraphs in the correct order.**
a The writer's feelings about the experience   [ ]
b An introduction to the experience   [ ]
What was the experience? Who was the writer with?
c A more detailed description of the experience   [ ]
Where was it? What happened before and during the experience? What did the writer do?

8 You are going to write three paragraphs about a good or bad experience you have had. First plan your paragraphs. Answer these questions using the ideas below, or your own ideas.

1 An introduction to the experience.
   • *What was the experience?*
   • *Who were you with?*

> climb a mountain   break a bone   go to a country
>
> go on a long journey   see something / someone famous
>
> visit a city   lose something important

2 A more detailed description of the experience.
   • *Where was it?*
   • *What happened before and during the experience?*
   • *What did you do?*

> the weather: hot / sunny / snowy / cold
>
> I cried.
>
> I shouted.   I laughed.

3 Your feelings about the experience.

> It was scary / sad / annoying / stressful.
>
> It was exciting / great / wonderful.
>
> It was the best / worst experience of my life.
>
> It was the most interesting / the most boring experience
> of my life.

9 Write three paragraphs about your experience in your notebook. Use the notes you made in exercise 8 and the model text in exercise 6 to help you. Use a variety of adjectives.

Vocabulary Builder Quiz 9

Download the Vocabulary Builder for Unit 9 and try the quiz below. Write your answers in your notebook. Then check them and record your score.

1   Complete the verbs in the sentences.
1 I always m.................. a mess when I'm cooking.
2 How many bags have you got to c.................. in?
3 I have to g.................. a speech at my sister's wedding.
4 Dad's hurt! We should c.................. an ambulance.
5 Are you sure we didn't t.................. the wrong train?
6 Be careful you don't l.................. your passport or you won't be able to fly.
7 I f.................. ill and I don't want to go out tonight.

2   Complete with the prepositions.
1 What time does your flight arrive .... New York?
2 My grandfather fell .... while he was walking along the road.
3 The cup fell .... the floor and broke.
4 Did you go .... the Eiffel Tower in Paris?
5 Have you ever been .... a helicopter?
6 I'm a big fan .... *Game of Thrones*.
7 There was a lot of traffic .... the motorway.

3   Complete the sentences with the words in the box.

> cooler   embarrassing   happen   check   sad   stressful

1 I find travelling quite .... There are so many things to remember!
2 I felt .... when my old cat died.
3 When did it ....?
4 It was really .... when I fell off my chair.
5 We're lost. Let's .... the map.
6 If you need some water, there's some in the ....

4   Match the beginnings (1–5) to the endings (a–e).
1 We went on a very exciting   a the zoo.
2 Every room has a view   b ride at the theme park.
3 The king used to live in   c when he hurt himself.
4 You can see lions at   d this palace.
5 The boy started crying   e of the beach.

Score ____ /25

**Wait a couple of weeks and try the quiz again.
Compare your scores**

VOCABULARY Trains and stations

1 Match the verbs (1–6) to the nouns (a–f) to make phrases.

1 buy
2 get
3 pay
4 cause
5 get off
6 change

a at the stop
b in cash
c a delay
d a ticket
e in Lille
f a discount

2 Complete the conversations with the words in the box.

cash	delay	direct	line	platform
return	single	second class		

1 A: Yes, I'd like a ticket to London, please. For today.
  B: ¹ *Single*?
  A: No, ² ...., please. I'm coming back on Thursday.
  B: OK. First or ³ ....?
  A: Second is fine.

2 A: That's £62.70, please. How would you like to pay?
    By ⁴ .... or card?
  B: Is Visa OK?
  A: Of course. Just enter your PIN here, please. Thank you.
  B: Which ⁵ .... is it?
  A: Number 3.
  B: Is it a ⁶ .... train?
  A: No, you have to change at Crewe.

3 A: You're late!
  B: I know. I'm really sorry. There was a ⁷ ....
  A: What happened?
  B: We stopped for nearly forty minutes. There was a cow
    on the ⁸ ....
  A: Oh, no.

3 ✪ 10.1 Listen and check your answers.

DEVELOPING CONVERSATIONS
Telling the time

Learner tip

We say *quarter past* (nine), *half past* (nine) and *quarter to* (nine), not *fifteen past* (nine), *thirty past* (nine) or *fifteen to* (nine). But we can say *nine fifteen* or *nine thirty*.

4 Look at the pictures and complete the times with the words in the box.

fifteen	half	o'clock	past	quarter
ten	thirty	thirty-five		

1 ten *thirty*
2 seven ....
3 four ....
4 .... to eight
5 six ....
6 .... to two
7 .... past nine
8 five .... eleven

5 Write the times in a different way.

1 quarter past five .... *five fifteen* ....
2 twenty past eleven ....
3 five forty-five ....
4 half past one ....
5 twenty-five past six ....
6 quarter to three ....

PRONUNCIATION *to*

6 ✪ 10.2 Listen and underline the phrase you hear, a or b.

1 a It's quarter to five.   b It's quarter past five.
2 a Ten to two.   b Ten past two.
3 a At twenty-five to four.   b At twenty-five past four.
4 a Quarter to nine.   b Quarter past nine.
5 a Five to eleven.   b Five past eleven.
6 a Come at five to nine.   b Come after five to nine.

7 Listen again and repeat the phrases.

LISTENING

8 🔊 **10.3 Listen to three conversations about travel. Match the pictures (a–c) to the conversations (1–3).**

Conversation 1   picture [   ]
Conversation 2   picture [   ]
Conversation 3   picture [   ]

a

b

c

9 Listen again and choose the correct information.

Conversation 1
1   The woman wants to go to the *station* / *city centre*.
2   The *bus* / *train* station is the next stop.

Conversation 2
3   They *have to* / *don't have to* change trains at the next station.
4   They *know* / *don't know* which platform they arrive at.

Conversation 3
5   The man *is* / *isn't* going to come back today.
6   He gets *15%* / *50%* off his ticket.

10 What do you remember about the conversations? Match the sentence beginnings (1–6) to the endings (a–f).

1   Which stop do I get off at   ....*c*........
2   Do you mean the bus station   ....
3   We have to change   ....
4   I don't know. Two   ....
5   Yes, I'd like a ticket   ....
6   Yes, you can buy a student card   ....

a   or maybe three.
b   for £15.00 and then you get 50% off.
c   for the station?
d   at the next station.
e   or the train station?
f   to Preston, please.

11 🔊 **10.4 Listen and check your answers.**

VOCABULARY Transport

1 Look at the pictures and complete the words with the missing vowels (*a, e, i, o, u*).

1 p l a n e
2 t r _ _ n
3 b _ s
4 b _ _ k _ _
5 t _ x _
6 c _ _ r

2 Choose the correct word.
1 He's a (taxi) / bike driver.
2 The car / plane broke down.
3 Is this the number 88 train / bus?
4 Hurry up! You're going to miss your train / bike!
5 I like to ride my car / bike to work.
6 Oh, no! The flight to Miami is delayed / missed.

3 Complete the sentences with the verbs in the box.

| book   lock   ~~park~~   pay   pick   run   stop   wait |

1 I always *park* my car outside my house. It's safe there.
2 Don't forget to .... your bike. You don't want someone to steal it.
3 Can you .... Robbie up from the train station?
4 Does the number 36 bus .... all night?
5 Can you .... the taxi driver? I forgot my money.
6 Did Rachel .... her flight on the internet?
7 How long did you .... for the bus? Was it very late?
8 Can we .... that taxi? I don't want to walk home.

4 Complete the text with the words in the box.

| station   catch   charge   get   number |
| run all night   ~~buses~~   taxis |

Transport in my city is OK. There isn't an underground system, but the ¹ *buses* are really good. The ² .... 3 bus goes into the centre of town from outside my flat. The only problem is that they don't ³ .... So if you're out late, you have to ⁴ .... a taxi. The official ⁵ .... are yellow. They're good because you know the driver can't ⁶ .... you too much. The trains are good too. You can ⁷ .... a train from the ⁸ .... and be in London in thirty minutes.

GRAMMAR *too much, too many* and *not enough*

5 Rewrite the sentences using the words in brackets.
1 He's driving fast. (too)
   He's driving too fast.
2 This bag isn't cheap for me. (enough)
   ....
3 It's early to go. (too)
   ....
4 This film is long. (too)
   ....
5 I can't buy it. I haven't got money. (enough)
   ....
6 You aren't walking fast. Hurry up! (enough)
   ....

6 Put the words in the box in the correct column.

| accidents   buses   crime   drivers |
| people   pollution   traffic   water |

countable	uncountable
.......*accidents*.......	....
....	....
....	....
....	....

7 Complete the sentences with *much, many* or *enough*.
1 There are *too many* people on this bus!
2 I didn't put .... sugar in my coffee. It's horrible.
3 You haven't given me .... money. There's only six euros here.
4 I have .... things to do today.
5 Do you think there's .... traffic on the roads?
6 There is too .... pollution in this city.

8 Read the text and choose the correct words.

Cycling in our cities is becoming ¹ *not enough / too much / (too)* dangerous. The problem is that there is just ² *too much / too many / not enough* traffic on the roads and there are ³ *n't enough / too much / too many* cycle lanes. Another problem is that car drivers don't pay ⁴ *too many / too much / enough* attention. They need to drive more carefully. And they drive ⁵ *too / too much / not enough* fast. ⁶ *Too much / Too many / Not enough* accidents involve bikes. The government needs to do something about it.

READING

9 Read about the three journeys. Which journey takes the longest?

10 Match the two halves of the sentences. Then read about the journeys again and check your answers.

1 Machu Picchu is also
2 Cuzco was
3 The Ottoman Express is
4 The Ottoman Express travels
5 The Terracotta Warriors are
6 The Silk Road was

a gold and blue.
b two thousand years old.
c a trade route to the West.
d the capital city of the Inca Empire.
e called The Lost City of the Incas.
f through seven countries.

11 Choose the correct answer.

Journey 1
1 The train climbs to *3,000m / 4,000m* between Cuzco and Puno.
2 The city of Puno is *on Lake Titicaca / high in the Andes.*

Journey 2
3 On the first day, the Ottoman Express goes through *two / three* countries.
4 Peleș Castle is in *Romania / Bulgaria.*

Journey 3
5 The train leaves Beijing in the *morning / evening.*
6 Xinjiang province is in the *east / west* of China.

Great train journeys

Andes Experience

The **journey** starts with a trip to Machu Picchu. On the way you stop in some beautiful villages. You can do some shopping there before you continue to Machu Picchu, the Lost City of the Incas, high in the Andes. You have four hours to enjoy the views and then you carry on to Cuzco, the **ancient** capital of the Inca Empire. On day two you **set off** early. As the train climbs slowly to 4,000m, you can relax in your armchair and enjoy the beautiful scenery of the Andes. After a short stop in La Raya, it's time for lunch. You arrive in Puno, the end of your journey, on Lake Titicaca, at around 6pm.

Trans-European luxury

The adventure starts as you arrive at the platform in Paris and see the gold and blue of the Ottoman Express. On the train, your **steward** shows you to your **compartment**, where you can rest while you travel through France, Germany and Austria. At breakfast the next morning, enjoy the scenery as your train enters Hungary and arrives in Budapest. On day three, you can enjoy the sights of the city and the beautiful River Danube, before you travel overnight into Romania. On day four, there's a trip to Peleș Castle. After a night in the Romanian capital, Bucharest, you travel through the beautiful scenery of Bulgaria, and cross into Turkey on the morning of day six. Arrival in Istanbul in the afternoon ends a six-day adventure across seven countries.

Silk Road

Before your evening departure from Beijing, you can enjoy a sight-seeing tour of the city, including the Temple of Heaven and the Forbidden City. You arrive in the ancient city of Xi'an, in central China, the next morning, where you can visit the 2,000-year-old Terracotta Warriors. Then the journey continues northwest, following the Silk Road, the ancient **trade** route leading to the West. From day eight to day fourteen, the tour explores Xinjiang province in the west of China. Sights include visits to the Mogao Caves and the Jiaohe Ruins. A flight back to the capital completes the tour of a lifetime.

Glossary

journey: an occasion when you travel from one place to another
ancient: very old
set off: to start a journey
steward: a waiter on a plane, train or boat
compartment: one of the separate spaces into which a railway carriage is divided
trade: the act of buying or selling goods

DEVELOPING CONVERSATIONS
Where's the best place?

1 Look at the words and phrases in the box and answer the questions.

1 Which word combines with *change*? ....
2 Which two words are verbs? .... and ....
3 Which three words combine with *go* to make leisure activities? .... , ... and ....
4 Which two words or phrases combine with *get* to make things you receive? .... and ....

| money | dancing | a haircut | stay | some exercise |
| eat | cycling | shopping | | |

2 Ewa is going to live with Liam and his family for a short time. Read the conversation and complete it with the words and phrases from exercise 1.

Liam: Welcome, Ewa. It's great you're going to ¹ *stay* with us for a few weeks. Is there anything you would like to know?

Ewa: Thank you. Yes, I have some questions. Where is the best place to ² .... ?

Liam: Well, the post office opposite here probably gives the best rate.

Ewa: Oh, great. And where's the best place to ³ .... ?

Liam: Try Baxter's Gym. It's good – with a great pool – but it's a bit expensive. Oh, and if you want to ⁴ .... there are lots of bike lanes.

Ewa: Thanks. That sounds really good.

Liam: And you can use our mountain bikes any time.

Ewa: Fantastic! Thanks. Oh, and where's the best place to ⁵ .... ?

Liam: In this house, of course! But in town try 'Bon Appétit'. The food is good there and so is the atmosphere.

Ewa: Great! I'm going to try it. And where's the best place to ⁶ .... ?

Liam: Hm, what sorts of things do you like buying?

Ewa: Clothes, maybe.

Liam: Right. Try 'Up Market', in the city centre. They have a great selection of different clothes there. And if you want to ⁷ ...., they have a good salon upstairs. Our daughter Sonia goes a lot. She comes back with a different style every time!

Ewa: Fantastic. Thank you very much. I have just one more question. Where's the best place to ⁸ .... ?

Liam: No idea, but you can ask Sonia. She knows where all the good clubs are. Sonia!

3 🔊 **10.5** Listen and check your answers.

GRAMMAR Superlatives

4 Complete the table.

	Adjective	Superlative
short adj.	....	the cheapest the hottest
-y → the -iest	.... dry	the easiest ....
the most + adj	expensive	.... the most interesting
irregular	.... bad	the best ....

5 Look at the information. Complete the sentences with superlatives from exercise 4.

1
> Death Valley, California 56.5°C
> El Azizia, Libya 58°C
> Oodnadatta, South Australia 50.7°C

El Azizia is .... place in the world.

2
> Sahara Desert 10 cm rain per year
> Atacama Desert .01 cm rain per year
> Mohave Desert 25 cm rain per year

The Atacama Desert is .... place on earth.

3
> Chery QQ £3,308
> Suzuki Maruti £3,455
> Tata Nano £2,115

The Tata Nano is .... car in the world.

4
> Azeda Beach, Brazil ☆☆☆ ☺
> Kapalua Beach, Maui ☆☆☆☆☆ ☺
> Cooden Beach, UK ☆ ☹

Kapalua Beach is .... beach in the world.

5
> cheetah 112 km/h
> antelope 98 km/h
> lion 80 km/h

The cheetah is .... animal on earth.

6 Make sentences from the prompts. Use the superlative form of each adjective.

1 The sloth is / slow / animal on earth.
The sloth is *the slowest animal on earth.*
2 Eddie 'The Eagle' Edwards was / bad / Olympic athlete of all time.
Eddie 'The Eagle' Edwards was ....
3 Vostok Station, Antarctica, is / cold / place on earth.
Vostok Station, Antarctica, is ....
4 The Bugatti Chiron is / expensive / car in the world.
The Bugatti Chiron is ....
5 Mawsynram, India, is / wet / place on earth.
Mawsynram, India, is ....

DEVELOPING WRITING
Building a text from notes

7 Read the email. Underline the answers to the questions below and number them 1–5.

```
○ ○ ○
[Sent] [Chat] [Attach] [Font]
From    calum.johnson@blueriver.co.uk
To      andrew@tiger.com
Subject Visiting London
```

Hi Andy

I'm really happy you're coming to stay. The first thing to tell you is how to find this place. [1] It's easy! Get off the coach at the Hilton Hotel, call Sarah and wait. She is going to pick you up from there. We're not very far from the city centre. It takes under half an hour to get to Oxford Street. Get the underground from Shepherds Bush.

Oxford Street and Regent Street are great places to go shopping. And go to Soho for lunch. Try Caldo – it does great food and there's a lovely atmosphere. There are lots of great little restaurants in Soho.

All the best
Calum

---

1 How do I get to your flat?
2 Do you live near the city centre?
3 How do I get to the city centre from your flat?
4 Where's the best place to go shopping?
5 Where's the best place to eat?

---

8 A friend is coming to stay with you.
Write notes to answer the questions in exercise 7.

station → 7C bus → walk → here
15 minutes from centre by bus

....
....
....

9 Write an email to a friend who is coming to stay. Tell your friend how to get to your place and recommend some things for your friend to do in your city. Use the notes you made in exercise 8 and any of the phrases below to help you.
- From the train station, get the 7C bus … / walk down the street to …
- Our house / flat is quite near / isn't near the city centre …
- From here, walk down the road … / get the 14 bus / take the underground …
- Try Harrods / Fanucci's / Carl's Gym – it's a great / the best / place for …
- The area is very safe / quite dangerous so don't worry / be careful …

Vocabulary Builder Quiz 10

Download the Vocabulary Builder for Unit 10 and try the quiz below. Write your answers in your notebook. Then check them and record your score.

1 Cross out the word in each group that doesn't collocate
1 catch   *the bus / a flight / home / my train*
2 taste   *delicious / like fish / well / horrible*
3 get off   *the train / a bus / a plane / a car*
4 lock   *the journey / your bike / a door / the car*
5 book   *a flight / some cash / online / the tickets*

2 Complete the compound nouns.
1 I got a hair.................. at the weekend. Do you like it?
2 I'd like a return .... to Manchester, please.
3 The taxi .... took the shortest route.
4 Do you like sea................... like prawns and squid?
5 They don't have enough money to fly first ....

3 Find words that are both verbs and nouns to complete the sentences.
1 Don't forget to .... your bike when you leave it.
   Oh no! My key has broken off in the ....
2 There's a car .... opposite the museum.
   Can we .... the car here, please?
3 There was a .... and our train was late.
   I'm sorry, but we have to .... the flight, due to the weather.
4 I've got a funny .... in my mouth.
   Does the cake .... nice? It looks delicious!
5 Ruby can .... in the next election because she'll be 18.
   Every .... counts, so please don't forget.
6 I'm afraid there's a .... for using the telephone.
   Do they .... extra for service here?

4 Choose the correct preposition.
1 Their car broke *down / up* and they're going to be late.
2 I prefer cycling *to / for* driving.
3 You need to get *off / up* at this stop for the hospital.
4 Do you want me to pick you *off / up* from work today?

5 Complete the sentences with the words in the box.

direct	journey	passengers
platform	transport	

1 Which .... does the train leave from?
2 There isn't a .... flight. You have to change in Paris.
3 Some taxi drivers won't take more than three ....
4 There are some .... problems in the city this morning.
5 How long is the .... by bus?

Score ___ /25

Wait a couple of weeks and try the quiz again. Compare your scores.

11 FOOD

VOCABULARY Restaurants

1 Complete these phrases you hear in a restaurant. Write the missing words in the puzzle. What is the hidden word?

1 We usually add 10% for ....
2 Would you like any ....?
  Ice cream, perhaps?
3 Can I .... you anything else?
4 We're very busy tonight.
  Have you ....?
5 Do you have a .... for two, please?
6 For my ...., I'd like the soup, please.
7 Are you ready to ....?
8 Can we have the ...., please?
9 We don't want any starters, thanks. Just
  a .... course.
10 Can we see the ...., please?

2 Look at the phrases in exercise 1 again and complete the table below. Write **C** if the customer said the phrase and **W** if the waiter said it.

1	2	3	4	5	6	7	8	9	10
W									

DEVELOPING CONVERSATIONS Ordering food and drink

3 Write the words in the correct order to make questions and answers. Who says each one, the waiter (W) or the customer (C)?

1 you / Are / order? / to / ready
....

2 any / like / Would / dessert? /you
....

3 course? / And / main / for / your
....

4 finished. / I'm / the / has / afraid / fish
....

5 the / I'd / please. / like / steak
....

6 some / get / Can / ice cream / I / please
....

7 have / starters, / I'll / the / For / please. / salad / Yes
....

8 have / I'll / chicken. / the / Then / OK.
....

4 Match the questions with the answers in 3.

W: *Are you ready to order?*
C: *Yes. For starters, I'll have the salad, please.*
W: ....
C: ....
W: ....
C: ....
W: ....
C: ....

5 🔊 11.1 Listen and check your answers.

LISTENING

6 Complete the food items with *a, e, i, o* or *u*.

1 __ c __ p __ f t __ __

2 s __ m __ st __ __ k

3 __ gl __ ss __ f
r __ d w __ n __

4 s __ m __ f __ sh

5 s __ m __ w __ t __ r

6 __ b __ ttl __
__ f w __ n __

7 __ c __ p __ f
c __ ff __ __

8 c __ ff __ __
__ c __ cr __ __ m

9 p __ st __
w __ th s __ __ ce

7 🔊 **11.2 Listen to Steve and Carol at a restaurant. As you listen, tick (✓) what they have from the pictures in exercise 6.**

8 Listen again and complete the sentences with *S* (Steve), *C* (Carol), *SC* (both of them) or – *N* (neither of them).

1 doesn't like red wine. ....
2 had a starter. ....
3 ordered extra vegetables. ....
4 asked for some water. ....
5 didn't enjoy the meal. ....
6 didn't have a dessert. ....
7 had a coffee. ....

9 Match the two halves of the phrases. Then listen again and check your answers.

1 A table   a some red.
2 Have   b for two?
3 Can I   c you booked?
4 I'd like   d to order?
5 Are you ready   e glass of water?
6 Are you OK for   f get you a drink?
7 Can I have a   g drinks?

10 Re-order the two short conversations below using words and phrases from *Listening* and *Developing Conversations*.

1 Don't you want a starter? ....
   Are you ready to order now, sir? ...*1*...
   No, thanks – just a main course and a glass
   of red wine. ....
   Yes, I'd like the steak and a salad please. ....

2 No problem. Can I pay by credit card? ....
   Can I get you anything else? ...*1*...
   Yes, sir, a credit card is fine. ....
   No, thanks. Can I have the bill please? ....
   Of course. We usually add 10% for service. ....

11

VOCABULARY Food

1 Complete the chart with the words in the box.

cream	bananas	beef	water	carrots	lamb
beer	apples	onions	cheese	oranges	pork
juice	milk	spinach			

meat	dairy	fruit	vegetables	drinks
chicken	butter	kiwis	garlic	wine
....	*cream*	....	....	....
....	....	....	....	....
....	....	....	....	....

2 Match the food items (1–7) to the pictures (a–g).

a

b

c

d

e

f

g

1 sugar ....
2 peas ....
3 rice ....
4 salt and pepper ....
5 steak ....
6 coffee ....
7 potatoes ....

3 Choose the correct word.
1 There isn't enough *sugar / salt* on this steak.
2 Spaghetti is a type of *potato / pasta*.
3 Indian cooking is famous for its *spices / pepper*.
4 The basic food of Asia is *bread / rice*.
5 Peas and soya are types of *nut / beans*.
6 Prawns and oysters are *fish / seafood*.

4 Complete the sentences with words from exercise 1.
1 How do you have your coffee – with ....
   and sugar?
2 No, this isn't lamb – it's .... You know,
   meat from a cow.
3 .... are the only vegetable that makes
   you cry.
4 I'm thirsty. I'd like a freshly squeezed orange
   .... , please.
5 A: Do you eat ....?
   B: No, we don't eat seafood or meat from a pig.
6 A: What's the name for solid food made from milk?
   B: It's ....

GRAMMAR *Me too, me neither* and auxiliaries

5 Choose the correct words to complete the rules.
1 We use *me too / me neither* to agree with an affirmative statement.
2 We use *me too / me neither* to agree with a negative statement.
3 To *agree / disagree* with a statement in the present simple we sometimes use *I do* or *I don't*.
4 To *agree / disagree*, we sometimes use other auxiliary verbs like *have* and *can*.

6 Complete the dialogue with *I do, I don't, Me neither* and *Me too*.

Aina: Oh, let's go to this fish restaurant. I like fish.
Jesús: Oh, [1]..................... I'm vegetarian!
Aina: Oh, right. OK. Well, how about that Chinese restaurant? I love Chinese food.
Jesús: [2]..................... It looks good.
Aina: But it's very crowded. I don't want to wait for a table.
Jesús: [3]..................... Let's eat somewhere else. How about that pizza restaurant over there?
Aina: I don't really like pizza.
Jesús: Oh, [4]..................... I love all Italian food – pizza, pasta ... But that's OK. Do you like Indian food?
Aina: Yes, I love curry.
Jesús: Great. [5]..................... Let's look for an Indian restaurant. And then we'll both be happy!

7 🔊 11.3 Listen and check your answers.

8 Complete the dialogues with the auxiliary verbs in the box.

am	can	didn't	don't	have	wouldn't

1 A: I want to cook that pie Jamie Oliver made on his programme.
   B: Oh, I .... It looked really difficult.
2 A: We had an amazing dinner at that new restaurant in town last night.
   B: Oh, really? We .... We went there last month and it was awful.
3 A: I'd really like to try sushi one day. It looks amazing.
   B: Oh, I .... I don't really like fish.
4 A: I want to make a cake for Dan's birthday tomorrow but I can't make cakes.
   B: Oh, I .... I'll help you.
5 A: I'm not going to watch the *Masterchef* final. It's boring.
   B: Really? I .... It's the best thing on TV!
6 A: I've never tried Polish food.
   B: Oh, I .... It's delicious! You should try it.

READING

9 Read the magazine article. Write the name of each restaurant under the correct photo.

Restaurant guide
by Celia Black

More and more people are choosing to eat out these days. And that's great news for restaurant owners. In this city we have more than forty restaurants. And that's great news for the people who live here. Two new restaurants opened last week – Mi Casa and Johnny B's. I visited them both.

Mi Casa, Ship Street
Mario and Isabella Fratelli already **run** the popular Mario's on George Street, which is one of my favourite restaurants. I was very excited when I heard about their new place, Mi Casa. It's in a great location on the river, and it's cheaper than Mario's. My friend Julie and I went on a Friday but we didn't book a table. That was a mistake because when we arrived they didn't have any free tables. **However**, we only had to wait ten minutes, and the waiter was very friendly and offered us drinks which we enjoyed on the **terrace** outside. For starters we had seafood, which was really delicious. For the main course, we couldn't decide what we wanted because the food sounded so good. In the end I had chicken with tomatoes and vegetables, and Julie had pizza. Both were excellent. The desserts were good too. I had ice cream and Julie had a lovely chocolate cake. We had a fantastic meal and the restaurant had a great atmosphere. I recommend it.

Johnny B's, Carlton Green
My experience at Johnny B's was very different. I went with my friend Omar to this smart modern restaurant. It's near the station, and it looked very nice. But it looked better than it was. First of all, the tables were very near each other, and the music was too loud. The restaurant was full, but there were only three waiters. And they weren't very friendly when we **complained** that we waited twenty minutes for the menu. For starters I had fish and Omar had a salad of beans and peas. It was nice, but the **portion** was very small. The menu had a large choice of meat **dishes**, but I was surprised that there wasn't much for vegetarians. I ordered steak, and it was OK, but the only thing they offered Omar was eggs. The wine was OK, but we didn't try dessert because we wanted to leave. It was a really bad experience. There was too much meat on the menu, the service was awful and the food was too expensive. We are never going to go there again!

Glossary
run: control
however: but
terrace: a flat place outside a house or restaurant where people can sit
complain: say that you do not like something or that you are unhappy about something
portion: the amount of food that one person gets
dish: a part of a meal

....

10 Are the statements true or false? Circle T or F. Read the article again and check.

1 The owners of Mi Casa have another restaurant. (T) F
2 Mi Casa was very busy on Friday. T F
3 The starters at Mi Casa were good, but the desserts were not. T F
4 Johnny B's had a great atmosphere. T F
5 Omar's starter at Johnny B's was too small. T F
6 Johnny B's is a good restaurant for vegetarians. T F

11 Read the article again and write what they ate at each restaurant.

	starter	main course	dessert
Mi Casa			
Johnny B's			

12 Complete the summary with the words in the box.

but	friendly	~~liked~~	nice	wasn't

The writer ¹ *liked* Mi Casa very much, ² .... she didn't like Johnny B's. Mi Casa had good food, and a ³ .... atmosphere and the waiters were ⁴ .... Johnny B's was too crowded, there ⁵ .... a good choice for vegetarians and the food was too expensive.

GRAMMAR Explaining quantity

1 Put the words in the box in the correct column.

apple	biscuit	chocolate	coffee	egg	fish
fruit	meat	soft drink	sugar	sweet	vegetable

Countable nouns	Uncountable nouns
apple	....
....	....
....	....
....	....
....	....
....	....

2 Complete the rules with the words in the box.

a lot of	any	many	much	some

1 We use ...., ... and .... with both countable and uncountable nouns.
2 We use .... only with countable nouns.
3 We use .... only with uncountable nouns.
4 We often use ...., ... and .... in questions and negative sentences.

3 Choose the correct words to complete the dialogue.

Aina: How [1] *much / many* coffee do you drink in a day?

Jesús: I don't drink [2] *much / many* cups of coffee in a day. Maybe one or two in the morning. That's all. But I'm enjoying this one.

Aina: Same here. I don't usually drink [3] *some / any* hot drinks. This is very unusual for me!

Jesús: What? Don't you drink tea?

Aina: No, I don't. But I drink [4] *much / quite a lot of* soft drinks.

Jesús: I don't drink [5] *much / many* soft drinks at all. You know, there's [6] *a lot of / some* sugar in soft drinks. Maybe six spoons in a glass.

Aina: I know! But I don't eat [7] *any / much* sweets.

Jesús: Well, that's good. I eat [8] *a lot of / much* chocolate.

Aina: I eat [9] *some / any* chocolate, but not a lot.

4 🔊 **11.4 Listen and check your answers.**

VOCABULARY Forming negatives by adding *un-*

5 Write the opposite form of the adjectives.

employed	....
....	unfair
....	unforgettable
friendly	....
happy	....
healthy	....
....	unpopular
tidy	....
....	unusual

6 Complete the sentences with the correct adjective from each pair in exercise 5.

1 John doesn't like his new job. He's very ....
2 Everyone loves that song. It's really ....
3 You should get more exercise. It's really .... sitting at your desk all day.
4 My dad was .... for a long time. He lost his job when he was 40.
5 Wow! Your room is very .... Where did you put all your stuff?
6 My neighbour is really .... He always stops to chat in the morning.
7 Ask your boss if you can leave early. It's .... that you're the only one working late.
8 The ending of that film was .... I'm still thinking about it today.
9 What an .... dog! I've never seen one like that before.

DEVELOPING WRITING
An email invitation

7 **Read the invitation and answer the questions.**

1 How does the writer begin the invitation?

2 How does she end it?

Sent	Chat	Attach	Font

From	Angela@torrent.fr
To	Kevin@clubnet.com
Subject	Party time

Hi Kevin

I hope you're well. It was good to see you at Kira's wedding in the summer.

I'm having a party on Saturday 10th March to celebrate my birthday.

It's at La Coupole on the corner of rue Dauphine and avenue Robespierre, from 8.00pm to midnight. You're welcome to bring a friend if you like.

Let me know if you can come. I hope to see you there.

Best wishes

Angela

Language note

Sometimes, on more formal invitations, the letters *RSVP* appear instead of the sentence *Let me know if you can come*. The two mean the same. If you see *RSVP*, you must reply and tell the person who invited you if you can or can't come.

---

8 **Look at the invitation again and answer the questions.**

1 What's the invitation to? .... *a party* ....

2 When is it? ....

3 What's the special occasion? ....

4 Where is it? ....

5 What time is it? ....

6 Who can Kevin bring? ....

9 **You are going to write an invitation to a friend. First write notes to answer these questions about your invitation.**

1 What's the invitation to? (for example: a party, a dinner, a lunch)

2 When is it?

3 What's the special occasion? (for example: a birthday, an anniversary, a wedding, the end of exams)

4 Where is it? (for example: a restaurant, a bar, at home, at someone's house)

5 What time is it?

6 Can the guest bring someone?

10 **Write an invitation to your friend. Use the notes you made in exercise 9 and the model text to help you.**

Vocabulary Builder Quiz 11

Download the Vocabulary Builder for Unit 11 and try the quiz below. Write your answers in your notebook. Then check them and record your score.

1 **Match 1–6 with a–f to make compound nouns.**

1	fried	a	drink
2	main	b	product
3	dairy	c	chicken
4	cookery	d	soup
5	soft	e	book
6	tomato	f	course

2 **Complete the adjectives in the sentences.**

1 The children were really h.................... at the end of the day. They ate a big dinner.

2 The decision was u................... as we had to pay more.

3 Who made this t................... mess in the kitchen?

4 I'm trying not to eat u................... food at the moment like biscuits and sweets.

5 We had an u................... lunch at that restaurant. It was amazing!

3 **Complete the sentences with words formed from the verbs in brackets.**

1 I want to lose some .... , so I'm eating healthily. (weigh)

2 Are you going to have the salad as a ....? (start)

3 My cousin is .... as a chef in a café in town. (employ)

4 Do you like plain food or unusual .... of flavours? (combine)

5 I think .... is included in the bill. (serve)

4 **Choose the correct verb to complete the sentences.**

1 If you pay by credit card, they *make / want / add* 5%.

2 I'd like to *order / have / want* some drinks.

3 I *recommend / avoid / include* the soup. It's very good.

4 I'm a vegetarian so I *suggest / avoid / enjoy* eating meat or fish.

5 Does the bill *have / include / need* service, or do we have to leave a tip?

5 **Complete the sentences with the words in the box.**

cream	nuts	pepper	pork

1 Add salt and .... to the soup to add flavour.

2 I don't eat dairy products like .... and butter.

3 Sausages are usually made of beef or ....

4 Vegetarians have to get protein from .... and beans.

Score ___ /25

Wait a couple of weeks and try the quiz again. Compare your scores.

VOCABULARY Health problems

Learner tip

When you learn new vocabulary, you can draw a little picture to show the meaning of new words.

head

1 Label the parts of the body with the words in the box.

arm	back	chest	foot	hand	~~head~~	leg	stomach

1 ....*head*.............
2 ....
3 ....
4 ....
5 ....
6 ....
7 ....
8 ....

2 Complete the sentences with the words in the box.

broken	burnt	cough	cut	headache	~~sick~~	stiff

1 That fish I ate was bad. I think I'm going to be *sick*.
2 Steve played computer games for four hours and now he's got a ....
3 Monika .... her hand on the hot grill.
4 I played tennis yesterday, and today my legs are really ....
5 Be careful of that broken glass. You're going to .... yourself.
6 I can't write. I've .... my arm.
7 You've got a terrible .... You should stop smoking.

3 Choose the correct word.

A: Are you ¹(OK)/ *fine*?
B: My stomach really ² *hurts / sick*.
A: Are you ³ *broken / hungry*?
B: Yeah. Maybe I should eat something.

C: Don't come near me! I've got a ⁴ *cold / cut* and I don't want you to get it.
D: Oh, OK. You sound really ⁵ *stiff / ill*. Are you sure you're OK?
C: Well, I've got a very bad cough.
D: You should see the doctor. Maybe you've got a chest ⁶ *hurt / infection*.

4 🔊 12.1 Listen and check your answers.

GRAMMAR *should / shouldn't*

5 Write the words in order to make sentences.

1 to / should / He / go / hospital.
   He should go to hospital.
2 the / They / day / should / take / off.
   ....
3 us. / should / with / You / come
   ....
4 the / shouldn't / cancel / party. / We
   ....
5 my / She / advice. / should / to / listen
   ....
6 too / You / much. / eat / shouldn't
   ....

6 Look at the pictures and write advice for each person with *You should / shouldn't* and the words in brackets.

1 *I feel sick.*
2 *I've got a really bad cough.*
3 *My back really hurts.*
4 *I've got a headache.*
5 *I burnt my arm.*
6 *I've got a terrible cold.*

1 (lie down)
   You should lie down.
2 (stop smoking)
   ....
3 (carry those heavy bags)
   ....
4 (get some fresh air)
   ....
5 (put cold water on it)
   ....
6 (go to work)
   ....

DEVELOPING CONVERSATIONS

Saying no

7 Match the beginnings (1–5) to the endings (a–e).
1 Maybe you should   a should take the day off.
2 It's just   b lie down.
3 Maybe you   c in a few days.
4 I just need   d a small cut.
5 I'll be OK   e to take an aspirin.

8 Number the lines in order to make four conversations.

1 a Maybe you should lie down.   [   ]
   b You look terrible. Are you OK?   [*1*]
   c No, really. I'm fine.   [   ]
   d Yes, I'm just a bit tired.   [   ]

2 a No, really. I'll be fine.   [   ]
   b Maybe you should go to the hospital.   [   ]
   c Oh, it's nothing.   [   ]
   d You've cut your hand! It looks really bad.   [   ]

3 a Are you sure?   [   ]
   b Would you like some more cake?   [   ]
   c Yes, thanks. It was delicious.   [   ]
   d No, thanks. I've had enough.   [   ]

4 a It's OK, thanks.   [   ]
   b Would you like me to come round tonight?   [   ]
   c No, really. I'll be fine on my own.   [   ]
   d But Mark's away and you're all alone in that big house.   [   ]

9 ◐ 12.2 Listen and check your answers.

10 Read these conversations. There are three mistakes in each one. Find and correct them.

1 A: Are you OK ? You look terrible.
   B: I got a headache.
   A: Maybe you take an aspirin.
   B: No, it nothing.

2 A: Are you OK?
   B: No, my stomach hurts and I sick.
   A: Maybe you lie down? Would you like some water?
   B: No, thanks. I be fine.

3 A: Ow! I burn my hand.
   B: You should some cold water on it.
   A: No, it's OK. I'll fine.

LISTENING

11 ◐ 12.3 Look at the pictures and listen to the conversations. Who needs to go to hospital, Makiko, Mike or Jenny?

12 Listen again and choose the correct words.

Conversation 1
1 Makiko's got a *headache* / *cough*.
2 Mrs Kells thinks she should *miss the meeting* / *go home*.

Conversation 2
3 Mike's *chest* / *back* hurts.
4 Liam thinks Mike *should go to the doctor* / *take more care of himself*.

Conversation 3
5 Jenny fell and hurt her *foot* / *hand*.
6 Piotr thinks she should *lie down* / *go to the hospital*.

13 What can you remember about the people? Write answers to the questions. Then listen again and check.
1 When was the meeting last week?
   On Friday.
2 How long has Makiko been ill?
   ....
3 Which parts of Mike's body hurt?
   ....
4 Does Mike do a lot of sport?
   ....
5 What did Jenny fall off?
   ....
6 What colour is her foot?
   ....

VOCABULARY Feelings

1 Find eight words for feelings in the wordsquare.
Look →, ↓ and ↘.

U	W	G	A	H	T	I	R	E	D
H	A	P	P	Y	E	W	R	X	I
L	N	N	P	T	I	M	E	C	H
O	G	A	N	T	E	T	L	I	O
L	R	M	B	O	I	U	A	T	H
N	Y	W	I	T	Y	R	X	E	B
R	I	E	N	Y	L	E	E	D	N
S	T	R	E	S	S	E	D	R	M
U	S	S	Y	I	O	S	I	H	S
U	P	S	E	T	B	D	A	V	N

2 Label the photos with the words in exercise 1.

3 Put the words in exercise 1 into two columns: positive and negative.

positive	negative
....	.... *upset* ....
....	....
....	....
....	....

4 Match the sentence beginnings (1–7) to the endings (a–g).

1 We all cried
2 I'm really looking forward
3 We have to do
4 He fell
5 We had to
6 I smiled when
7 She really shouted

a wait an hour for the train to arrive.
b a really difficult test tomorrow.
c at the man who caused the accident.
d when Fluffy died.
e I heard the good news.
f asleep during the film.
g to my holiday in Finland.

5 Write the feeling to describe the sentences in exercise 4.

1 .... *upset* ....   5 ....
2 ....   6 ....
3 ....   7 ....
4 ....

1 .... *tired* ....

2 ....

6 ....

3 ....

4 ....

7 ....

5 ....

8 ....

READING

Language note

An *agony aunt* is a woman whose job is to give advice on personal problems in a newspaper or magazine by answering people's letters. The part of the newspaper or magazine where you find these letters is called an *agony column* or *advice column*.

6 Read the problems and write the person's name.
1 Who is annoyed? ....*Kim*........
2 Whose back hurts? ....
3 Who is worried? ....
4 Who is sad? ....
5 Who is stressed? ....

7 Match the problems (1–5) with the pieces of advice (a–e).

8 Read the problems again and choose the correct answer.
1 Tony has smoked for *ten / eleven* years.
2 Ellie's boss is a *man / woman*.
3 Lara can't think about her *boyfriend / studies* at the moment.
4 Pritpal's doctor *helped / didn't help* him get better.
5 Kim's boyfriend wants to *continue / end* their relationship.

9 Read the advice again and complete these statements.
1 The most important thing for Tony to do is
....
2 Ellie should tell her boss how ....
3 Lara should forget about ....
4 Pritpal should ask .... for help.
5 Kim should tell her boyfriend ....

What's your problem?

Write in and share your problems with Agony Aunt Annie

Health advice

1 Every morning when I get up I cough for about ten minutes. I think it's getting worse. I started smoking when I was fifteen and I'm now twenty-six. I'm worried that this cough is because of my smoking. What should I do?

Tony

2 I'm having a difficult time at work at the moment. My boss is not a patient person and she is making me do more and more. I'm feeling really stressed and I don't know if I can continue like this.

Ellie

3 I have a bad back. It hurts a lot when I am sitting at my desk or in an armchair. I can't carry anything. I've seen my doctor but he just told me to take an aspirin. I don't know what to do.

Pritpal

Relationship advice

4 My boyfriend left me recently and **broke my heart**. I can't think about my studies and I can't stop crying. I don't want to speak to anyone at the moment. When is it going to stop hurting?

Lara

5 I don't love my boyfriend anymore. I've met someone else, who I want to be with. I want to **finish with** him but every time I try to tell him he gets upset and cries, and when he cries I feel annoyed. What can I do?

Kim

a It should stop when you finally **accept** it, and move on. You should think about the future and start enjoying your **freedom**. You should meet other people and forget about the past.

b First, you should see your doctor and find out if there is a problem. Second, you should stop smoking. You can look forward to a happy and healthy life, if you stop now.

c Nobody wants to be with someone who doesn't love them, so you should tell him the truth. It isn't going to be easy and he may get upset, but in the end it's the best thing for both of you.

d You should maybe try to sit down with her and tell her how you feel. Maybe she doesn't know you feel stressed at the moment.

e So many people have this problem. You should go back to your doctor and tell him you want to see a **specialist**. And maybe you shouldn't leave until he agrees.

Glossary

break someone's heart: to upset someone very much
finish with someone (informal): to end a relationship
accept (something): to understand that you can't change something
freedom: the right to do what you want, make your own decisions
specialist: a person who knows a lot about a subject

GRAMMAR *because, so* and *after*

1 Complete the sentences with *so, because* or *after*.

1 Jon was stressed *because* his boss gave him a lot of work.
2 .... the class, Ahmed and Carmen went for a coffee.
3 Belen was tired, ... she went to bed early.
4 Yoshiko was upset .... Hiro shouted at her.
5 .... lunch, Serena and I went for a walk.
6 I'm going out tonight, ... I'm feeling quite excited.
7 I'm happy .... it's the weekend!

VOCABULARY In the news

2 Match the words in the box with collocating phrases.

build	cause	~~celebrate~~	damage
hit	kill	open	protest

1 *celebrate*.
   your birthday / Independence Day / a win.
2 ....
   to the public / a new library / a restaurant
3 ....
   with eggs / your head / the car in front
4 ....
   someone in an accident / two people / animals for sport
5 ....
   more houses / a new stadium / 1,000 new homes
6 ....
   your health / the environment / a public building
7 ....
   against pay cuts / against poor working conditions / job cuts
8 ....
   a lot of problems / serious damage / delays on the roads

3 Complete the headlines with words from exercise 2.

1 Snow *causes* huge delays.
2 Train accident .... 10 and injures 22 more.
3 Crowds gather as royal palace .... to the public for one week.
4 Air travel .... your health <u>and</u> the environment.
5 Prime Minister .... his head on low doorway.
6 Government plans to .... 20,000 new homes by the end of the decade.
7 Doctors and nurses .... against plans to extend hours.
8 Millions gather in city centre to .... the New Year.

DEVELOPING WRITING

A letter of advice

4 Read the letter Daniel wrote to an advice column. Circle the information in the letter that answers these questions.

1 What's the problem?
2 When did it start?

5 Read Agony Aunt's reply and circle 1, 2 or 3.

1 In which paragraph does Agony Aunt offer the main advice?   1   2   3
2 In which paragraph does she sympathise with Daniel?   1   2   3
3 In which paragraph does she summarise Daniel's problem?   1   2   3

30 Shipt Way
Portsmouth
PO16 4TY

15 October

Dear Agony Aunt,
I don't know what to do or how it happened, but I have fallen in love with my best friend's girlfriend. We were good friends and everything was fine, but then about four months ago we started to have feelings for each other. I know she likes me and she has told me she wants to finish with my friend. But she hasn't done anything yet. I don't know what to do. Should I tell my friend what has happened or should I walk away?

Regards,
Daniel

15 Walk Place
Harrogate
HG6 2TT
21 October

Dear Daniel,
You are in a difficult situation and I really feel for you. Naturally, you need to think carefully about what you're going to do.
Firstly, if you tell your friend you love his girlfriend, you're probably going to lose his friendship. I don't think you want that to happen. Secondly, if she isn't happy with your best friend or doesn't love him anymore, she should finish with him. It's not your problem – it's hers.
Here's my advice, Daniel. You should walk away and leave them alone. Go and spend time with other people, and wait and see what happens between your friend and his girlfriend. Be patient – I wouldn't like you to lose your friend and the girl you love.
Best wishes,
Agony Aunt

6 You are going to be an agony columnist and give Gabriella some advice. First, underline the problems in her letter.

> 100 Port Way
> Portsmouth
> PO16 4TY
> 10 October
>
> Dear Agony Aunt/Uncle,
> A friend introduced me to someone just over six months ago. His name is Paolo and he's a musician. We quickly fell in love. But there's a problem. Well, two problems, actually. He's married with a child, and he's in prison at the moment. Paolo is thirty-two and I'm twenty-one, but we love each other. He says he is going to leave his wife when he gets out of prison (four months from now). I don't know what to do. Should I wait for him or should I find someone else?
> Regards,
> Gabriella

7 Write a letter of advice to Gabriella. Choose some phrases in the box to help you write your letter, or create your own.

First part of letter:
- Paolo is in prison.
- What is Paolo's crime?
- Is he going to end up in prison again?
- Is life with Paolo going to be difficult for you?

Second part of letter:
- He is someone's husband.
- He is someone's father.
- Is the difference in your ages a problem?
- Is there a future for you both?

Main advice:
- Wait and see if he is telling you the truth.
- You shouldn't wait for him.
- You should find someone of your own age.
- You should give him a chance – he may be a good person.

> 15 Walk Place
> Harrogate
> HG6 2TT
> 23 October
>
> Dear Gabriella,
> You are in a difficult situation and you need to think carefully about what you're going to do.
> Firstly, ...
> Secondly, ...
> Here's my advice, Gabriella. You should ....
> ....
> ....
> Agony Aunt

Vocabulary Builder Quiz 12

Download the Vocabulary Builder for Unit 12 and try the quiz below. Write your answers in your notebook. Then check them and record your score.

1 Match the adjectives (1–5) to the nouns (a–e).
1 frying   a storm
2 stiff   b pan
3 big   c air
4 fresh   d goal
5 winning   e neck

2 Complete with the past tense verb forms in the box.

burnt	cancelled	carried	earned	joined

1 I .... the animal's trust over a period of weeks.
2 My cousin .... the army when he turned 18.
3 He .... his arm while he was cooking dinner.
4 I .... those bags all the way from the supermarket.
5 They .... the meeting because of the weather.

3 Choose the correct preposition.
1 Are you looking forward *of / to* your holiday?
2 We couldn't stop in time and hit the car *in / at* front.
3 You should always warm *to / up* before going for a run.
4 It's sunny today. Don't forget to put *on / out* some suncream.
5 I'm taking a day *up / off* on Friday.

4 Find words that are both verbs and nouns to complete the sentences.
1 You've got a big .... on your face. Why are you so happy? Don't forget to .... when he takes the photograph!
2 I'm going to .... against this decision. It's unfair! There's a .... about government cuts at the weekend. Shall we go?
3 I didn't .... properly before the game and I hurt my leg. We always do a five-minute .... before our run.
4 How did that .... get on the carpet? Don't .... yourself. That pan is really hot.
5 That's a nasty .... Have you got some medicine for it? Try not to .... during the film. You'll annoy everyone.

5 Match the beginnings (1–5) to the endings (a–e).
1 You can read about the concert   a alone so I can think.
2 We got the best seats   b when we won the World Cup.
3 There were huge celebrations   c in the entertainment section.
4 Sometimes I like to be   d after the accident.
5 He struggled to find work   e right in front of the band.

Score ___ /25

Wait a couple of weeks and try the quiz again. Compare your scores.

VOCABULARY Weather

1 Find the words in the wordsnake and write them next to the correct picture.

wetdrycoldcloudystormhotrainsnowicesunnywarmwindy

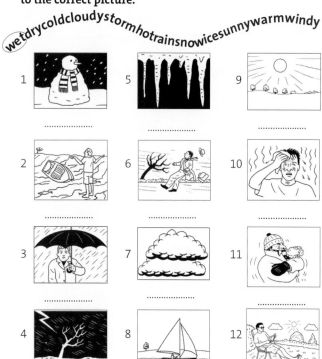

1 ....
5 ....
9 ....

2 ....
6 ....
10 ....

3 ....
7 ....
11 ....

4 ....
8 *wet*
12 ....

2 Complete the dashes to make words from exercise 1.
1 The sky is clear and it's very s _u n n y_ and w __ __ __.
2 We've had a lot of d __ __ __ weather. I like it but the vegetables and flowers don't.
3 It's very h __ __ in here. Can you open a window, please?
4 It's w __ __ outside, so we should take the umbrella. I think there's going to be more r __ __ __.
5 What a pity! We wanted to go to the beach but it's very c __ __ __ __ __ __ today.
6 What a terrible s __ __ __ __. It broke two windows.
7 I love playing in the s __ __ __ but I'm c __ __ __ __ now.

3 Complete the sentences with the words in the box.

autumn	summer	spring	winter

My favourite season is ¹ .... , when the flowers are starting to come out. I like ² .... , too. I like sitting warm in front of a fire and looking outside at the snow. The only season in my country is ³ .... We can go to the beach every day of the year. ⁴ .... is beautiful, but it makes me sad when it starts to feel colder.

GRAMMAR *might* and *be going to*

4 Read Sam's proposed plans for next week and complete the sentences.

1 On Monday *I'm going to meet* Lily in the Blue Boar.
2 We *might have* a walk in the park.
3 On Tuesday .... coffee with Sian in Café Coco.
4 In the evening we .... to the cinema.
5 On Wednesday .... my hair cut.
6 In the evening .... dinner for Ed and Jana.
7 On Thursday .... Mr Mackie at the bank.
8 I .... some shopping in the afternoon.

5 Choose the correct words.
1 I*'m going to / might* stay in tonight, but I haven't decided yet.
2 We*'re going to / might* go to Mai's house for dinner tonight. I'm really looking forward to it.
3 Will and Tania *are going to / might* open a new shop next month. They're really excited.
4 I'm not sure but I*'m going to / might* be busy on Friday.
5 The sky looks clear, so it*'s going to / might* be a nice day tomorrow, but I'm not sure.
6 Oh, no! Look at the sky! It*'s going to / might* rain.

6 Look at the prompt in brackets and write the sentence using *might* or *be going to*.
1 We / have to leave early.   (possible)
  We might have to leave early.
2 They / phone us when they arrive.   (definite plan)
  ....
3 Lin / not see her friends next week.   (decided)
  ....
4 You / not get the job.   (not sure)
  ....
5 It / be cold and wet tomorrow.   (certain)
  ....
6 It / snow tomorrow.   (not certain)
  ....

LISTENING

7 🔊 **13.1 Listen to the report. Is the weather going to be good or bad later ?**

8 Listen again. Match the weather with a photo of how it is at the moment.
1 North ....
2 South ....
3 East ....
4 West ....

a

b

c

d

9 Are the statements true or false? Circle T or F.
1 The rain affected the entire region.   T   F
2 The storms affected the south.   T   F
3 The entire region is going to be sunny.   T   F
4 Last night was windy but not cold.   T   F
5 There might be some more storms this week.   T   F

DEVELOPING CONVERSATIONS
Short questions

10 Match a short question with a short response.

1	Why?	a	Lou.
2	How?	b	Because I want you to.
3	Who with?	c	The beach.
4	What time?	d	By train.
5	How long for?	e	To do some shopping
6	Where?	f	At two o'clock.
7	What for?	g	An hour or two.

11 Complete the dialogue with the questions from exercise 10.

Chloe: Come on, Jack. Why don't we go out?
Jack: Mmm? [1] ....
Chloe: Nobody. Just you and me.
Jack: [2] ....
Chloe: I don't know. To the city centre?
Jack: [3] ....
Chloe: Um, why don't we walk?
Jack: Maybe. [4] ....
Chloe: What do you think? A couple of hours, maybe?
Jack: [5] ....
Chloe: Because it's not good to stay inside all the time.
        Hey – we can go to the market.
Jack: [6] ....
Chloe: To get something for lunch. And then why don't we
        go to the cinema?
Jack: [7] ....
Chloe: I think there's a Bourne film on at five thirty. What
        do you think? Come on, Jack. Stop watching that TV
        and get off the sofa!

12 🔊 **13.2 Listen and check your answers.**

13

VOCABULARY The countryside and the city

1 Complete the crossword with things you can find in the countryside and the city.

Across

2. not in a good state (2,3,9)
5. (5)

7. too many people in one place (7)
9. waste, things that you throw away (7)
11. dirty air, water or land (9)

12. (5)

14. an illegal action (5)

15. (7)

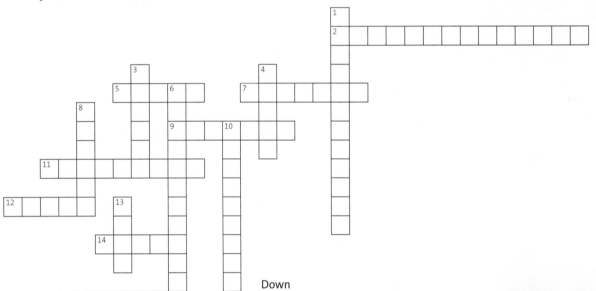

Down

1. groups of people who want to hurt people (7,5)
3. (6)

4. a soft, green plant that covers the ground (5)
6. to have things around on all sides (10,2)
8. places to keep animals or grow food (6)

10. (5,2,5)

13. (4)

15. the opposite of covered in hills, uneven (4)
16. easy to use, easy to get to or near where you live (10)

READING

2 Read the descriptions and tick (✓) the things that are mentioned.

traffic [ ]   shopping [ ]   factories [ ]

animals [ ]   weather [ ]

Why I love the country
Carlo

I have always preferred living in the country – never in a town or city, and not even in a village. I was born here on my parents' farm, and although I **went away** to study, I always knew I wanted to come back. Now I work on the farm too. When I was at university, I lived in the city. I found it crowded, noisy and smelly. There was too much traffic and pollution. And even with all those people around, I felt lonely. I was so happy when I came back here. Life is just slower and more relaxed. And I am a person who likes peace and quiet. People think it's boring, but it's not. I know everyone around here, and there are lots of young people. Another thing is, you really see the weather in the countryside. You **notice** the little differences in the way the seasons change from spring to summer and autumn to winter. When I look out of the windows I see hills and fields. Who wouldn't want that? I am never going to live in a city – I just know it!

Why I love the city
Shannon

I haven't always lived in this city. I come from a small town, where it's very quiet. But I moved here when I got my first job, and I liked it so much I stayed! I just love everything about city life: the people, the noise, the taxis and buses. There's always something to do. I never feel bored. You can go to a restaurant, go to see a film or visit a museum. You can buy anything you like, and the shops are open **24/7**. Some people say that people who live here are unfriendly, but I know all the people who live in my building and the people who run the shops and restaurants in my street. They all say 'hello' when they see me. Living here I sometimes feel as if I'm in a film. When I'm going to work, walking along the street, or riding the subway, I feel that I'm part of something important – part of a big, busy international city. I am happy to be here. I know it's noisy and crowded, but to me, this city is just beautiful. It's always going to be that way. I'm just a city person.

Glossary

go away: go to another place
notice: see
24/7: 24 hours a day, 7 days a week

3 Read the descriptions again. Are the sentences true or false? Circle T or F.

1 Carlo was born in the city.   T (F)
2 He didn't like the city because he felt lonely.   T   F
3 The weather in the country is worse than in the city.   T   F
4 Shannon came to the city to study.   T   F
5 She doesn't know many people.   T   F
6 She finds the city exciting.   T   F

4 Who are these sentences about? Write *C* for Carlo and *S* for Shannon. Then read the descriptions again and check.

1 His / Her parents are farmers.   [C]
2 He / She comes from a small town.   [ ]
3 He / She knows a lot of young people.   [ ]
4 He / She can go shopping whenever he / she feels like it.   [ ]
5 He / She likes looking at hills and fields.   [ ]
6 His / Her neighbours are friendly.   [ ]

5 Complete the summary with the words in the box.

bored	crowded	didn't like
happy	prefers	slow

Carlo likes living in the country because it's quiet and peaceful. He [1] *didn't like* the city because it was [2] .... , noisy and smelly. He enjoys the [3] .... pace of life and noticing the changes in the countryside around him.

Shannon lived in a small town, but she [4] .... the city. She likes everything about city life and she never feels [5] .... She doesn't want to live in the country because she feels [6] .... in the city.

VOCABULARY Animals

1 Look at the pictures and unscramble the words to make the names of the animals.

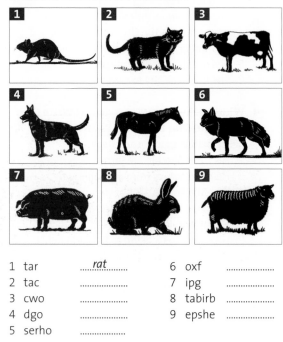

1 tar   *rat*
2 tac   ....
3 cwo   ....
4 dgo   ....
5 serho   ....

6 oxf   ....
7 ipg   ....
8 tabirb   ....
9 epshe   ....

2 Answer the quiz with some of the words for animals in exercise 1.

Animal quiz

Can you guess which animals we're talking about?

1 Most people hate these misunder-stood animals. People believe they are dirty and spread disease. You can often see them in rubbish bins.   *rat*

2 These bushy-tailed animals hunt at night. They are usually red, but the ones that live in the Arctic are white!   ....

3 People keep these animals on farms and we eat their meat. Their wool is used to make clothes.   ....

4 People keep these animals as pets. They can also do work, for example on farms or saving people's lives.   ....

5 These animals live on farms and are black, brown or white. They give us milk.   ....

6 These animals are very strong and can run fast. They can carry people and pull heavy things.   ....

GRAMMAR Present perfect to say *how long*

3 Complete the rule with the words in the box. There are two extra words.

be	past simple	has/have	past participle

We form the present perfect with the auxiliary verb .... + a ....

4 Write the past participles of the verbs.
1 be   *been*
2 study   ....
3 live   ....

4 know   ....
5 work   ....
6 have   ....

5 Complete the sentences using the correct form of the verbs in brackets.
1 I *have worked* .... in my company for ten years.   (work)
2 I .... my best friend for twenty years.   (know)
3 I .... in this city for fifteen years.   (live)
4 I .... together with my partner for two years.   (be)
5 I .... my mobile phone for six months.   (have)
6 I .... English for ten years.   (study)

6 Make questions from the sentences in exercise 5.
1 *How long have you worked in your company?*
2 How long .... ?
3 How .... ?
4 .... ?
5 .... ?
6 .... ?

7 Write true short answers to the questions in exercise 6. It isn't necessary to use *for*.
1 ....
2 ....
3 ....
4 ....
5 ....
6 ....

PRONUNCIATION

8 🔊 13.3 Listen to the sentences and underline the weak forms of *has* and *have*.
1 How long have you had your cat?
2 They have been together for years.
3 Has he known her for long?
4 We have studied English for more than ten years.
5 How long has she lived here?
6 Have you worked here for a long time?

9 Listen again and repeat the sentences.

DEVELOPING WRITING A description of where you live

10 Look at the phrases 1–12 below and put each number into one of the groups below, City or Country.

1 exciting and busy
2 a lot of problems like crime
3 lots of things to do
4 there aren't many shops
5 a lot of traffic and pollution
6 boring – nothing to do
7 lots of fresh air
8 peaceful and quiet
9 crowded and noisy
10 shops open 24/7
11 relaxing
12 you need a car to go anywhere

City	Country
....	....
....	....

11 Read the text. Match each paragraph (1–3) to the descriptions (a–c) in the box.

a summary   b description of the place   c introduction

Paragraph 1 ....   Paragraph 2 ....   Paragraph 3 ....

The place where I live

[1] I live in a big city. I like living here, but there are good and bad things about city life.

[2] I like the city because it is exciting and busy. There are lots of things to do and the shops are open 24/7. But sometimes it can be crowded and noisy. There is a lot of traffic and pollution, and other problems like crime.

[3] I think the country is boring. For me, city life is more exciting and interesting. I prefer living in the city.

12 You are going to write about the place where you live. Look back at exercise 10 and tick (✓) the phrases that describe the place where you live.

13 Write three paragraphs about the place where you live. Use the phrases you ticked in exercise 12 and the model text in exercise 11 to help you.

The place where I live
[1] I live in
[2] I like
But sometimes
[3] For me,

Vocabulary Builder Quiz 13

Download the Vocabulary Builder for Unit 13 and try the quiz below. Write your answers in your notebook. Then check them and record your score.

1 Cross out the word in each group that doesn't collocate.

1	wet	*day / weather / floor / flood*
2	empty	*road / glass / building / forest*
3	limited	*choice / amount / house / number*
4	crowded	*street / animal / bar / house*
5	perfect	*home / condition / hill / weather*

2 Complete the phrases with the prepositions in the box.

by	down	in	of	on (x2)

1 They're pulling that old church .... and building flats there.
2 Would you like to live .... a farm?
3 The school is surrounded .... buildings.
4 The tower is .... top of the hill, and you can see it for miles.
5 The buildings are all .... bad condition and need repair.

3 Complete the sentences with a / an, the, or put – if there is no article.

1 It's .... lovely sunny day. Let's go for a picnic.
2 What's .... scenery like in your country?
3 You don't need .... reason to want a holiday.
4 What did .... weather forecast say about tomorrow?
5 You should pick up .... rubbish in the countryside.
6 There's .... limited number of tickets, so hurry.

4 Complete the verbs.

1 We are going to c................... a mountain tomorrow. The view will be amazing!
2 Pooh! Those socks s................... bad. Put them in the wash.
3 My dogs like to run and c................... each other when we go to the park.
4 Temperatures today could r................... as high as 40 degrees.

5 Complete the sentences with the words in the box.

attention	chemicals	scary	invited	flooding

1 When my cat wants .... , she pushes my hand with her face.
2 Those cows are .... ! Let's go now.
3 There is a risk of .... after the recent heavy rain,
4 Many farmers put too many .... on their fields
5 I've .... my parents for dinner on Friday.

Score ____ /25

Wait a couple of weeks and try the quiz again.
Compare your scores.

VOCABULARY Describing films, plays and musicals

1 Choose the correct words.

1 It's a typical Hollywood *film* / *concert* with a happy ending.
2 We're doing a *cinema* / *play* at college. I'm in it.
3 The singing in that *cinema* / *musical* was great.
4 I saw 'The Killers' at a *concert* / *film* last summer. They're my favourite band.
5 John Boyega is appearing this month as Othello at the *musical* / *theatre*.

2 Look at the pictures and unscramble the words to describe the four films.

1 yunfu   *funny*

2 rascy

3 das

4 nivlote

3 Complete the sentences with the words in the box.

brilliant	depressing	entertaining
predictable	~~strange~~	terrible

1 What a *strange* and unusual film. I didn't know what was happening at all.
2 That was pretty .... I'm going to feel bad for days now!
3 That film had such a .... ending. You know what's going to happen after the first half hour.
4 *Hairspray* is one of the most .... musicals I've ever seen. It was fun.
5 Sylvester Stallone was .... in *Creed*. He gave his best performance ever.
6 That play was probably the worst thing I've seen in a long time. It was ....!

DEVELOPING CONVERSATIONS

What's it like?

4 Match the questions (1–6) to the follow-up questions (a–f).

1 What's your sister like?   a Has he been at the school long?
2 What was the film like?   b Is she older or younger than you?
3 What was the band like?   c Is it red, like the old one?
4 What's the new teacher like?   d Did they play all their new songs?
5 What's the acting like?   e Did it have a happy ending?
6 What's his new car like?   f Did she play her role well?

5 Read and complete the conversations with the words in the box.

the food	~~like~~	nice	What was

1 A: What's Kelly's new boyfriend ¹ *like*?
  B: Really ² ....
  A: I've heard he's a bit loud.
  B: No, I didn't think so. I liked him.

2 C: ³ .... your holiday like?
  D: Lovely. The beaches were beautiful and the people were really friendly.
  C: What was ⁴ .... like? I've heard it's really good.
  D: Yeah, delicious. We didn't have one bad meal the whole time we were there.

6 🔊 14.1 Listen and check your answers.

LISTENING

7 🔊 **14.2 Listen and tick (✓) the words the people use to describe the film.**

Aisha: boring   exciting   violent   funny
Julie: strange   entertaining   funny   long
Rashid: funny   terrible   fantastic   silly

8 Listen again. Are the sentences true or false? Circle T or F.

1 There are a lot of people outside the cinema.   (T)   F
2 Two thousand people got free tickets for the film.   T   F
3 Aisha liked the film very much.   T   F
4 Julie thought some parts of the film were very sad.   T   F
5 Rashid thought the acting was terrible.   T   F
6 He got a free ticket.   T   F

9 Do you remember who said what? Write _A_ for Aisha, _J_ for Julie and _R_ for Rashid. Then listen again and check.

1 It was probably one of the best films I've ever seen.   ...._A_.........
2 It was very funny, though.   ....
3 It's not my kind of film at all.   ....
4 The acting was brilliant.   ....
5 It was very entertaining.   ....
6 I didn't get a free ticket.   ....

10 Read the three reviews below, about _Kelly's Pirates_. Which review best matches what you heard in _Listening_ about the film?

1

> There were only 200 people at the premiere of _Kelly's Pirates_ in Leicester last night. Many people didn't go out because of the snow. The main actors were James McTavish and Lila Peroni, but the acting was terrible. The film wasn't very good and it wasn't very funny. The main characters were cows and they lived in a hot air balloon.

2

> Many people went out in the cold weather last night to see the premiere of the new McTavish/Peroni movie at Leicester Square. The film was funny and made the audience laugh, but some people thought the story was strange in parts, especially when the characters went up in the air in a hot air balloon with some cows. But everyone thought that the acting was good.

3

> THERE were 2000 free tickets to see _Kelly's Pirates_ at the Princes Cinema last night. Everyone who saw it hated it. They didn't like the film because it wasn't very funny. The story was silly, with some cows in a hot air balloon! And the acting wasn't good: Lila Peroni and James McTavish were both really terrible.

11 Listen again and check your answers.

GRAMMAR *will / won't* for predictions

1 Choose the correct verb for the phrases.
1 (speak) / *live* Chinese
2 *be / find* life on other planets
3 *win / own* the World Cup
4 *work / find* abroad
5 *look for / look after* the environment
6 *be / have* rich
7 *live / become* to be 100

2 Complete the sentences with the *will* form of the verbs and nouns in exercise 1. Use contractions where possible.
1 Half of babies born in the UK today *will live to be 100*.
2 Many people think that Brazil ....
3 Do you think you .... or stay in your country?
4 We believe that people .... and save the Earth.
5 Experts say that 15% of the world's population .... by 2050.
6 If he works hard and saves money, he .... one day.
7 One day, scientists ...., but not on the Moon.

3 Choose the correct verb form, positive or negative.
1 John probably *will* / (won't) come to work tomorrow. He's feeling very ill.
2 The new law *will / won't* help everyone, including old people.
3 I expect Alison *will / won't* be late, as usual. She never arrives on time.
4 They *will / won't* go on holiday this year. They haven't got any money.
5 I don't think she *will / won't* get the job. She doesn't have enough experience.
6 We *will / won't* see you at the party tonight. We're going to stay at home.

4 Complete the text with *will* or *won't*.

GOVERNMENT'S PLANS FOR PENSIONS

A NEW study [1] *will* be published tomorrow about the government's plans for pensions. It is expected to say that more and more people [2] .... live longer in the next few years. Because of this, there [3] .... be enough money to pay for pensions from the age of sixty. Pensions will be cut and everyone [4] .... need to work until they are older. The situation [5] .... be difficult for younger people who [6] .... be able to stop working until they are sixty-five or above.

5 Correct the mistakes in the sentences, if necessary, or write OK.
1 I'll to see you tomorrow.
   I'll see you tomorrow.
2 Do they will arrive before the party tonight?
   ....
3 There won't not be enough money to pay for the tickets.
   ....
4 I think Liam will make a good leader.
   ....
5 We'll be probably a bit late.
   ....
6 Do think you'll ever be rich?
   ....

PRONUNCIATION

6 🎧 14.3 Listen and tick (✓) the sentence you hear, a or b.
1 a They'll come at ten o'clock   b They come at ten o'clock.
2 a We'll want to sit outside.   b We want to sit outside.
3 a I'll see you on Thursday.   b I see you on Thursday.
4 a You'll need to bring some money.   b You need to bring some money.
5 a We'll finish later tonight.   b We finish later tonight.
6 a I think they'll bring their children.   b I think they bring their children.

7 Listen again and repeat the sentences.

READING

8 Read the newspaper stories. Match each story to the part of a newspaper where you would expect to find it.

- Sports
- National news
- International news
- Financial news
- Show business

1 ....

Dan Smitt and Valentina Solice are going to get divorced. The couple married only two years ago in a $2 million **ceremony** in Los Angeles. They have three children, Chien, Nami and Seisoo. Smitt and Solice met when they were making *Take My Wife*, a romantic comedy set in Rome.

2 ....

After a better result than they expected in last night's local elections, the Democrats are optimistic about their chances of winning next week's national elections. The Socialists said that they hope people will support them, but with only 23% of the vote at present, it looks **unlikely**.

3 ....

Two weeks before one of the most important competitions of the year, Universe star player Gianfanco Pizzi has been injured and will probably be out of the European Cup. Universe captain Marc van Rijn said yesterday it was a terrible **blow** for the team, but they will still do everything they can to win the cup.

4 ....

There have been angry scenes outside the offices of one of the country's largest companies. Muntz, maker of sweets and chocolates, lost €3 million last year. It says it is going to close down its largest factory and cut 80,000 jobs. Employees are **protesting** outside the factory.

5 ....

Suleman Singh, the Suritanian president, has **accused** the Rinastani prime minister of telling lies. The two countries have been unable to **resolve their differences** for more than sixty years and it was hoped that these talks would be the beginning of a process towards peace.

9 Answer the questions.

1 How long have Dan Smitt and Valentina Solice been married?
2 How many children do they have?
3 Do the Democrats think they can win the election?
4 Who is the captain of Universe?
5 How much money did Muntz lose last year?
6 How many jobs are going to be lost?
7 When did the problems between Rinastan and Suritan start?

10 Look back at these highlighted words in the text and try to work out what they mean. Answer the questions. Don't use a dictionary.

1	*ceremony* (noun)	Does it happen in front of other people?
2	*unlikely* (adjective)	Is it going to happen?
3	*blow* (noun)	Is this a good or a bad thing to happen?
4	*protest* (verb)	Are the people doing this happy or unhappy?
5	*accuse* (verb)	Do you accuse someone of something good or something bad?
6	*resolve your differences* (verb)	If you need to resolve your differences, do you agree with each other?

11 Match the highlighted words in exercise 8 with the definitions (a–f).

a an event that stops you from being successful   [*3*]
b take action to show you disagree with something   [   ]
c to try to agree with each other   [   ]
d a formal public event with special customs   [   ]
e to say that someone did something wrong   [   ]
f probably not going to happen   [   ]

VOCABULARY Life and society

1 Complete the table with the words and phrases in the box.

wages	open	insurance	unemployment
safe	treatment	cold	violence
dry	don't talk to you much		

Economy	Crime	People	Climate	Health system
jobs	murder	friendly	warm	
wages				

2 Choose the correct answer.

1 It's very cold and wet. The climate's not very *nice / open*.
2 They invite you into their homes. The people are very *friendly / strong*.
3 There's a lot of unemployment. The economy is quite *problem / weak*.
4 The health system isn't good. Treatment is expensive and you need *service / insurance*.
5 You have hardly any free time. Your quality of life is not very *good / friendly*.
6 You don't need to lock your door at night. Crime is not a *bad / problem*.

3 Complete the text with the words and phrases in the box.

wages	open	problem	very good
talk	lock	strong	

We live in an expensive part of town. The people aren't very
¹ *open* – they don't ² .... to you much, but
crime is not a ³ .... You don't need to
⁴ .... your house during the day. We like the
country we live in. The climate is ⁵ .... – it's
always warm and sunny. At the moment the economy is
⁶ ...., so almost everyone's ⁷ ....
are high, which makes them happy.

GRAMMAR Adjective + verb

4 Match the beginnings (1–7) to the endings (a–g) to make phrases.

1 Pleased —   a to hear about Ken.
2 It's difficult   b not to say anything.
3 It's good   c to say.
4 We were sad   d to meet you.
5 I'll help you if you agree   e to be alive.
6 It was close. I'm lucky   f to say I did it. Sorry.
7 I'm embarrassed   g to see you again.

5 Write the words in the correct order to make sentences.

1 find / It's / to / work. / difficult
It's difficult to find work.
2 to see / easy / a doctor / when / you're ill. / It's
....
3 to / really nice / have / a close / It's / community.
....
4 helpful / It's / another language. / to / learn
....
5 important / It's / not to / your neighbours. / criticise
....
6 the same / good / meet / It's / someone / from / place. / to
....

6 Complete the second sentences so that they mean the same as the first sentences.

1 Keeping your house warm is cheap.
It's cheap *to keep your house warm*.
2 Having people you can talk to is great.
It's great ....
3 Living in a warm climate is important.
It's important ....
4 Learning something new is interesting.
It's ....
5 Helping other people feels good.
It ....
6 Sitting in the garden on a warm day is lovely
It's ....

DEVELOPING WRITING A film review

7 Quickly read the review. What's the name of the film and who are the stars?

Prejudice (2011)
Prejudice is a new film starring Juan Santinez and Carter Jones. It is set in the present day in San Francisco. Mafia boss Pablo Guerrero, played by Santinez, is trying to escape from police detective Lou Rivers, played by Jones. *Prejudice* isn't very good and it isn't very bad – it's an average film which will probably disappear from the cinemas quickly and reappear online.
My rating: ★ ★ ★ ☆ ☆

8 Read the film review again and choose the correct answers.

1 When is it set?
   a the 19th century   b the 20th century
   c the present day   d the future
2 Where is it set?
   a on the moon   b in San Francisco
   c in Thailand   d in Rome
3 What is the story about?
   a a romance between old friends
   b an alien comes to Earth
   c a group of soldiers in a war   d a chase
4 What did the reviewer think of the film?
   a Excellent b Very good c OK d Not very good
   e Bad   f Terrible

Language note

We often write a summary of a film or book in the present simple.
Rivers is an ex-police officer who is trying to escape from Mafia boss Guerrero.

9 Write a review of a film you've seen. Answer the questions and write your review in under 100 words. Use the answers in exercise 8 or choose your own.

1 What's the name of the film and who are the stars?
2 When and where is it set?
3 Give a brief description of the story.
4 Say what you think about the film.
5 Give your rating (a mark out of five).

1 The film is called ....
2 It is set in ....
3 ....
4 ....

My rating: ☆ ☆ ☆ ☆ ☆

Vocabulary Builder Quiz 14

Download the Vocabulary Builder for Unit 14 and try the quiz below. Write your answers in your notebook. Then check them and record your score.

1 Complete the opposites of the words.
1 war   p...................
2 beginning   e...................
3 terrible   b...................
4 employment u...................
5 weak   s...................

2 Complete the sentences with nouns formed from the verbs in brackets.
1 The .... covered the damage to the car caused by the crash. (insure)
2 The .... for your illness will require a few visits to hospital. (treat)
3 There was too much .... in the film. It was really violent. (kill)
4 The .... continued for several months, until there was peace. (fight)
5 The .... in the film was fantastic. (act)

3 Complete the sentences with the verbs in the box.

expect	injure	win	play	see	support

1 The family had to .... each other after the terrible event.
2 I didn't .... to see you here.
3 Can you come and .... the play at the theatre on Friday?
4 Do you want to .... the role of the queen in our show?
5 I'm quite sure that their party will .... the election.
6 Be careful you don't .... yourself up that ladder!

4 Which of the following adjectives
1 is NOT negative?
bad / depressing / predictable / brilliant
2 does NOT collocate with *film*?
entertaining / open / wonderful / predictable
3 does NOT collocate with *food*?
strong / bad / brilliant / predictable
4 is NOT positive?
brilliant / wonderful / open / depressing
5 does NOT collocate with *economy*?
strong / weak / growing / clear

5 Match the questions (1–4) to the answers (a–d).
1 Is it easy to get a job in computing? a It was wonderful!
2 What was the party like? b No, we lost!
3 Do you think the treatment is working? c Yes. He seems to be getting better.
4 Did you win the election? d Yes, there are a lot of tech jobs.

Score ___ /25

Wait a couple of weeks and try the quiz again.

VOCABULARY Machines and technology

1 Label the photos (1–6) with words from the box. There are four extra words.

digital camera	dishwasher	keyboard	hairdryer
mobile phone	plug	screen	tablet
vacuum cleaner	washing machine		

1 ....   2 ....   3 ....

4 ....   5 ....   6 ....

2 Complete the definitions with words from exercise 1.

1 I need a new one. Mine doesn't suck up the dirt any more.
   vacuum cleaner
2 You can do lots of things with it, but I just use it to make calls.
   ....
3 I use it every day to dry my hair.
   ....
4 You can't charge your phone without putting this into a socket first.
   ....
5 I read books on it, go online, listen to music and look at my photos. I can't make calls on it.
   ....
6 It only does one thing – it takes really good photos.
   ....

GRAMMAR be thinking of + -ing

3 Write the words in the correct order to make sentences.

1 of / house. / thinking / buying / They're / a
   They're thinking of buying a house.
2 thinking / £500 / to charity. / I'm / of / giving
   ....
3 tomorrow. / coffee / coming / Sue's / for / of / thinking
   ....
4 in concert. / We're / of / thinking / him / seeing
   ....
5 thinking / giving up / John's / smoking. / of
   ....
6 of / Are / the country? / thinking / leaving / you
   ....

4 Complete the sentences with *be thinking of* + a verb from the box in the *-ing* form. Use contractions where appropriate.

write	join	go	sell	take	buy	learn

1 I*'m thinking of joining* a gym.
2 Ana .... her brother a birthday present.
3 We .... to Paris this year. Interested?
4 Dominic .... another language.
5 .... you .... your exams again?
6 They .... their car.
7 I .... a book about my life.

DEVELOPING CONVERSATIONS *Do you know much about ...?*

5 Write the words in the box under the headings you associate them with.

oceans	countries	DVD	grass	milk
engine	tyres	email	net	balls

cars	geography	tennis	cows	computers
tyres	....	....	....	....
....	....	....	....	....

6 Read the dialogues. Complete each one with a question. Use the headings in exercise 5.

1 A: [1] *Do you know much about geography?*
   B: Not really. Why?
   A: Well, do you know where Malta is?
   B: Malta? I'm afraid I don't know which country it's in.

2 A: [2] ....
   B: A bit. I know that if you sit down and turn the little key you can get to the shops really quickly.

3 A: [3] ....
   B: Yeah, quite a lot. What do you need to know?
   A: Can I save documents on to this DVD?
   B: Yeah. You can save anything on to it.

4 A: [4] ....
   B: A bit. I know they eat grass and drink milk.
   A: They drink water.
   B: Mmm?

5 A: [5] ....
   B: Yeah, quite a lot. Players hit a ball over a net. I'm kidding! Go ahead.
   A: Why is the score 15, 30 and 40?
   B: I have no idea.

7 🔊 15.1 Listen and check your answers.

READING

8 Look at the photos and label the sections with the words in the box. There are two extra words.

> barcode   battery   biro   camera   cleaner   dishwasher   photographic film

9 Read about the inventions. Which items in the pictures are mentioned?

Inventions that have changed the world

Since the first humans existed, people have made discoveries and inventions that have changed the world. Scientists recently made a list of the top 100 inventions. Here are some of them.

1 ....
In 1938, a Hungarian journalist, László József Biró, created a pen which used the same **ink** that was used in books. Before then, people used pots of ink for writing, which were difficult to carry around. Biró sold his invention to a Frenchman, Baron Marcel Bich, in 1950. Today, around 14 million Bic Biros are sold every day.

2 ....
Josephine Cochran was rich, and she probably never washed dishes in her life. But her **servants** did, and they damaged the plates and cups. In 1886, she invented a machine which could wash dishes. She showed her invention at the 1893 World Fair, but only hotels and restaurants liked it. In the 1920s, William Howard Livens invented a small dishwasher for the home, but not many people bought it. It was not until the 1950s, when people had more money, that dishwashers became popular.

3 ....
The first barcode, invented in 1949 by Americans Norman Woodland and Bernard Silver, was made of circles, not lines. It was a way of processing things more quickly at supermarket **checkouts**. In the 1970s, barcodes were introduced all over the world. After some supermarkets started using barcodes, their sales increased by 10–12% and stayed there.

4 ....

The first photographs were taken in the early 19th century, but they were not **permanent**. Early cameras used metal plates to record the picture, but the cameras were big and heavy. In 1885, George Eastman Kodak first made paper film to use in cameras. In 1888, he invented the first camera, called 'the Kodak', to take film. The camera was very simple and quite cheap. It had film inside which could take up to 100 pictures. The film had to be sent back to the factory to be processed. Now, film cameras are not as popular and most people use digital cameras.

5 ....

A battery makes electricity. In the 1780s, an Italian, Luigi Galvani, discovered that a dead **frog's** leg moved when he touched it with two pieces of metal. In 1800, his friend, Professor Alessandro Volta, used Galvani's discovery to make the first battery from pieces of metal and thick paper in salty water. Today we use batteries in computers and many other machines.

Glossary

ink: a coloured liquid for writing or printing
servant: someone who cooks and cleans in your house
checkout: where you pay in a shop
permanent: something that does not change
frog: a small animal that lives in or near water

10 What do you remember about the inventions? Match the names of the people (1–6) to the things about them (a–f). Then read the texts again and check.

1	Luigi Galvani	a was a journalist.
2	Marcel Bich	b invented the barcode.
3	George Eastman Kodak	c made a dead frog's leg move.
4	László József Biró	d had a problem with her servants.
5	Josephine Cochran	e made cameras.
6	Norman Woodland	f bought an invention.

11 Read the text again. Are the sentences true or false? Circle T or F.

1	Biros were the first pens.	T	F
2	After they started using barcodes, some supermarkets sold more.	T	F
3	Josephine Cochran sold a lot of dishwashers.	T	F
4	Dishwashers became popular in the home in the 1950s.	T	F
5	Professor Volta made a battery from metal, paper and water.	T	F
6	'Kodak' cameras had to be sent back to the factory.	T	F

VOCABULARY Computers and the internet

1 **Cross out the word in each group that doesn't collocate.**

1 *search / send / check* an email.
2 receive *a link / a website / an email.*
3 download from *the internet / a website / online.*
4 delete *the internet / a document / an email.*
5 go *to a link / a search / online.*
6 save documents *on to a memory stick / online / a link.*

2 **Use words from exercise 1 to complete the dialogue.**

Paul: Hi Sue. Did you get my [1] *email*?

Sue: Hi. No. I haven't [2] r.. any emails this morning.

Paul: It's not that important. I had a problem last night. I [3] d .... one of your documents. Could you [4] s.. it to me again?

Sue: Of course I will. Or I could save it on to a [5] m.. if you have one.

Paul: I don't have one on me.

Sue: No problem. Give me one minute. I'm just going to [6] c.. my emails. Oh, yes, here's yours. But we don't need it now, do we?

Paul: No. I can tell you exactly what I want. It was a document about the history of the mobile phone.

Sue: Oh, I know the one. But I got all of that from Cellnet. You can download it from their [7] w.. .

Paul: Oh, great. Could you send me the [8] l..?

Sue: Sure. I'll do it now. Oh, now what's going on? I can't go [9] o.. Aren't these machines supposed to make our lives easier?

3 🔊 **15.2 Listen and check your answers.**

PRONUNCIATION Spelling addresses

4 🔊 **15.3 Listen to these sounds and write the letters you hear.**

1 /eɪ/	2 /iː/	3 /aɪ/	4 /əʊ/	5 /juː/	6 /e/	7 /ɑː/
a	b	i	....	q	....	....
....	c	....		....	....	
....	d			....	....	
....					....	
					....	
					....	
					....	
					....	

5 **Match 1–3 with a–c.**

1 home address: a www.evritour.com
2 website: b ricardotema@nslt42.co.it
3 email address: c Avenida Santa Fe 2694

6 🔊 **15.4 Listen to the spelling of these addresses. Tick (✓) the address you hear.**

1 a www.asulikeit.net.au ☐
   b www.asulikit.net.au ☐

2 a 24a Hurst Drive ☐
   b 24–8 Hirst Drive ☐

3 a yodeejay@pkan.com ☐
   b yodwejay@pkan.com ☐

4 a Aceveda 4268 ☐
   b Acebeda 4628 ☐

5 a baz2@ndubz.co.ir ☐
   b baz2@ndubz.com.ir ☐

6 a www.anderextee.org.nz ☐
   b www.anderxt.org.nz ☐

7 **Write *h* (home address), *w* (website) or *e* (email address) for each address in exercise 6.**

1 ....*w*....
2 ....
3 ....
4 ....
5 ....
6 ....

DEVELOPING WRITING Describing an invention

8 Read the text quickly and choose the best heading.

1

FUTURE CARS

2

Last century's finest

3

The car – we all love it!

1 I think the best invention of the 20th century is the car. I don't understand how it works, but I know I couldn't live without mine!

2 People all over the world use their cars to get to work and go places quickly. The police use cars, and when you have a problem you can use your car to get to hospital.

3 I use a car every day in my job. I couldn't do my job without one! I visit people and talk to them. I also use my car a lot in my personal life. I use it to visit friends and family and go away at weekends.

4 In my opinion the car is the best invention of the 20th century because it changed the way people travel. It's useful and quick. It can even save your life!

9 Look at the text again. Match each paragraph (1–4) to its purpose (a–d).

a How the writer uses his car. ....
b Introduction: what the invention is. ....
c Conclusion: why it's the best invention. ....
d What it is used for and how it helps people. ....

10 You are going to write an essay with the title 'What is the best invention of the 20th century, and why?'. First choose one of these inventions, or use your own idea.

| computer | television | mobile phone | MP3 player |

11 Make notes about the invention under these headings.

1 Introduction: say what the invention is.
telephone

2 Say what it is used for and how it helps people.
Talk to friends and families – used all over the world.
Can call police or hospital.

3 Say how you use it.
Every day in my job. Also in personal life.

4 Conclusion: summarise why you think it's the best invention.
Everyone has one. Useful for many things

12 Now write your description. Write four paragraphs.

LISTENING

1 🔊 **15.5 Listen to Eric talking to a shop assistant. Tick (✓) the items he asks to see.**

hairdryer	☐	vacuum cleaner	☐
digital camera	☐	laptop	☐
washing machine	☐	mobile phone	☐
games console	☐		

2 Listen again and choose the correct answer.

1 The camera costs *£800 / £1,800*.
2 The camera comes with a free *bag / memory card*.
3 The computer is *light / heavy*.
4 The battery lasts for *six / eight* hours.
5 Eric wants a mobile for *listening to music / making calls*.
6 The mobile costs *£300 / £400*.
7 Eric buys the *mobile / games console*.

Learner tip

Words often occur in groups as set phrases connected to specific subjects. Below are some phrases connected to technology. The first is *the latest model*, a 3-word phrase often used when talking about technology.

3 Draw a line to complete phrases about technology. Then listen again if necessary and check your answers.

1	this is the latest	Net
2	with software fully	model
3	it's Wi-Fi	art
4	surf the	ready
5	send text	loaded
6	state-of-the-	messages

4 Match the definitions (a–f) to the phrases (1–6) in exercise 3.

a the most recent in a range of machines ....*1*.........
b look at websites on the internet ....
c the newest and most advanced ....
d includes internet and email software in the price ....
e send short messages from a mobile phone ....
f it can connect to the internet without using a cable ....

VOCABULARY What technology does

5 Match verbs from box A with nouns from box B to make a phrase which means the same as each explanation.

A	B
check	~~electricity~~
control	energy
create	everything
develop	problems
keep	vocabulary tests
~~produce~~	your heart rate
save	your files in one place
solve	your own apps

1 make power
produce electricity
2 build your own applications
....
3 find the answer to difficult issues
....
4 monitor cardiac activity
....
5 have power over all things
....
6 not use electrical power
....
7 make sure your documents are together
....
8 make vocabulary tests
....

6 Write the missing verbs from exercise 5 to complete the crossword and the sentences.

Across

1 We can *create* tests for the vocabulary that we've learned. (6)
2 I can .... electricity, using solar technology. (7)
5 It's possible to .... problems quickly, using your computer. (5)
6 We .... all our files in one place. (4)

Down

1 I use my mobile to .... everything in my house. (7)
3 We .... apps quickly and very easily. (7)
4 He uses his watch to .... his heart rate. (5)
5 The smart meter in my house helps me .... energy. (4)

GRAMMAR Adverbs

7 Write the adverbs in the column.

adjective	adverb
1 bad	*badly*
2 early	....
3 good	....
4 hard	....
5 late	....
6 loud	....
7 quick	....
8 quiet	....
9 slow	....

Language note

Adverbs tell us more about verbs. Adverbs describing frequency (how often we do something) often come before the verb. For example *I **always go** to work by train.* Adverbs of manner (that tell us how we do things) usually come after the verb. For example *She **speaks quietly**.*

8 Put the adverbs in exercise 7 in pairs of opposites. One adverb doesn't have an opposite.

1 .... – ....
2 .... – ....
3 .... – ....
4 .... – ....
5 .... doesn't have an opposite.

9 Complete the sentences with the adverbs in exercise 7.

1 My neighbours play their music too *loudly*. I can hear it all over the house.
2 We have to get up .... if we want to catch the train.
3 She speaks French really .... She's brilliant at languages.
4 I arrived .... for the film and missed the beginning.
5 He drives really .... He's going to have an accident one day.
6 She works too .... and she isn't going to finish in time.
7 You're working too .... these days. You need to relax more.
8 Please speak .... The students are doing an exam.
9 You're walking too .... for me. Please slow down!

Vocabulary Builder Quiz 15

Download the Vocabulary Builder for Unit 15 and try the quiz below. Write your answers in your notebook. Then check them and record your score.

1 Complete the sentences with the correct prepositions.
1 I deleted the files *by / on* accident.
2 Did you read that interesting article *about / for* the economy?
3 You can store documents *in / on* a memory stick.
4 Could you plug the laptop *in / off*? You're nearest the socket.

2 Complete the compound nouns with the words in the box.

camera	machine	cleaner	power	stick

1 solar .... 4 washing ....
2 memory .... 5 vacuum ....
3 digital ....

3 Complete the verbs.
1 Don't p................ that button! It'll turn everything off.
2 Solar panels can p................ a lot of electricity.
3 Did you d................ those files on my computer? I can't find them.
4 You should s................ energy by turning off appliances.
5 I want to d................ my own apps.
6 Is that your jacket? I saw it d................ on the ground.

4 Find words that are both verbs and nouns to complete the sentences.
1 I did a .... for 'Miami hotel' online and found a great place.
   Did you .... the internet for that book you want?
2 I can't go shopping without a .... My memory is really bad!
   Can you .... all the things that were stolen?
3 You can .... some free software from their website.
   I hope this isn't an illegal .... on your computer.
4 I'm going to .... a new layout for my blog.
   The .... of this website is terrible.
5 That cat .... you shared is really funny.
   I'll .... your speech so you can post it online later.

5 Match the sentence beginnings (1–5) to the endings (a–e).

1 Do you know how to change   a computer software on the internet.
2 You can learn how to install   b the latest version of the software?
3 Remember to read   c the computer.
4 Sometimes, you need to restart   d the brightness on my phone?
5 Did you download   e the instructions before you use it.

Score ___ /25

Wait a couple of weeks and try the quiz again.
Compare your scores.

16 LOVE

VOCABULARY Love and marriage

1 Find nine words in the wordsquare to complete the sentences. Look →, ↓ and ↘.

A	U	D	I	V	O	R	C	E	D	M
P	N	M	E	Y	E	U	J	A	S	O
P	W	N	U	Q	A	R	E	K	E	F
R	L	W	I	F	E	O	A	R	P	S
O	E	S	E	V	O	R	L	R	A	E
V	U	J	N	R	E	P	O	I	R	S
E	C	R	E	U	T	R	U	A	T	I
A	U	I	D	S	P	E	S	D	N	L
W	E	D	D	I	N	G	N	A	E	N
Y	A	T	A	B	R	N	S	P	R	O
H	E	V	T	O	G	A	I	W	E	Y
D	H	U	S	B	A	N	D	B	P	O
X	W	T	A	R	Z	T	Y	E	O	I

1 Your **partner** is another word for your boyfriend or girlfriend.
2 When a man marries a woman, she becomes his ....
3 A woman is .... when she is going to have a baby.
4 When a woman marries a man, he becomes her ....
5 My parents don't .... of my friends.
6 A .... is when two people get married.
7 A .... person is afraid that someone is trying to take their partner away from them.
8 Your .... is the day each year when you celebrate the date of your wedding.
9 You are .... when your marriage legally ends.

2 Complete the phrases with the verbs in the box.

get (x2)	have (x3)	save

1 *get* married   4 .... money
2 .... a baby   5 .... a date
3 .... divorced   6 .... a partner

3 Complete the sentences with the phrases in exercise 2.

1 I was sad to hear they're going to **get divorced**. They were a lovely couple.
2 Do you think couples should .... before marriage?
3 Lucia is pregnant. She's going to .... in the spring.
4 Sol and Anna .... on Friday. They're going to the cinema together.
5 We're going to .... next year. The wedding will be in September.

> **Learner tip**
>
> Many verbs in English are followed by a preposition. When you learn these verbs, learn them with the preposition.
> For example: *get up, look after, turn off*

4 Choose the correct preposition or adverb.

1 If you like Mia, why don't you ask her *off* / *out*?
2 My dad doesn't get *up* / *on* with Tony. He doesn't like him at all.
3 Olivier is going to move *in* / *up* with his girlfriend.
4 Sara and Tim broke *off* / *up* last week. She's very upset.
5 My parents think we should try to save *up* / *on* some money before we get married.

DEVELOPING CONVERSATIONS
Did I tell you ...?

5 Match the beginnings (1–6) to the endings (a–f).

1 Did I tell you Lucy and Chris have   a saw Marina last week?
2 Did I tell you Mark and I are going   b get married?
3 Did I tell you Layla is   c broken up?
4 Did I tell you I   d having a party and you're invited?
5 Did I tell you Paul has got   e to go to Brazil?
6 Did I tell you Charles is going to   f a new girlfriend?

6 Complete the conversations with the words in the box.

get	going	got	has	have	is	meet	saw	seen

1 A: Did I tell you Max and Hana are ¹*going* to move to Hong Kong?

B: Wow! Did I tell you that Max's sister Lin ² .... broken up with Tom?

A: I know! I hear she's going to ³ .... married to a workmate.

2 C: Did I tell you I ⁴ .... Mr Foster the other day? With a new girlfriend!

D: No! Mr Foster? Did I tell you I'm going to ⁵ .... his ex-wife on Tuesday?

E: Did I tell you Mrs Foster's going to ⁶ .... a baby?

C and D: What?

3 F: Did I tell you Amy and Ben ⁷ .... divorced last month?

G: Oh, that's a shame. Did I tell you Ann ⁸ .... three months' pregnant?

F: What? But she hasn't ⁹ .... her husband for six months!

7 🔊 **16.1 Listen and check.**

LISTENING

8 🔊 **16.2 Listen. Who are the two people in the photos?**

9 Listen again and match the names to the relationships.

1 Rob   Shelley's old boyfriend
2 Mum   Rob's wife
3 Shelley   Rob's mother
4 Kevin   Shelley's father
5 Pam   Rob's daughter

10 Listen again and choose the correct information.

1 Rob is calling with some *bad / good* news.
2 Shelley *is / isn't* going to get married.
3 Shelley met a man at *work / a party*.
4 He's a *student / professor* at the university.
5 They're going to get married *on a beach / in a church*.
6 Rob and Pam are going to visit Brazil for a few *weeks / days*.

11 Complete the summary of the conversation with the words in the box.

known	sure	~~get married~~	divorce
surprised	broke up	fell in love with	

Rob is phoning his mother to tell her that his daughter, Shelley, is going to ¹ *get married*. Granny thinks Shelley is going to marry Kevin, but Rob tells her that Shelley and Kevin ² .... three months ago. Shelley was working in Brazil when she ³ .... a Brazilian man. He's a professor at the university. She hasn't ⁴ .... him very long. Rob was ⁵ .... about the wedding, but he's going to go out to Brazil with his wife, Pam. Granny isn't ⁶ .... about the marriage. She thinks it will end in ⁷ ....

GRAMMAR Past continuous

1 Complete the sentences with the past continuous form of the verbs in the box.

have	listen	eat	shop	stay	visit

1 She *was having* lunch with her family.
2 He .... to music in his bedroom.
3 I .... with friends in Jakarta.
4 They .... at the mall opposite the cinema.
5 I .... the packet of biscuits that you gave me.
6 You .... your family on the farm.

2 Rewrite the sentences in exercise 1 as negative sentences.
1 .... *She wasn't having lunch with her family*
2 ....
3 ....
4 ....
5 ....
6 ....

3 Make questions from the statements.
1 You were talking about me.
   Were you talking about me?
2 She was walking to work.
   ....
3 They were buying some new clothes.
   ....
4 He was calling his sister on the phone.
   ....
5 Your parents were having a nice time.
   ....
6 I was spending too much time online.
   ....

4 Look at the pictures and complete the sentences with the past continuous and past simple forms of the verbs in brackets.

I *was watching* TV when the cat *came* in.
(watch / come)

We .... in Egypt when we .... this.
(live / buy)

He .... the house when it .... to rain.
(leave / start)

They .... to a party when the car .... down.
(go / break)

5 Complete the text with the past simple or past continuous form of the verbs in brackets.

I [1] *was living* in Spain when I met Miguel. I [2] .... (work) as a teacher at a language school in Granada. One day, I [3] .... (sit) at a table in the café next door to the school when he [4] .... (come) in. I [5] .... (notice) him at once because I [6] .... (think) he was very good looking. I [7] .... (walk) to the door when he [8] .... (look) right at me and smiled. He [9] .... (have) lovely eyes. We [10] .... (get married) six months later.

PRONUNCIATION Sentence stress and weak forms

6 🔊 16.3 Listen to how *was* and *were* are pronounced in these sentences. Are they weak or stressed? Write *W* for weak and *S* for stressed.
1 I was watching TV at home. ....*W*.......
2 What were you thinking about? ....
3 She wasn't looking for a boyfriend. ....
4 I was making a coffee in the kitchen. ....
5 They were eating outside under the trees. ....
6 We weren't playing tennis when you saw us. ....

7 Now listen again and underline the stressed words in each sentence.

8 Listen again and check. Repeat the sentences.

READING

9 Read the love stories. How many of the couples got married?

Great love stories

ORPHEUS AND EURYDICE

Orpheus and Eurydice fell in love, married and lived together happily until Eurydice was bitten by a **snake** and died. Orpheus travelled to **the Underworld**. He sang beautiful songs to Hades, the god of the dead. Hades agreed to let Eurydice return with Orpheus. But he told Orpheus that he must not look at her until they were both back in their world. But Orpheus turned around just before they got back and Eurydice disappeared forever.

SHAH JAHAN AND MUMTAZ MAHAL

Emperor Shah Jahan was fifteen when he married 14-year-old Mumtaz Mahal in 1607. They were together for seventeen happy years and had fourteen children before Mumtaz died. The emperor was heartbroken. The following year, he started construction of the Taj Mahal, a huge white building in memory of his wife. It took nearly twenty-one years to complete. When Jahan died, he was **buried** next to his wife in the Taj Mahal.

LAYLA AND MAJNUN

Layla and Qays fell in love when they were young. Qays wrote love poems about Layla, and when they were older he asked Layla's father if they could get married. Her father said no. Qays was heartbroken. He ran into the desert and stayed there. He started **behaving** very strangely and people called him 'Majnun', meaning 'mad man'. Layla married another man and moved away. Majnun followed her, but they were never together in life. But when they died, they were buried side by side, together **at last**.

Glossary

snake: a long, thin animal with no legs and a smooth skin

the Underworld: in old stories, a place below the earth where people go when they die

bury: to put a person who has died in the ground

behave: to do things in a particular way

at last: used when something which you have been waiting for finally happens

---

10 Read the stories again and circle the correct answers.

1 Eurydice was killed by a *dog / snake*.
2 Orpheus went *to the Underworld / abroad* to get Eurydice back.
3 Shah Jahan married Mumtaz Mahal when he was *fourteen / fifteen*.
4 Construction of the Taj Mahal took *under / over* twenty years.
5 *Qays / Layla* went mad.
6 Layla married *Majnun / another man*.

11 Are statements 1–6 true or false? Circle T or F.

1 Hades agreed to let Orpheus take Eurydice with him.	T	F
2 Eurydice disappeared because Orpheus turned and looked at her.	T	F
3 Shah Jahan and Mumtaz Mahal had seventeen children.	T	F
4 Shah Jahan and Mumtaz Mahal are buried together.	T	F
5 Layla's father wanted Qays to marry his daughter.	T	F
6 Layla and Majnun were reunited in death.	T	F

GRAMMAR *will / won't* for promises

1 Write the words in the correct order to make promises.

1 me / Will / every day? / call / you

....

2 tell / more news. / I'll / I hear / when / you

....

3 worry. / anyone. / I / tell / Don't / won't

....

4 I / be / See / late. / later. / you / won't

....

5 I / I / a mess. / make / promise / won't

....

6 I'll / tomorrow. / pay / promise / back / you / I

....

Language note

We can use *I hope so* and *I hope not* to respond and agree with statements about the future. We use *I hope so* to agree with positive statements and *I hope not* to agree with negative statements. For example:

A: *I promise I'll pay you back tomorrow.*

B: **I hope so.**

A: *I won't do that again.*

B: **I hope not.**

2 Match sentences (1–6) with responses (a–f).

1 Will you marry me?
2 Please don't tell anybody.
3 I'll be back by ten. Promise.
4 You will call me, won't you?
5 I really will do better next year.
6 I won't see her or talk to her ever again.

a Don't worry. I won't.
b I hope not.
c It's nice of you to ask, but I don't think I'm ready.
d I'll be here, waiting.
e I hope so.
f Yes, sure. I'll do it as soon as I get home.

3 Correct the mistakes in the sentences.

1 A: Bye. Take care.
   B: I'll. Bye.
   ....*I will. Bye*...................

2 Don't worry. I won't to forget.

....

3 You will call me?

....

4 He wills be here by five o'clock.

....

5 Why you won't help?

....

DEVELOPING WRITING Writing a story (with time sequencers)

4 Look at the notes on the story of Romeo and Juliet. Then read the story and circle the phrases in the box that help to describe the sequence of events.

- Romeo and Juliet lived in Verona.
- Their families were enemies.
- They met at a party and fell in love.
- They got married.
- Juliet's cousin killed Romeo's friend in an argument.
- Romeo killed Juliet's cousin.
- Juliet's father wanted her to marry someone else.
- Juliet pretended to be dead but she was only sleeping.
- Romeo thought she was dead, so he killed himself.
- Juliet woke up, saw Romeo dead and killed herself.
- The two families stopped fighting and became friends.

One night / day,	Finally,	A short time later,	Then

The greatest love story

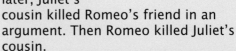

Romeo and Juliet lived in Verona. Their families were enemies. One night, they met at a party and fell in love. Then they got married.

A short time later, Juliet's cousin killed Romeo's friend in an argument. Then Romeo killed Juliet's cousin.

Juliet's father told her he wanted her to marry someone else. Juliet pretended to be dead but she was only sleeping. Romeo thought she was dead, so he killed himself. A short time later, Juliet woke up, saw Romeo dead and killed herself.

Finally, the families of the two lovers stopped fighting and became friends.

5 You are going to write a love story. Look at the notes. Choose sequencers from the box in exercise 4 and write the story.

- Mark Antony was a Roman General and Cleopatra was the Queen of Egypt.
- They met and fell in love.
- Mark Antony returned to Rome and married Octavian's sister.
- Mark Antony left Octavian's sister and returned to Cleopatra.
- Antony and Cleopatra got married.
- Octavian was angry and sent an army to fight Antony and Cleopatra.
- Antony and Cleopatra lost.
- Antony thought Cleopatra was dead, so he killed himself.
- Cleopatra killed herself after seeing Antony dead.

The love story of Antony and Cleopatra

Mark Antony was a Roman General and Cleopatra was the Queen of Egypt. One day, they met and fell in love. ....
....
....
....
....
....
....
....
....
....
....
....
....
....
....

Vocabulary Builder Quiz 16

Download the Vocabulary Builder for Unit 16 and try the quiz below. Write your answers in your notebook. Then check them and record your score.

1 Match the words (1–5) to (a–e) to make compound nouns.
1 wedding   a appointment
2 mother   b club
3 night   c anniversary
4 hospital   d present
5 birthday   e -in-law

2 Cross out the word in each group that doesn't collocate.
1 *tall / high / good-looking / nice* person
2 *trouble / big / good / bad* influence
3 hold *the baby / an anniversary / a cup / my hand*

3 Complete the sentences with the correct preposition.
1 I've just heard that Katy and Mike have broken ....
2 This is the holiday .... my dreams.
3 When she saw the house, it was love .... first sight.
4 Jake! Please let go .... your sister's hair!
5 The book had a big influence .... Sasha.
6 Pip's parents don't approve................... her new boyfriend.
7 She writes books .... a living.

4 Find words that are both verbs and nouns to complete the sentences.
1 What flowers shall we .... in the garden?
  I want to buy a .... for my mum's birthday.
2 She isn't the kind of person who would .... a promise.
  We'll have a .... at ten before the second part of the lesson.
3 Sorry to .... you, but do you know where the station is?
  My brother often got into .... at school.
4 We took the .... to the fourteenth floor.
  Can you help me .... this box? It's heavy.
5 You have to keep your .... and come to the party.
  Do you .... to write to me every day?

5 Match the beginnings (1–5) to the endings (a–e).
1 Will you help me remove   a of my sister's boyfriend.
2 My parents always encouraged   b this paint from the carpet?
3 Mum doesn't approve   c an appointment to see the dentist.
4 I thought I heard someone knock   d each other to follow their dreams.
5 I'm afraid you need to have   e at the door.

Score ___/25

Wait a couple of weeks and try the quiz again. Compare your scores.

AUDIOSCRIPT

Unit 1

⏺ 1.1
1 What's your first name?
2 What's your surname?
3 Where are you from?
4 Which part?

⏺ 1.2
1

L = Lily, B = Brad
L: Hi, I'm Lily. What's your name?
B: Hi, I'm Brad. Nice to meet you.
L: Yeah. Nice to meet you, too. Where are you from?
B: I'm from the USA.

2

D = Doctor, J = Julio
D: What's your name?
J: Julio.
D: Is that your first name?
J: Yes.
D: Right. And what's your surname?
J: da Silva.
D: OK. Thanks.

3

K = Ken, Y = Yolanda
K: Hi, Come in. Sit down. My name's Ken. I'm a teacher here.
Y: I'm Yolanda. Nice to meet you.
K: Nice to meet you, too. Are you from Spain, Yolanda?
Y: No, I'm not. I'm from Argentina.
K: Oh, sorry. Which part?
Y: Posadas. It's in the north.

⏺ 1.3
Japan
Kenya
Italy

⏺ 1.4
China
Mexico
Brazil

Unit 2

⏺ 2.1

M = Man, W = Woman
M: Do you want to go to dinner?
W: That sounds nice. Where do you want to go?
M: I like Thai food. What about you?
W: Yeah, great. What time do you want to meet?
M: Is 7.30 OK?
W: Good. See you later then.
M: See you. Oh, where do you want to meet?
W: At the bus stop.
M: OK. See you there at 7.30.

⏺ 2.2

A = Ana, J = Joshua
A: Who's that?
J: Him? Oh, that's Jack. He's funny.

A: He looks good. Does he like doing sports?
J: No, he doesn't, but he loves music. He plays the piano. He listens to his music all the time.
A: And who's next to him in the photo?
J: That's Will. He's Emily's brother. That's Emily. They are very different. Emily loves studying but her brother loves watching TV.
A: Who's this? The woman with black hair.
J: That's Grace.
A: OK … I think *Grace* likes doing sport. Am I right?
J: Almost. She likes dancing.
A: Oh, OK. Doesn't *anyone* like doing sport?
J: *I* do!
A: I know, Joshua! But what about your *friends*?
J: And Daniel likes sport. That's Daniel there. And that's Chloe.
A: Wow! She looks great. Is she Daniel's sister?
J: No, she isn't, but they look similar. She looks good because she *loves* shopping and she knows where to go to find all the *best* clothes!
A: I want to meet her!

⏺ 2.3
1 scissors
2 window
3 relax
4 manager
5 cathedral
6 dictionary

⏺ 2.4
1 homework	relax	money
2 early	tonight	arrange
3 exercise	cinema	computer

Unit 3

⏺ 3.1
S = Sue, M = Meena
S: I need to get some stamps from the post office.
M: I want to go to the post office, too. I need to mail a package to my sister. It's her birthday next week.
S: Ah, that's nice. Oh, yes and I want to exchange some money for our skiing holiday, too.
M: OK. And then we can eat lunch. I'm hungry!
S: I don't want to eat but I'm cold. I want to drink a coffee.
M: OK! … Then I'd like to go to the chemist's. I want to buy some aspirins for Anil. And is there a clothes shop near here?
S: Yes, there's one opposite the cinema. Why?
M: I need to purchase a jacket for our holiday. It's cold in the mountains.

⏺ 3.2
A = Agent, J = Jane
A: Hello? Gibbs Properties, Paul speaking. Can I help you?
J: Hello. Is that Gibbs Properties?
A: Yes, it is.
J: Hello. My name's Jane Dreyfus. I want to rent a flat in north Selfield. Do you have anything available?
A: Let me see … Yes, we have a one-bedroom flat in north Selfield from June 1st.

J: Where exactly?

A: The address is 12 Wharton Drive. That's W-H-A-R-T-O-N.

J: And how much is it?

A: It's 590 pounds basic rent plus 40 pounds for gas and electricity, which makes a total of 630 pounds per month.

J: Mm. I don't want to pay more than £600.

A: But it is a beautiful flat. You can call the landlord and arrange to see the property if you like.

J: Yes, good idea. What's his phone number?

A: It's 09146 71903.

J: Thanks. And are there any local facilities?

A: There's a supermarket and a café next to the flat.

J: OK, thanks.

A: Thank you. Goodbye.

⏺ 3.3

1 I can come next week.

2 He can't help us.

3 They can't see the film.

4 We can drive there.

5 She can watch TV in here.

6 I can't make you a sandwich.

Unit 4

⏺ 4.1

L = Lee, A = Aisyha

1

L: So, how was New York?

A: Great! We stayed in the Waverley Hotel.

L: That sounds nice.

A: Yes, it was very comfortable.

2

B = Ben, H = Hassan

B: Do you want to come to the park with me tomorrow? There's a free concert with Kasabian.

H: Hmm. That sounds interesting. I really like them. What time is it?

B: I think it starts at two o'clock.

3

P = Phil, G = Gudrun

P: How was your weekend?

G: Andreas was ill. He stayed in bed *all* weekend.

P: That sounds bad. Is he OK now?

G: He's fine. It was only a cold.

⏺ 4.2

/t/   walked

/d/   played

/ɪd/ visited

⏺ 4.3

cooked	wanted	chatted	showed	liked
rained	needed	tried	relaxed	

⏺ 4.4

1 The fourth of July

2 The twenty-fifth of April

3 The third of November

4 The twelfth of October

5 The first of May

⏺ 4.5

1

S = Sam, B = Bella

S: Hi, Bella. Sorry I'm late. How was your weekend?

B: Oh, great, thanks. It was my birthday on Saturday, so we went out for dinner.

S: Happy Birthday! Did you go anywhere nice?

B: Yeah. That new restaurant in Bank Street.

S: Oh, the Italian one?

B: That's right. I had fish, and Mark had pizza. It was really good!

S: Mmm. Sounds good.

B: And I got a lot of great presents. Mark gave me a lovely new jacket. Anyway, how about you? How was your weekend?

S: Well, not so good, actually, my dog ran away...

2

A = Ann, C = Claire

A: What did you do at the weekend, Claire?

C: I went to see my sister. It was really nice.

A: Oh, where does she live now?

C: In Dublin.

A: Oh, yes. I remember.

C: Yeah, we went to a rock festival in the park. And, well – we saw Julie!

A: What? Julie from here? From the office?

C: Yes.

A: At the rock festival?

C: Yes, at the rock festival. And she was with a new man!

A: Really! That sounds interesting. Where were they ...

3

Rc = Ricardo, R = Rob

Rc: Where were you yesterday? You missed the football match.

R: Yeah, I know.

Rc: Why? What happened?

R: Well, I thought it started at two o'clock, so I left home at one.

Rc: It started at twelve!

R: Yes, I know that now.

Rc: Well, we waited for you. Carlos stayed outside for twenty minutes after the game started.

R: Oh, no. Really? I saw the last fifteen minutes of the game on TV in a shop window.

Rc: Oh, that sounds really bad.

R: Yeah. I spent *all* my money on that ticket. It was a lot.

Rc: Oh, no. Well ... I took some photos. Do you want to see them?

R: OK. Why not?

Unit 5

⏺ 5.1

W = Woman, M = Man, S = Shopkeeper

W: I want this one.

M: Yeah, that one is the nicest. ... Excusez moi.

S: Can I help you?

M: Oh, you speak English. Great. We're from the United States!

S: Ah, yes.

M: How much are the Eiffel Towers?

S: These ones?

M: Not those. Those ones over there.

S: OK. They are thirty euros each.

M: Wow. That's too expensive. And those, near you? The small ones.

S: These are ten euros each.

W: Can we have two of those, please?

S: Two small ones. OK. That's twenty euros, please.

2

W = Woman, M = Man

W: Hello. Do you want some fruit?

M: Yes. It looks lovely.

W: What would you like?

M: How much are the bananas?

W: Sixty-four baht for one kilo.

M: And how many bananas are there in a kilo?

W: About eight.

M: OK, a kilo of bananas, please. And how much are the mangos?

W: Thirty baht each.

M: OK. Thanks. Can I have that one and those two, please?

W: Do you want a pineapple?

M: No, thanks. Just the mangos and the bananas, please.

3

W = Woman, S = Shopkeeper

W: Excuse me. What's this dress made of?

S: Cotton.

W: Do you have it in small?

S: No. Just medium or large.

W: And this shirt?

S: Also cotton but we only have it in medium and large.

W: And this jacket? What's it made of?

S: Leather.

W: OK. How much is it please?

S: Three thousand five hundred rupees. Fifty pounds. Are you British?

W: No, I'm Australian. So that's around eighty Australian dollars. It's too much. Would you take three thousand rupees?

S: hmm ... Three thousand four hundred. It's *very* good quality.

W: I'm afraid I can't pay more than three thousand two hundred for it.

S: OK. I can give it to you for three thousand two hundred. Cash?

🍂 5.2

W = Woman, S = Shopkeeper

W: Excuse me. How much are the cakes?

S: These white ones?

W: No, those yellow ones.

S: These? Three for a quid.

W: What are they made of?

S: Eggs, sugar and flour, of course.

W: Oh, OK.

S: How many would you like?

W: Three, please.

S: Anything else?

W: Can I have some bread, please?

S: How much would you like?

W: One loaf is fine.

S: That's two quid. Thanks, love.

🍂 5.3

1 thirteen

2 one hundred and fifty

3 three hundred and sixteen

4 five hundred and ninety

5 two thousand and forty

6 fourteen thousand

🍂 5.4

1 One hundred twenty

2 Three hundred and eighteen

3 Two hundred and fourteen

4 Three thousand sixty

5 One thousand and thirty

6 Nine thousand forty

🍂 5.5

S = Steve, M = Mary

S: OK, Mary. He's coming this way.

M: Where are you, Steve?

S: I'm next to the lifts. Can you see me?

M: No, I'm looking at the lifts but I can't see you.

S: I'm walking towards him.

M: Oh, yes. OK, I see you. And I think I see him. Is he wearing jeans?

S: Yes. He's wearing jeans and a white shirt.

M: Yes, I can see him. He's carrying a bag.

S: Yes, that's him. I'm following him. He's leaving the store.

M: In a white jacket?

S: No, not white. BLACK! It's one of our black jackets!

M: A black jacket? And an umbrella?

S: Yes.

M: Ah, yes, he's wearing a black jacket ...

S: No! He's *holding* the jacket and he's got a black bag.

M: Oh, YES. I see him! Yes, that's him. Stop him, Steve! He's going out of the door with *our* jacket!

S: It's OK. I'm closing the doors now.

🍂 5.6

1

Can I try these on?

Of course. The changing rooms are over there.

2

Can I pay here?

Sorry, this till's closed. Could you use that one?

3

How do I get to the second floor?

There's an escalator just here.

4

Where's womenswear, please?

It's on the fourth floor.

5

Do you sell books for children?

Yes, there are some down there, on the bottom shelf.

6

When does the sale end?

On Saturday. There are some great bargains.

UNIT 6

☻ 6.1

1 How are you?
2 Are you working?
3 What are you studying?
4 What class are they in?
5 Are you hungry?
6 Where are you staying?

☻ 6.2

1
H = Hassan, B = Brendan
H: How's the course going?
B: Really well. I'm really enjoying it.
H: What's good about it?
B: Well, the teacher is very good. I really like her. And the other students are very friendly.
H: Wow. It sounds great! Is there anything you don't like?
B: No. I'm really happy!

2
L = Lucy, A = Ahmed
L: How's the course going?
A: Not very well. It's really boring. And it's a lot of work.
L: Oh, dear.
A: I think I chose the wrong subject.
L: Oh, no.
A: Yes. I don't really like chemistry. I'm not sure it's what I want to do.

☻ 6.3

1
I = Interviewer, F = Felix
I: What do you do, Felix?
F: I'm a student at Sheffield University.
I: Right. So, what are you studying?
F: I'm doing a degree in law.
I: Wow. Are you enjoying it?
F: Not really. It's not going very well.
I: Oh, why not?
F: I didn't do very well in my exams.
I: Oh, no.
F: Yes, I was lazy and I didn't work. The exams were really difficult. I think I chose the wrong subject.
I: Oh, dear.

2
I = Interviewer, K = Keiko
I: What do you do, Keiko?
K: Well, I'm a doctor, but I'm not working at the moment.
I: Oh, what are you doing?
K: I'm doing an English course.
I: Really? How's the course going?
K: It's great! It's really varied. I'm learning so much!
I: Are the other students nice?
K: Oh, yes. They're really friendly. And the teachers are very helpful.
I: Oh, that's nice.
K: Yes. I'm really enjoying it. I don't want to go back to work!

3
I = Interviewer, L = Luis
I: What are you studying, Luis?
L: Engineering.
I: Oh, OK. And how's the course going?
L: It's a lot of work, but I'm enjoying it. It's really interesting.
I: What year are you in?
L: My second year. I've got exams next month.
I: Oh, good luck!

UNIT 7

☻ 7.1

I = Inge, M = Marco
I: Do you have any brothers and sisters, Marco?
M: Yes. Two brothers and a sister.
I: Older or younger?
M: My sister is two years older than me and my brothers are both younger.
I: And are your parents in Italy?
M: Yes, they are ... in Perugia. All the family lives there.
I: What do they do?
M: My mum's a school teacher and my dad works in the university.
I: What do they teach?
M: Dad teaches Italian and Mum teaches English.
I: Oh, right. That's why you're so good at languages. You're definitely the best at English in our class. How many languages do you speak?
M: Well, there's English, French, German, some Arabic and, of course, Italian. That's five. I love learning languages. What about you?
I: Me too, but I only speak German, English, and a bit of Italian. Just three. My parents are teachers, too.
M: Are they? What do they teach?
I: Skiing.
M: Wow. How old are they?
I: They're both forty this year.
M: Oh, they are young. So how old are you?
I: How old do you think? And what about your parents – how old are they?
M: My dad is fifty and my mum is forty-eight. They aren't so sporty, though.
I: Do you live with them?
M: No, I don't but we – my wife and I – live in the same city.
I: Wife? Your wife! You're married!
M: Yes, I am. Her name's Sonia.
I: er ... Do you have any children?
M: Yes, we do. A son, Luca.
I: Do you? er ... Wow! That's great.
M: Are you OK?
I: Oh, yes, yes. ... Sure. ... Is that the time? I have to go.
M: OK, Inge. See you later.

☻ 7.2

1 Sean and Caitlin can speak Mandarin Chinese.
   Can they?
2 We only paid €2 for this.
   Did you?

3 Look. It's snowing.
   Is it?

4 We are about thirty minutes late.
   Are we?

5 Fiona was off work all last week.
   Was she?

6 James has a Porsche and a Ferrari.
   Does he?

🎧 7.3

K = Karl, L = Luke

K: So, Luke. Do your parents live here in New York?

L: No, sir. They live in Ohio.

K: I see. So do you live in a college dormitory?

L: No, sir. I share an apartment with two other students.

K: Is that right? And tonight you want to take Britney there?

L: No, sir. There's a party at our college.

K: Is there? And will there be any teachers at this party?

L: Oh, yes, sir. It's our graduation party.

K: Is it? Good. And what about the future, do you have plans to return to Ohio?

L: No, sir. I want to work here in New York City.

K: Do you? And do you know exactly what you want to do?

L: Oh, yes, sir. I have a job at the Bank of America.

K: Really? Son, I think it's time you started calling me Karl ...

🎧 7.4

W = Woman, M = Man

W: So, what did you think of them?

M: Well, they were all very nice. It's so difficult to choose.

W: I liked Jason best.

M: Who was he? The first one?

W: Yes. He was very friendly, and quite funny. I liked his joke about the dog and the cat.

M: Hmm. Do you think he'll fit in here?

W: What do you mean?

M: Well, this is a quiet office. I like it that way. I thought Jason was a bit loud.

W: Hmm. Maybe. He was certainly very confident.

M: Confident? Yes, he talked non-stop! It was difficult for anyone else to say anything!

W: But he really knows what he's good at. He's got a lot of experience even though he didn't go to university.

M: Well, I don't think he would get on well with the others here ... What about Luis?

W: The Spanish guy? Yeah ...

M: He speaks English really well.

W: Yes, he does. But do you think he's too young?

M: How old is he? Let me see. Twenty-three. He left university six months ago.

W: Hmm. Younger than Jason. He's twenty-six.

M: He was very different to Jason. He was quieter, for a start. He was a really nice guy. I liked him.

W: I agree he's nice, but he doesn't have a lot of experience.

M: Well, he speaks three languages, and he studied IT at university, so he's obviously very good with computers.

W: Hmm. What did you think of Kerry? I liked her a lot. She went to a very good university.

M: Well, I thought she was OK. Very clever, obviously, but...

W: What?

M: Well, I thought she was a nice woman. And she answered our questions really well, but she was a bit quiet. She didn't say much at all.

W: Jason was too loud for you and Kerry was too quiet! Kerry has more experience than Jason or Luis and I think she would be more reliable. She worked at Miller's for two years, you know.

M: I'm not sure.

W: Well, we have to decide by the end of the day so let's talk to ...

UNIT 8

🎧 8.1

R = Richard, J = Jan

R: Is it going to be sunny at the weekend?

J: Yes, I think so. That's what I heard on the radio.

R: Good! Then we're going to have the party outside.

J: OK. But we're going to need some more chairs.

R: I'm going to see John later. I can ask him to bring some.

J: Good idea. Is he going to bring some extra plates and glasses, too?

R: Yes, he is.

🎧 8.2

K = Katrina, J = Julia

K: Hello, Julia. It's Katrina.

J: Yeah, hi Katrina. How are you doing?

K: Fine, thanks. Hey, listen, What're you doing tomorrow night? Do you want to come to the cinema with me and Christian? We're going to see that new Matt Damon film.

J: Tomorrow? That's Friday, right? Oh, I can't. I'm going to meet some friends for dinner. Actually, I think you know them. Do you remember Sophie and Rob?

K: Your friends from Scotland?

J: That's right. They're here for a wedding this weekend, and Friday night's the only night they're going to be free.

K: Oh, that's a shame. How about another time? What're you doing over the weekend? Are you busy?

J: Well, on Sunday I'm going to visit my parents. But I'm free on Saturday.

K: Well, I'm going to London on Saturday. Do you want to come? I'm going to go shopping in Covent Garden.

J: Good idea. Are you going to get the train?

K: Yes. Sometime in the morning. I think there's one at around nine thirty. Let me see .... Yes, here it is. Nine thirty-seven.

J: That sounds great! I need to get a new coat for the winter. Do you want to meet at the station?

K: OK. But I'm going to drive to the station and leave the car in the station car park. Do you want to come with me?

J: Oh, yes, please.

K: OK. I'll pick you up at nine.

J: Great. See you then! Bye, Katrina.

K: Bye.

8.3

1 So, are you gonna cook dinner for me tonight?
2 It's going to be so romantic!
3 I'm not gonna go to bed early!
4 Are you going to do your homework now?
5 Tonight we're gonna watch football on TV.
6 Is he gonna clean his room?

8.4

1 It's gonna be great!
2 I'm gonna go now.
3 Are you gonna eat that?
4 We're gonna leave at eight.
5 They're gonna lose the match!

8.5

L = Lee, D = Dagmara

L: What're you doing tonight?
D: Nothing. Why?
L: Do you want to go out somewhere?
D: Yeah. We can go to the cinema in town.
L: Good idea. What do you want to see?
D: There's a new film with George Clooney. I love him. I think it starts at eight.
L: OK. Do you want to go for a coffee first?
D: That sounds great. Do you know a good place to meet?
L: How about at Michel's Café at seven o'clock?
D: Perfect. See you there!

UNIT 9

9.1

M = Maya, D = Didi

D: Do you know where you're going on holiday this summer?
M: I can't decide. I'm thinking of going to France.
D: You should! It's a beautiful place. We're thinking of going to Venice.
M: Don't! It's a beautiful place but there are too many people there in summer!
D: OK, we're also thinking of going to Miami.
M: You should! We've been there lots of times. It's great! The weather is fantastic!
D: Have you? Oh yes, I thought we could go shopping there.
M: Don't! It's boring. The European styles are more interesting.
D: Oh, OK. So where do you want to go in France?
M: I thought I'd go to Paris.
D: Don't! It's full of tourists! Why don't you go south?
M: Yes, maybe. A friend of mine, Tina, told me I should go to Bordeaux.
D: You should! It's so relaxing and the food is amazing! My friend, Carla, told me we should go to *Le Petit Chat* for a good meal in Miami.
M: Don't!
D: Why this time?
M: It's awful! If you want a really good meal in Miami, go to Gianni's. It's a wonderful Italian restaurant.
D: Why don't I just go to Italy?
M: Oh, you should! The Italians are so stylish and the shops are full of beautiful clothes!
D: But you just told me not to. Oh, forget it!

9.2

E = Egyptian man, V = Veronica

E: Have you been to Egypt before?
V: No, I haven't. This is my first time, but my husband has – he was in Alexandria, in the north of Egypt.
E: It's a very beautiful place. Well, I hope you're enjoying my country. Have you seen any famous places yet?
V: Oh, yes! We've been to Luxor.
E: Oh, very good. Did you like it?
V: Yes, we loved it. It was very romantic. And we saw the Valley of the Kings.
E: It's a beautiful place. And very important for Egyptians. Have you been to the Pyramids and seen the Sphinx here?
V: No, we haven't, but we want to see them. I went to St. Catherine's Monastery a few days ago.
E: Did you and your husband enjoy it?
V: Well, actually my husband was ill so I went on my own.
E: Oh, and what did you think of it?
V: It took a very long time to get there – and back. And we were only there for a very short time, so I wasn't very happy.
E: That's a pity. But it's true, it's a long way from here. It's near the beach. Have you been to the Red Sea?
V: Yes, we have. It was amazing! We love swimming and we spent two weeks at the beach before we came to Cairo. And I'm going back next week. My husband is going to Jordan for two days to see a friend so I'm going back to the beach!

9.3

1 The train is cheaper.
2 We love it!
3 She arrived two weeks ago.
4 We slept in a tent.
5 It was a great experience.
6 He fell and broke his arm.

UNIT 10

10.1

1
A: Yes, I'd like a ticket to London, please. For today.
B: Single?
A: No, return, please. I'm coming back on Thursday.
B: OK. First or second class?
A: Second is fine.
2
A: That's £62.70, please. How would you like to pay? By cash or card?
B: Is Visa OK?
A: Of course. Just enter your PIN here, please. Thank you.
B: Which platform is it?
A: Number 3.
B: Is it a direct train?
A: No, you have to change at Crewe.

3

A: You're late!

B: I know. I'm really sorry. There was a delay.

A: What happened?

B: We stopped for nearly forty minutes. There was a cow on the line!

A: Oh, no.

10.2

1 It's quarter to five.

2 Ten past two.

3 At twenty-five to four.

4 Quarter past nine.

5 Five to eleven.

6 Come at five to nine.

10.3

1

A: Excuse me. Is this the stop for the station?

B: Sorry?

A: For the station. Is it this stop?

B: Oh, no. Not for the station. This is the city centre.

A: Oh. Which stop do I get off at for the station?

B: Do you mean the bus station or the train station?

A: The train station.

B: Oh, erm … it's not the next one – that's the bus station. I think it's the one after that. Yeah, the one after that. That's right.

A: Thank you.

2

C: Oh, the train's stopping.

D: Oh no! We aren't moving at all.

C: Don't worry. It's a direct train.

D: No, it isn't. We have to change at the next station. We're going to miss our connection.

C: Oh, dear. What time does it leave?

D: Er, twelve forty-two, from platform 8.

C: It's twelve twenty now. Which platform do we arrive at?

D: I don't know. Two or maybe three.

Driver: Ladies and gentlemen. We are sorry for the delay. There is a problem with the train. We are waiting for another train …

3

E: Can I help you?

F: Yes, I'd like a ticket to Preston, please. For today.

E: Single or return?

F: Return. I'm coming back on Thursday.

E: OK. First or second class?

F: Second is fine.

E: OK. That's £62.00, please.

F: Oh, I forgot. I'm a student. Can I get a discount?

E: Yes, you can buy a student card for £15.00 and then you get 50% off.

F: That sounds good.

E: OK. One student railcard, and your ticket. That's £46.00, please. How would you like to pay?

F: Is a credit card OK?

E: Of course. Just enter your PIN here, please. Thank you.

10.4

1 Which stop do I get off at for the station?

2 Do you mean the bus station or the train station?

3 We have to change at the next station.

4 I don't know. Two or maybe three.

5 Yes, I'd like a ticket to Preston, please.

6 Yes, you can buy a student card for £15.00 and then you get 50% off.

10.5

L = Liam, E = Ewa

L: Welcome, Ewa. It's great you're going to stay with us for a few weeks. Is there anything you would like to know?

E: Thank you. Yes, I have some questions. Where is the best place to change money?

L: Well, the post office opposite here probably gives the best rate.

E: Oh, great. And where's the best place to get some exercise?

L: Try Baxter's Gym. It's good – with a great pool – but it's a bit expensive. Oh, and if you want to go cycling there are lots of bike lanes.

E: Thanks. That sounds really good.

L: And you can use our mountain bikes any time.

E: Fantastic. Thanks. Oh, and where's the best place to eat?

L: In this house, of course! But in town try Bon Appetit. The food is good there and so is the atmosphere.

E: Great! I'm going to try it. And where's the best place to go shopping?

L: Hmm, what sort of things do you like buying?

E: Clothes, maybe.

L: Right. Try Up Market, in the city centre. They have a great selection of different clothes there. And if you want to get a haircut, they have a good salon upstairs. Our daughter Sonia goes a lot. She comes back with a different style every time.

E: Fantastic. Thank you very much. I have just one more question. Where's the best place to go dancing?

L: No idea, but you can ask Sonia. She knows where all the good clubs are. … Sonia!

UNIT 11

11.1

A = Waiter, B = Woman, C = Man

A: Good evening. Are you ready to order?

B: Yes. For starters, I'll have the salad, please.

C: And I'll have the soup.

A: And for your main course?

B: I'd like the steak, please.

C: And I'd like the fish.

A: Oh, I'm afraid the fish has finished.

C: Oh, OK. Then I'll have the chicken.

A: Would you like any dessert?

B: Can I get some ice cream, please?

A: Ice cream. Yes. And for you, Sir?

C: Oh, just a coffee for me please. Black, no sugar.

A: Of course.

🔊 11.2

A = Waiter, S = Steve, C = Carol

A: Good evening. A table for two?

S: Yes, please.

A: Have you booked?

S: Yes, we have. The name's Lawson.

A: Ah, yes. We have a nice table for you by the window. You can see the gardens from here.

C: That's beautiful. Thank you.

A: Can I get you a drink?

S: Could I see the wine list?

A: Yes, it's right here.

S: Oh, right. What would you like? A glass of red?

C: No, you know I don't like red wine, Steve. A glass of white.

S: I'd like some red. No, I've changed my mind. Can we have a bottle of white, please? Sauvignon Blanc.

A: Of course. And here are your menus. Today's special is pasta with a seafood sauce. It's very good. ...

A: Are you ready to order?

C: Yes, please. I'd like the fish.

A: You don't want a starter?

C: No, thanks.

S: Me neither. I'm going to have some steak. And can I have some extra vegetables, please?

A: Sure. Are you OK for drinks?

C: Can I have a glass of water, please?

A: No problem. ...

S: What's the fish like?

C: I don't really like it. It doesn't taste of anything. I don't know why I didn't have the pasta. And yours?

S: I like the vegetables but the steak isn't great. It's quite dry. I don't really want to come back here again. ...

A: How was your meal?

C: Fine, thank you.

S: OK. Thanks.

A: Would you like a dessert? Or tea or coffee?

C: I'm full. Just a tea, please.

S: I'd like to try the coffee ice cream, please. Oh ... then can we have the bill, please? ...

C: How much are you going to leave?

S: Eight?

C: That's more than ten per cent. Why do you want to give such a big tip?

S: The service was good. It's only the food that wasn't so great.

C: OK. Do you want to go?

🔊 11.3

A = Aina, J = Jesús

A: Oh, let's go to this fish restaurant. I like fish.

J: Oh, I don't. I'm vegetarian!

A: Oh, right. OK. Well, how about that Chinese restaurant? I love Chinese food.

J: Me too. It looks good.

A: But it's very crowded. I don't want to wait for a table.

J: Me neither. Let's eat somewhere else. How about that pizza restaurant over there?

A: I don't really like pizza.

J: Oh, I do. I love all Italian food – pizza, pasta ... But that's OK. Do you like Indian food?

A: Yes, I love curry.

J: Great. Me too. Let's look for an Indian restaurant. And then we'll both be happy!

🔊 11.4

A = Aina, J = Jesús

A: How much coffee do you drink in a day?

J: I don't drink many cups of coffee in a day. Maybe one or two in the morning. That's all. But I'm enjoying this one.

A: Same here. I don't usually drink any hot drinks. This is very unusual for me!

J: What? Don't you drink tea?

A: No, I don't. But I drink quite a lot of soft drinks.

J: I don't drink many soft drinks at all. You know, there's a lot of sugar in soft drinks. Maybe eight spoons in a glass.

A: I know! But I don't eat any sweets.

J: Well, that's good. I eat a lot of chocolate.

A: I eat some chocolate, but not a lot.

UNIT 12

🔊 12.1

1

A: Are you OK?

B: My stomach really hurts.

A: Are you hungry?

B: Yeah. Maybe I should eat something.

2

C: Don't come near me! I've got a cold and I don't want you to get it.

D: Oh, OK. You sound really ill. Are you sure you're OK?

C: Well, I've got a very bad cough.

D: You should see the doctor. Maybe you've got a chest infection.

🔊 12.2

1

A: You look terrible. Are you OK?

B: Yes, I'm just a bit tired.

A: Maybe you should lie down.

B: No, really, I'm fine.

2

C: You've cut your hand! It looks really bad.

D: Oh, it's nothing.

C: Maybe you should go to the hospital.

D: No, really. I'll be fine.

3

E: Would you like some more cake?

F: No, thanks. I've had enough.

E: Are you sure?

F: Yes, thanks. It was delicious.

4

G: Would you like me to come round tonight?

H: No, really. I'll be fine on my own.

G: But Mark's away and you're all alone in that big house.

H: It's OK, thanks.

🎵 12.3

1

M = Makiko, MK = Mrs Kells

M: Excuse me, Mrs Kells. Can I speak to you for a minute?

MK: Come in, Makiko. What is it? Are you OK?

M: I'm sorry, but I don't feel well. I've got a terrible headache. I just can't concentrate.

MK: You had a cold last week, didn't you?

M: Yes, I missed the meeting on Friday because I had to go home.

MK: Have you been to the doctor?

M: No, it's just a cold.

MK: But you've had it for more than a week now. Maybe it's an infection. You should go home and call the doctor.

M: OK. But I think I just need to get some sleep. I'll be fine by the end of the week.

2

L = Liam, M = Mike

L: That's another point to me!

M: Ooh! Oh, that hurts!

L: Are you OK, Mike?

M: Oh. Yeah, yeah. I think I'm OK. But my chest hurts.

L: Your chest? Oh ... Oh, dear. Well, maybe you should lie down.

M: OK. Ooof. Oh. That's better. I haven't done any sport for years, you know.

L: Are you sure you're OK?

M: Yeah, I'm fine. But my leg hurts too. *And* my arm! But I'll be fine in a moment.

L: Hmm. Your arm and leg too, huh? Maybe you should take more care of yourself. Do some more sport.

M: Yeah. I'll be fine.

3

J = Jenny, P = Piotr

J: Ahhh. Oww.

P: Jenny! What are you doing on the floor? What happened?

J: What do you think? I fell off the chair. Owwww.

P: You fell off the chair?

J: Yes ... I needed to get the pan off the cupboard and I fell off the chair.

P: Are you OK?

J: Do I look OK!?

P: You've hurt your hand.

J: No! My hand's fine. I've hurt my foot. Look!

P: Ooh, yes. I see what you mean. It looks strange. It's blue.

J: I just need to rest it. Oww.

P: Maybe it's broken. You should go to the hospital.

J: Yes. I think you're right. Maybe I should.

UNIT 13

🎵 13.1

G = Gregg, D = Dan

G: We have Dan Goodman with the weather news for the region.

D: Thanks, Gregg. Good morning. We had some heavy rain over the entire region last night with some big storms in the south. These are now in the east of the region – it's still pretty bad over there. In the north it's raining right now. But the rain is going to move out of the region in the next two hours.

G: Oh boy, Dan. Those storms last night *were* bad! It was cold and very windy. The wind blew down a tree in our street!

D: Yes, those storms were bad all right, Gregg. But the west is sunny now and it's going to stay good. The south is cloudy at the moment but the clouds are clearing away and it's going to be sunny by the end of the afternoon. It's the same for the east – it's going to be dry, sunny and warm later. Gregg.

G: Thanks, Dan. Good news. So, are we going to have any more storms?

D: Not this week. That's for sure. We might see some next week but it's too early to say.

G: Many thanks, Dan Goodman. Sport now ...

🎵 13.2

C = Chloe, J = Jack

C: Come on, Jack. Why don't we go out?

J: Mmm? Who with?

C: Nobody. Just you and me.

J: Where?

C: I don't know. To the city centre?

J: How?

C: Um, why don't we walk?

J: Maybe. How long for?

C: What do you think? A couple of hours, maybe.

J: Why?

C: Because it's not good to stay inside all the time. Hey - we can go to the market!

J: What for?

C: To get something for lunch. And then why don't we go to the cinema?

J: What time?

C: I think there's a Bourne film on at five thirty. What do you think? ... Come *on*, Jack! Stop watching that TV and get off the sofa!

🎵 13.3

1 How long have you had your cat?

2 They have been together for years.

3 Has he known her for long?

4 We have studied English for more than ten years.

5 How long has she lived here?

6 Have you worked here for a long time?

UNIT 14

🎵 14.1

1

A: What's Kelly's new boyfriend like?

B: Really nice.

A: I've heard he's a bit loud.

B: No, I didn't think so. I liked him.

2

C: What was your holiday like?

D: Lovely. The beaches were beautiful and the people were really friendly.

C: What was the food like? I've heard it's really good.

D: Yeah, delicious. We didn't have one bad meal the whole time we were there.

🔊 14.2

P = Presenter, H = Holly, A = Aisha, J = Julie, R = Rashid

P: And now it's over to Holly McKenzie, who's at the premiere of the new film *Kelly's Pirates* tonight in Leicester Square. Good evening, Holly!

H: Well, hi, Dave. I'm standing outside the Prince's Cinema in Leicester Square for the world premiere of *Kelly's Pirates*. It's snowing at the moment, but that hasn't stopped the many people here who have waited hours to see the stars of the film, James McTavish and Lila Peroni. There are about two thousand people here, and a lucky 200 of them got free tickets to see the film tonight. And I think the film has just ended. Yes, people are starting to come out now. Let's ask someone what they thought of the film. Excuse me, ladies? Can I talk to you for a minute?

A: Yeah, sure.

H: Can I ask your name?

A: It's Aisha.

H: Hi, Aisha. You've just come out of the cinema, right?

A: That's right. We got two of the free tickets.

H: What was the film like?

A: Oh, it was great! It was probably one of the best films I've ever seen.

H: Really?

A: Yes. It was exciting, and funny. The acting was brilliant. James McTavish is just oh, ... he was fantastic.

H: And your friend? What's your name?

J: Julie.

H: What did you think of the film, Julie?

J: Well, it was very entertaining. But I found some parts a bit strange.

H: What do you mean, strange?

J: I didn't really understand some of it. There's a bit when they were in a hot-air balloon with some cows! It was very funny, though.

H: Well, that sounds ... interesting! Thank you very much. Sir, sir? What's your name?

R: Rashid.

H: Hi, Rashid. Can I ask you about the film? What did you think of it?

R: I thought it was terrible. I didn't like it at all.

H: Oh, dear. Was there anything about it that you liked?

R: Well, the acting was quite good, but the story was stupid. I mean, there's this bit where they're in a hot-air balloon with these cows. It was just silly. It's not my kind of film at all. In fact, it's one of the worst films I've seen in a long time.

H: At least you didn't pay for the ticket.

R: Unfortunately, I did. I'm a journalist. I didn't get a free ticket.

H: Oh, well, thank you very much. And now I can see ... is that Lila Peroni? Yes, it is. Lila, Lila, over here!

🔊 14.3

1 They'll come at ten o'clock.
2 We want to sit outside.
3 I'll see you on Thursday.
4 You'll need to bring some money.

5 We finish later tonight.
6 I think they'll bring their children.

🔊 15.1

1
A: Do you know much about geography?
B: Not really. Why?
A: Well, do you know where Malta is?
B: Malta? I'm afraid I don't know which country it's in.

2
A: Do you know much about cars?
B: A bit. I know that if you sit down and turn the little key you can get to the shops really quickly.

3
A: Do you know much about computers?
B: Yeah, quite a lot. What do you need to know?
A: Can I save documents onto this DVD?
B: Yeah. You can save anything onto it.

4
A: Do you know much about cows?
B: A bit. I know they eat grass and drink milk.
A: They drink water.
B: Mm?

5
A: Do you know much about tennis?
B: Yeah, quite a lot. Players hit a ball over a net. I'm kidding. Go ahead.
A: Why is the score 15, 30 and 40?
B: I have no idea.

🔊 15.2

P = Paul, S = Sue

P: Hi Sue. Did you get my email?

S: Hi. No. I haven't received any emails this morning.

P: It's not that important. I had a problem last night. I deleted one of your documents. Could you send it to me again?

S: Of course I will. Or I could save it onto a memory stick if you have one.

P: I don't have one on me.

S: No problem. Give me one minute. I'm just going to check my emails. Oh, yes, here's yours. But we don't need it now, do we?

P: No. I can tell you exactly what I want. It was a document about the history of the mobile phone.

S: Oh, I know the one. But I got all of that from Cellnet. You can download it from their website.

P: Oh, great. Could you send me the link?

S: Sure. I'll do it now. Oh, now what's going on? I can't go online. Aren't these machines supposed to make our lives easier?

🔊 15.3

1 /eɪ/ a h j k
2 /iː/ b c d e g p t v
3 /aɪ/ i y
4 /əʊ/ o
5 /juː/ q u w
6 /e/ f l m n s x z
7 /aː/ r

🔊 15.4

1 www.asulikit.net.au
2 24a Hurst Drive
3 yodeejay@pkan.com
4 Aceveda 4268
5 baz2@ndubz.com.ir
6 www.anderxt.org.nz

🔊 15.5

A = Shop assistant, E = Eric

A: Do you need any help?

E: Oh, yes. I'm thinking of buying a laptop but these cameras are really nice. Can you tell me something about them?

A: Sure. Well, these two are good – this is the latest model. It takes really good, sharp photos and it's a fantastic price.

E: Oh, good. How much is it?

A: That one is ... eighteen hundred pounds.

E: Wow! That's a lot of money.

A: Well, it is a lot of camera. Professional photographers use this one. Oh, and it comes with a free bag, but you have to pay for the memory card.

E: Right. Maybe I should just look at the laptops.

A: Yes, over here we've got this one. It's very popular and it comes with software fully loaded.

E: You mean I can use it immediately?

A: Yep. Straight out of the box. It isn't very heavy and the battery lasts for eight hours. All for the special price of £400. You won't find better than that anywhere.

E: Mm. That's very good. I think I'll come back later for that. Oh, and I see you have some games consoles here. What is the difference between these two?

A: They're almost the same, but the buttons on this one are easier to use, and it's wi-fi ready.

E: What does that mean?

A: It connects to the internet without using a cable.

E: Ah, yes. I see. Yes, I think it is better. I think I'm going to take this one, but ... do you have any mobile phones?

A: Mobiles? Sure. They're over here. Now, what do you want to do with it? Take photos? Listen to music? Surf the Net?

E: Well, I just want to make calls and maybe send text messages.

A: OK, there's this one. It's beautiful. State-of-the-art.

E: There aren't any buttons. Is it touchscreen?

A: Exactly. You just touch the screen. Everyone's buying this model. We've almost sold out.

E: How much is it?

A: Three hundred pounds.

E: Oh, OK, maybe I'll just take the games console now and come back later for the other things ...

UNIT 16

🔊 16.1

1

A: Did I tell you Max and Hana are going to move to Hong Kong?

B: Oh! Did I tell you that Max's sister Lin has broken up with Tom?

A: I know! I hear she's going to get married to a workmate.

2

C: Did I tell you I saw Mr Foster the other day? With a new girlfriend!

D: No! Mr Foster? Did I tell you I'm going to meet his ex-wife on Tuesday?

E: Did I tell you Mrs Foster's going to have a baby?

C and D: What?

3

F: Did I tell you Amy and Ben got divorced last month?

G: Oh, that's a shame. Did I tell you Ann is three months' pregnant?

F: What? But she hasn't seen her husband for six months!

🔊 16.2

R = Rob, G = Granny

R: Hello, Mum. It's Rob here.

G: Rob, dear. How are you?

R: Fine, thanks. I'm just calling with some news.

G: Oh, really? Good news, I hope?

R: Well, yes, I think so. Shelley's just told us she's getting married.

G: Shelley? Oh! That's lovely news. Did Kevin ask her, or did she ask Kevin?

R: No, Mum. It's not Kevin.

G: What? What do you mean?

R: She's not going to marry Kevin.

G: Oh. I thought they were serious. He's such a nice boy.

R: Yeah, Pam and I liked him too, but they broke up about three months ago.

G: Three months ago? Oh, dear. I liked Kevin. So, who is this man?

R: Well, you know she's working in Brazil at the moment? Well, she met someone there, a Brazilian man. She met him at work.

G: Oh. So how long have they known each other?

R: Two months.

G: Two months?

R: Yes, I know. It's a surprise. But she sounds really happy. And he sounds nice. He's a professor at the university.

G: So, where are they having the wedding? Here in O'Kelly's Creek?

R: Er, no. Not here. On a beach in Brazil.

G: Brazil! A beach? What on earth ...?

R: Yes, Pam and I are going to book the flights this afternoon. You're coming, of course?

G: Well, I don't know ... I suppose I will. I can't miss Shelley's wedding.

R: It's a long flight, but we can stay a few days. See a bit of the country, maybe?

G: I can't believe it – little Shelley! I can still remember the first time I saw her when I visited you and Pam just after she was born. That little baby was pink, screaming and tiny. But to me she was the most beautiful thing in the world. It was love at first sight!

R: Yeah. It seems like yesterday. She'll always be my little girl. But she's twenty-six now, Mum, and she has to live her own life.

G: Well, I'll come to the wedding, but I'm not happy about it. They'll be divorced within the year ... I'm telling you!

16.3

1 I was watching TV at home.
2 What were you thinking about?
3 She wasn't looking for a boyfriend.
4 I was making a coffee in the kitchen.
5 They were eating outside under the trees.
6 We weren't playing tennis when you saw us.

ANSWER KEY

UNIT 1

GRAMMAR *be*

1
1 Hi   2 'm   3 's   4 meet

2
1 is   3 is   5 are
2 are   4 are   6 is

3
1 's   3 's   5 're
2 're   4 're   6 's

4
1 What's your first name?   3 Where are you from?
2 What's your surname?   4 Which part?

6
a 2   b 3   c 1   d 4

LISTENING

7
1 c   2 b   3 a

8
1 USA   3 da Silva   5 Argentina
2 Julio   4 teacher   6 the north

VOCABULARY Countries

9
1 Brazil   3 Italy   5 Kenya
2 Japan   4 China

10
1 Poland   3 Canada   5 Spain
2 Mexico   4 Saudi Arabia

11
Africa: Kenya
Asia: China, Japan
Europe: Poland, Italy, Spain
the Middle East: Saudi Arabia
North America: Canada
Central America: Mexico
South America: Brazil

PRONUNCIATION

12
Japan: 2 syllables   Kenya: 2 syllables   Italy: 3 syllables

13
Ja<u>pan</u>   <u>Ken</u>ya   <u>It</u>aly

14
Bra<u>zil</u>   <u>Chi</u>na   <u>Mex</u>ico

DEVELOPING CONVERSATIONS *Which part?*

15
1 I'm from   3 are you   5 your mum
2 It's in   4 the capital   6 Which part

16
1 capital   3 north   5 middle
2 east   4 south   6 west

VOCABULARY Jobs and workplaces

1
1 nurse   4 shop assistant   7 waiter
2 teacher   5 civil servant   8 police officer
3 receptionist   6 designer

2
a 4   c 8   e 2   g 6
b 5   d 1   f 7   h 3

3
1 What *are / do* you do?   I *do / 'm* a teacher.
　What *are / do* you teach?   I *'m / teach* English
2 What *is / do* your job?   I *'m / work* a designer.
　Where *are / do* you work?   I *'m / work* in a studio in Tokyo.
　Are / Do you enjoy your work?
　I / *I'd* love it.

GRAMMAR Present simple

4
1 Where does he live?
2 Who do you live with?
3 What time do they get up?
4 What do you do in your free time?
5 How do they travel here?
6 How many languages do / can you speak?

5
a 3   b 1   c 5   d 6   e 2   f 4

6
1 Do you work in an office?
2 Do they work in a secondary school?
3 Does she speak Italian?
4 Does he play football?
5 Do you and your family live in Scotland?

7
1 No, I don't   4 No, he doesn't.
2 No, they don't.   5 No, we don't.
3 No, she doesn't.

DEVELOPING WRITING An application form

8
1

9
1 Mancini   3 restaurant   5 Italy
2 waiter   4 Verona   6 London
　　　　　　　　　　7 English

10
Job application

First name:	**Ben**
Surname:	**Herman**
Address:	**24 Lime Street, Oxford, OX12 1LS**
Telephone:	**01842 71204**
Current occupation:	**Art teacher**
Email address:	**hermanb@art.com**
Country of origin:	**England**
Position applied for:	**designer**

Describe yourself in 20–30 words.
　I'm an *art teacher*. I work in **an art college / a college** in **Oxford**, a beautiful city in the centre of **England**. I want to work as a **designer** in **Cape Town**.

READING

11

2

12

1 a Angelika   b Jianyu   c Salima
2 a Germany   b China   c Morocco
3 a in a school   b in a government office   c in a hospital

13

1 S   2 J   3 A   4 J

VOCABULARY Describing places

1

1 river	4 church	7 cathedral
2 traffic	5 factory	8 restaurant
3 palace	6 university	9 park
		10 beach

2

1 rivers	3 parks	5 traffic (has no plural)
2 beaches	4 factories	6 palaces

GRAMMAR *there is / there are*

3

1 There are	3 There aren't	5 There are
2 There's	4 There isn't	

4

1 There isn't	4 There's	7 There aren't
2 There are	5 There isn't	8 There are
3 There aren't	6 There are	

VOCABULARY BUILDER QUIZ 1

1

1 waiter	3 designer	5 assistant
2 servant	4 student	

2

1 in   2 of   3 in   4 for   5 in

3

1 a job	3 long hours	5 at the police station
2 there	4 at night	

4

1 b   2 c   3 e   4 a   5 d

5

1 cathedral	3 beach	5 museum
2 university	4 factory	

UNIT 2

VOCABULARY Free time activities

1

Across

4 swimming   5 walking

Down

1 studying   2 dancing   3 reading   4 shopping

2

1 c   2 e   3 a   4 g   5 b   6 h   7 f   8 d

3

1 watching TV	5 playing the guitar
2 going to the cinema	6 going out to dinner
3 doing sport	7 meeting new people
4 listening to music	8 playing computer games

GRAMMAR Verb patterns

4

1 want   2 like   3 want   4 like   5 want   6 want

5

1 meeting	3 swimming	5 to go
2 wants	4 Do (you) like	6 doesn't (really) like

DEVELOPING CONVERSATIONS Arrangements

6

1 want	4 What	7 where
2 sounds	5 What	8 At
3 Where	6 Is	9 at

LISTENING

8

Jack	d	Emily	b	Daniel	c
Will	f	Grace	e	Chloe	a

9

1 F	3 F	5 F
2 T	4 F	6 T

VOCABULARY Daily life

1

have	go	get
breakfast	out for dinner	up
a shower	out dancing	home from work
a coffee	to bed	
lunch	to a concert	

2

1 get	3 have	5 have	7 go	9 go
2 have	4 have	6 get	8 go	10 go

3

1 get   2 drink   3 have   4 go   5 go

GRAMMAR Adverbs of frequency

4

100% always
        usually
        sometimes
        occasionally
        hardly ever
0% never

5

1 always	3 usually	5 occasionally
2 hardly ever	4 never	

6

1 I usually do my homework before dinner.
2 She always goes out dancing on Saturdays.
3 They sometimes have lunch at home.
4 We never watch TV at weekends.
5 He hardly ever gets home from work before 9pm.

READING

7

1 B   2 C   3 A

8

1 F	3 T	5 F	7 F
2 T	4 F	6 T	

9

1 premiere   2 club   3 message   4 sofa

VOCABULARY In an English class

10

a 3   b 1   c 5   d 8   e 9   f 2   g 7
h 10   i 4   j 6

11

2 pencil   4 dictionary   6 rubber
3 window   5 paper   7 paper

12

1 c   2 d   3 f   4 a   5 b   6 e

PRONUNCIATION

1

1 <u>sci</u>ssors   3 re<u>lax</u>   5 ca<u>thed</u>ral
2 <u>win</u>dow   4 <u>man</u>ager 6 <u>dic</u>tionary

2

1 relax   2 early   3 computer

GRAMMAR Countable and uncountable nouns

4

2 C   3 U   4 C   5 U   6 U   7 C   8 U

5

2 some   3 a lot   4 an   5 some   6 a lot

6

2 an   5 a   8 many
3 any   6 much   9 a
4 some   7 a lot   10 an

DEVELOPING WRITING Writing a description of yourself

7

1 name   3 live with   5 do you like
2 live   4 you do   6 do at the weekend

8

1 Jack Jenkins
2 Location: Sheffield, UK
3 with my flatmates, Dave and Andy
4 Occupation: Student
5 Hobbies: swimming, playing computer games, chatting with friends on the internet
6 Favourite weekend activities: going to the cinema, watching football on TV, playing football with friends.

9

1 I live in   4 In my free time, I like
2 I live with   5 At the weekend, I usually
3 I'm a

10

Student's own answers.

11

Student's own answers.

VOCABULARY BUILDER QUIZ 2

1

1 your mobile phone   3 a conversation
2 TV   4 homework

2

1 c   2 f   3 d   4 b   5 a   6 e

3

1 notebook   3 games   5 ticket
2 life   4 station

4

1 learn   3 film   5 scissors
2 new words   4 sounds

5

1 any kids   3 lunch   5 a coffee
2 go to the theatre 4 a short sleep

UNIT 3
VOCABULARY Local facilities

1

1 bank   4 sports centre   7 post office
2 café   5 clothes shop   8 shoe shop
3 bookshop   6 chemist

2

a 5   c 4   e 8   g 7
b 2   d 1   f 3   h 6

3

1 café   3 bookshop   5 chemist
2 post office 4 bank   6 clothes shop

GRAMMAR Prepositions of place

4

1 at   3 on   5 between   7 on
2 on   4 next to 6 opposite

5

1 The hotel is *on the left / on the right*.
2 The hotel is *between / opposite* the cinema and the department store.
3 The university is *at / on* the end of this street.
4 The chocolate factory is *at / on* the right.
5 The church is *opposite / between* the cinema.
6 The museum is *next to / opposite* the internet café.

6

1 on, opposite   3 on   5 between
2 at   4 next to 6 opposite

DEVELOPING CONVERSATIONS Asking for information

7

1 **send** a package / some money
2 **get** lunch / a package / some stamps / a jacket / a coffee / some money / some aspirins
3 **change** some money
4 **have** lunch / a package / some stamps / a jacket / a coffee / some money / some aspirins

8

1 send   3 have   5 get
2 exchange   4 have   6 get

LISTENING

9

3

10

1 Gibbs   3 Wharton   5 0914671903
2 June   4 630   6 café

VOCABULARY In the house

1
Across
1 TV   4 cupboard   9 fridge
2 alarm clock 7 sofa
Down
1 towel   5 bed   8 sink
3 mirror   6 table

2
1 living room 2 kitchen 3 bedroom 4 bathroom

3
1 kitchen   4 sink   7 TV
2 fridge   5 living room 8 bathroom
3 table   6 sofa   9 bed
                             10 bedroom

GRAMMAR Pronouns, possessive adjectives and 's

4

Subject	Object	Adjective	Pronoun
I	me	my	mine
You	you	your	yours
He	him	his	his
She	her	her	hers
We	us	our	ours
They	them	their	theirs

5
Conversation 1
1 My   2 We
Conversation 2
1 our   2 her
Conversation 3
1 our   2 Our   3 his   4 their

6
1 mine   3 Bella's (jacket) 5 Dave's (toothbrush)
2 theirs 4 hers   6 ours

7
1 mine   3 hers   5 My
2 John's 4 ours   6 his

READING

8
3

9
1 G   2 G   3 R   4 R   5 G   6 R

10
1 going out   3 living room 5 the countryside
2 near   4 small   6 old

VOCABULARY Collocations

1
1 e   2 f   3 a   4 b   5 d   6 c

2
1 plates   3 sandwich   5 make up
2 hair   4 dog   6 music

3
1 clean   3 table   5 on
2 put   4 set   6 sink

GRAMMAR can / can't

4
1 can't   3 can   5 can
2 can't   4 can't 6 can't

5
1 Can you   3 Can you   5 Can I
2 Can I   4 can you   6 Can you

6
1 He **can** come to the meeting tomorrow.
2 **Can you** help me with this homework, please?
3 You can't **smoke** in here.
4 Can **I use** this towel?
5 We **can't** use this room today.
6 I can't **find** my keys.

PRONUNCIATION can / can't

7
1 a   2 b   3 b   4 a   5 a   6 b

DEVELOPING WRITING

A note to your friend describing where you live

9
1 b   2 c

10
1 on the corner   3 by bus   5 along the road
2 opposite the house   4 two

11
1 Hi   4 café   7 bus
2 33   5 pub   8 clothes shop
3 Lime   6 restaurants 9 *Student's own name*

VOCABULARY BUILDER QUIZ 3

1
1 buy   3 brush   5 share
2 send   4 change   6 wash

2
1 on   2 up   3 down   4 up   5 off

3
1 dinner   2 tidy   3 your room   4 bread   5 the sea

4
1 b   2 e   3 a   4 d   5 c

5
1 study   2 balcony   3 sink   4 apartment

UNIT 4
GRAMMAR The past simple

1
1 was / were   3 did   5 came   7 show   9 read
2 had   4 go   6 see   8 play   10 needed

2
The irregular verbs are: *be, have, do, go, come, see* and *read*.

3
1 had   3 read   5 did
2 saw   4 came   6 played

4

1 spent	4 stayed	7 bought
2 was	5 watched	8 took
3 were	6 went	9 cooked

DEVELOPING CONVERSATIONS *That sounds …*

5

Conversation 1: photo b
Conversation 2: photo c
Conversation 3: photo a

6

1 nice   2 interesting   3 bad

PRONUNCIATION Past simple forms

9

/t/	/d/	/ɪd/
cooked	showed	wanted
liked	rained	chatted
relaxed	tried	needed

READING

10

1

11

	Review 1	Review 2	Review 3
The weather was good	✓	✗	✓
Maui was nice	✓	✓	✓
The food was good	✓	✓	✗
The rooms were clean	✓	✓	✗
The staff were friendly	✗	✓	✓

12

1 Hiro went to Hawaii *alone* / *with his family*.
2 Hiro thought his hotel was *good* / *bad* for families.
3 Elisa had a *good* / *bad* holiday.
4 Elisa was *happy* / *unhappy* when her holiday ended.
5 Manny *liked* / *didn't like* the sea and the beaches in Maui.
6 Manny spent a *day* / *week* in bed.

VOCABULARY Months, seasons and dates

1

T	J	A	N	U	A	R	Y	N	E
E	A	P	I	O	Y	O	H	O	K
A	S	R	M	B	R	C	L	V	T
J	E	I	M	A	E	T	A	E	E
J	U	L	Y	O	P	O	I	M	S
N	F	N	P	G	E	B	E	B	E
D	E	C	E	M	B	E	R	E	P
E	B	T	P	W	A	R	E	R	T
P	R	A	L	F	R	R	S	A	E
A	U	G	U	S	T	D	C	S	M
M	A	Y	C	N	R	N	G	H	B
S	R	V	A	E	P	B	O	Y	E
O	Y	E	L	I	C	T	B	E	R

In order: January, February, March, April, May, June, July,
August, September, October, November, December

2

1 spring   2 summer   3 autumn   4 winter

3

1 b   2 e   3 f   4 a   5 c   6 d

4

1 The fourth of July.   3 The third of November.
2 The twenty-fifth of April.   4 The twelfth of October.
                              5 The first of May.

GRAMMAR Past simple negatives

6

1 I didn't get up early.
2 She didn't have a great holiday.
3 They didn't take me out for dinner.
4 There wasn't a large dog on the table.
5 We didn't go to the cinema last Friday.
6 You didn't do your homework at the weekend.

7

1 That film wasn't very long.
2 There wasn't anything to do.
3 There wasn't anyone I knew at the party.
4 I didn't buy anything at the shops.
5 We didn't go anywhere last weekend.
6 She wanted it but she didn't have any money

8

1 didn't go	5 was	9 didn't get
2 went	6 didn't rain	10 weren't
3 didn't take	7 didn't do	11 had
4 stayed	8 bought	12 didn't want

LISTENING

9

Conversation 1: photo b
Conversation 2: photo c
Conversation 3: photo a

10

Bella: had fish for dinner, got some presents
Claire: visited her sister, went to a rock festival
Rob: left home at one, saw some of the football match
         on TV

11

1 F	3 T	5 F
2 T	4 T	6 T

VOCABULARY Going on holiday

1

a hotel	c taxi	e money	g car
b sightseeing	d train	f boat	h swimming

2

1 sightseeing	3 a taxi	5 a hotel
2 a day in Rome	4 to Tokyo	6 with friends

3

1 fly	3 stay	5 rent
2 spend	4 go	6 take

DEVELOPING WRITING Describing a holiday

4

2

5

1 b   2 e   3 f   4 a   5 d   6 c

6

Hi Evie

We got back from **Japan** this morning. We **had** a great time! On Monday we went **sightseeing**. We **saw** Tokyo Tower (it's like the Eiffel Tower, but it's red!) and the Imperial Palace. It was really interesting.

The next day we spent **two hours** walking around the Meiji Shrine. Then we went shopping in Harajuku. We loved it! In the evening we **went** to a restaurant. We had **sushi**. It was delicious!

On **Wednesday** we rented a **car** and went to Tokyo Disneyland. I enjoyed it but James didn't **like** it. The weather was **good** all the time – it was sunny every day!

I hope **you** and the family are well.

See you soon,

Love Sophie

GRAMMAR Past simple questions

7
1 Did Sean cook lunch?
2 Did you go to a concert?
3 Was Paul ill?
4 Did they watch TV?
5 Were her earrings expensive?
6 Did Brenda stay in bed yesterday?

8
1 Did you go on holiday anywhere?
2 Was the food good?
3 How was your summer?
4 Was it very expensive?
5 Where did you stay?

9
1 Where did you go (on holiday)?
2 Who did you go with?
3 Was the weather good?
4 Were the people friendly?
5 Did you have a good time?
6 How long were you there for?

VOCABULARY BUILDER QUIZ 4

1
1 free	3 sunny	5 warm
2 clear	4 rainy	6 fun

2
1 a taxi	3 a bed and breakfast	5 to Rome
2 fire	4 a taxi	

3
1 snow   2 stay   3 laugh   4 rain

4
1 the   2 a   3 a   4 The   5 a

5
1 e   2 d   3 a   4 c   5 b

UNIT 5
VOCABULARY Describing what you want to buy

1

colour	material	clothes	food	shape
red	wool	jacket	fruit	long
white	wood	shoes	meat	small
green	plastic	shirt	cake	short
yellow	leather	jeans	cheese	square
brown	cotton	dress	fish	round

2
Across
3 cake   4 jacket   5 shirt   6 fish
Down
1 dress   2 meat   3 cheese   4 jeans

3
1 jeans	3 jacket	5 meat
2 cheese	4 fish	6 cake

4
1 meat   2 short   3 white   4 cotton   5 yellow

GRAMMAR *this, that, these, those*

5
1 This	3 This	5 This
2 These	4 These	6 This

6
1 those	3 those	5 that
2 that	4 Those	6 that

7
1 this	3 these	5 this
2 those	4 that	6 this

LISTENING

8
Conversation 1:   picture b
Conversation 2:   picture c
Conversation 3:   picture a

9
Items ticked: 1, 3, 4, 9

10
Conversation 1
1 T   2 F
Conversation 2
3 T   4 F
Conversation 3
5 T   6 F

DEVELOPING CONVERSATIONS Questions in shops

11
1 How much are the	4 Anything else?
2 What are they made of?	5 Can I have some
3 How many	6 How much

PRONUNCIATION Numbers

13
1 13	3 316	5 2040
2 150	4 590	6 14,000

14

	American English	British English
1 120	✓	
2 318		✓
3 214		✓
4 3060	✓	
5 1030		✓
6 9040	✓	

GRAMMAR Present continuous

1
1 They are sleeping. They're sleeping.
2 He is doing the shopping. He's doing the shopping.
3 We are studying at university. We're studying at university.
4 I am watching TV. I'm watching TV.
5 You are working hard. You're working hard.
6 She is growing fast. She's growing fast.

2
1 They aren't sleeping.
2 He isn't doing the shopping.
3 We aren't studying at university.
4 I'm not watching TV.
5 You aren't working hard.
6 She isn't growing fast.

3
1 We're having
2 'm talking
3 are staying
4 aren't selling
5 's watching
6 is doing
7 isn't working / 's not working
8 are (you) going

4
1 We're having a sale this week.
2 They're watching TV.
3 We're doing well.
4 Are you studying at university?
5 How are you feeling today?
6 I'm working hard.

LISTENING

5
2

6
3

READING

7
2

8
1 1838   3 nineteenth   5 2009
2 1852   4 300   6 14

10
1 Paris   3 sells   5 popular
2 good value   4 large   6 work at Shinsegae
                                        Centum City

DEVELOPING WRITING Writing a postcard

1
1 Brad. In Japan.   2 Suchart. In New York.

2
a 2   b 3   c 4   d 1

3
Student's own answers.

4
Model answer:

Dear Isabella We're having a great time here in Japan. I'm writing this postcard from a restaurant. We're eating dinner and looking at the city. The view is amazing. There's a lot to do here. We're staying in a hotel and can walk to most of the interesting places. Yesterday we visited an art gallery. It was fun. But the best thing about this place is the shopping! We went shopping yesterday afternoon. I bought a T-shirt. We got something for you too! Love, Francesco	Isabella Conti via Venezia 89 Verona 9800 Italy

VOCABULARY Department stores

5
1 menswear   5 sports
2 security guard   6 womenswear
3 beauty department   7 changing rooms
4 shop assistant

6
1 b   4 d   7 f
2 h   5 e   8 g
3 a   6 c

7
1 b   2 e   3 d   4 a   5 c   6 f

VOCABULARY BUILDER QUIZ 5

1
1 unhappy   3 down
2 top   4 go in

2
1 cheese   2 customer   3 bananas   4 department

3
1 jumper   3 an unusual   5 growing
2 bottom   4 leather   6 toy

4
1 on   2 of   3 up   4 in   5 for   6 by

5
1 e   2 d   3 a   4 c   5 b

UNIT 6
VOCABULARY School and university

1
1 friendly   3 popular   5 lazy   7 helpful
2 boring   4 strange   6 nice   8 difficult

2
positive: friendly, popular, nice, helpful
negative: boring, strange, lazy, difficult

3
1 friendly 2 difficult 3 popular 4 lazy 5 strange

4
1 helpful 2 expensive 3 friendly 4 varied 5 lazy

5
1 varied   3 modern   5 friendly
2 patient   4 expensive   6 popular

6
1 Chemistry   3 Law   5 Medicine
2 Geography   4 Maths 6 Biology

7
1 Marketing   3 IT   5 Engineering
2 Literature   4 PE   6 History

8
1 IT   2 Medicine   3 Literature

PRONUNCIATION *are*

9
1 How are   3 What are   5 Are you
2 Are you   4 class are 6 Where are

10
3 Sentences 1, 3, 4, and 6 contain the weak form of 'are'.

DEVELOPING CONVERSATIONS *How's the course going?*

11
bad – good
boring – interesting
difficult – easy
friendly and *nice* don't have opposites here.

12
1 It's very interesting
2 I don't like the teacher.
3 It's quite difficult.
4 She's not very well.
5 The other students are really friendly.
6 I did very well in my exams.

13
1 going   3 good   5 very   7 sure
2 enjoying   4 like   6 subject

LISTENING

15
1 c   2 e   3 a   4 b   5 d

16
1 Law   2 English   3 Engineering

17
1 F   2 F   3 T   4 T   5 T   6 F

READING

1
2

2
1 d   2 e   3 a   4 b   5 c

3
1 university   3 2.5   5 eighteen   7
2 30   4 1636   6 Iceland   8 private

VOCABULARY Courses

4
1 c   2 e   3 f   4 b   5 d   6 a

5
1 did   6 finished   11 enjoyed
2 started   7 lasted   12 had
3 finished   8 cost   13 failed
4 lasted   9 paid   14 passed
5 started   10 borrowed

6
2 When did the course start?
3 When did it/the course finish?
4 How long did it/the course last?
5 How much did it/the course cost?
6 Did you have an exam?
7 Did you pass it/the exam?
8 Did you enjoy it/the course?

GRAMMAR Modifiers

7

✓✓	✓	✗	✗✗
very / really	quite	not very	not

8
1 James is quite lazy.
2 The other students are very nice.
3 These books are really interesting.
4 My classmates are quite friendly.
5 My university is very expensive.
6 My new teacher is really good.

9
1 aren't very friendly   4 isn't very good
2 's not very popular   5 aren't very interesting
3 aren't very expensive   6 isn't very difficult

10
1 really   2 quite   3 great   4 very

GRAMMAR Comparatives

1

	Adjective	Comparative
1 syllable	old	older
	tall	taller
	big	bigger
-y ⟶ -ier	easy	easier
	funny	funnier
	lazy	lazier
more + adj	expensive	more expensive
	interesting	more interesting
	creative	more creative
irregular	far	further
	good	better
	bad	worse

2
1 older   3 more expensive   5 further
2 taller   4 better   6 easier

3
1 younger   3 cheaper   5 nearer
2 shorter   4 worse   6 more difficult

4

1	taller	4	better	7	slower
2	more intelligent	5	faster	8	worse
3	older	6	higher	9	more creative
				10	more interesting

VOCABULARY Languages

5

1	Chinese	4	Russian
2	German	5	Spanish
3	Japanese	6	Turkish

6

1	Spanish	3	Turkish	5	Japanese
2	Chinese	4	Russian	6	German

DEVELOPING WRITING Describing your favourite teacher

7

1 The writer liked the teacher.
2 The writer thought the lessons were interesting.

8

Student's own answers.

9

Model answer:

My favourite teacher was called **Takako Yamada**, my **English** teacher. I **loved** the subject and I was a **good** student. She was a **big** woman with **black** hair. She was **friendly**, which is why I liked her.
What made her a good teacher was that her lessons were **interesting** and she was very **creative**. The time always went by quickly in her classes. I'll never forget **Takako Yamada**!

VOCABULARY BUILDER QUIZ 6

1

1	impatient	3	unimportant	5	unfriendly
2	unpopular	4	unhelpful		

2

1	decision	3	problem	5	grade	7	idea
2	break	4	skill	6	half	8	grade

3

1 with   2 in   3 –   4 for   5 in   6 –

5

1 f   2 c   3 e   4 a   5 d   6 b

UNIT 7
VOCABULARY Relationships

1

1	grandfather	5	son	9	brother
2	grandmother	6	daughter	10	sister
3	husband	7	uncle	11	cousin
4	wife	8	aunt		

2

1	grandfather	4	husband	7	cousin
2	daughter	5	wife	8	grandmother
3	uncle	6	sister		

3

1	Keira	4	Ben	7	Kate
2	Alexa	5	Judy and Alan	8	Paolo
3	Carlo and Beatrice	6	Sam		

GRAMMAR Auxiliary Verbs

4

1	Can you swim?	5	Does she speak English?
2	Did you go out yesterday?	6	Is he Sue's brother?
3	Are they married?	7	Are you a student?
4	Can you hear me?		

5

1	can	3	are	5	does	7	am
2	didn't	4	can't	6	isn't		

6

1	Do	3	Did	5	Is	7	Does
2	Am	4	is	6	were		

7

1	main	3	main	5	auxiliary
2	auxiliary	4	main	6	auxiliary

LISTENING

8

2

9

1	a sister	3	five	5	doesn't live
2	mother	4	forty	6	and son

10

1	or sisters	5	How old
2	your parents	6	Do you live
3	How many languages	7	Are you
4	do they (your parents)		

PRONUNCIATION Showing surprise

11

1 b   2 c   3 f   4 a   5 d   6 e

DEVELOPING CONVERSATIONS Adding information

13

1 They live in Ohio.
2 I share an apartment with two other students.
3 There's a party at our college.
4 It's our graduation party.
5 I want to work here in New York City.
6 I have a job at the Bank of America.

VOCABULARY Jobs and activities in the home

1

1	games	6	the dog
2	a story at bedtime	7	the cat
3	the dishwasher	8	jokes
4	the light switch	9	a story
5	games	10	my baby brother

2

1 empty the dishwasher
2 pick up my son from school
3 repair the light switch
4 read a story at bedtime
5 feed the dog

3

1 look after   2 tell   3 read   4 sing   5 play   6 feed

GRAMMAR *have to / don't have to*

4

	necessary	not necessary
I You We They	have to	don't have to
He She It	has to	doesn't have to

5

1 don't have to
2 has to
3 doesn't have to
4 don't have to
5 have to
6 has to
7 have to
8 doesn't have to

6

1 You don't have to
2 I don't have to
3 We have to
4 Tim has to
5 Daisy doesn't have to
6 Mia and Betty have to

7

1 They **have** to go to school on Saturdays.
2 We **don't** have to do any homework tonight.
3 I **have** to see the doctor today.
4 I emptied the dishwasher, so John doesn't **have** to.
5 Toby **doesn't** have to go to work today.
6 A teacher **has** to work very hard.

READING

8

Paul: oldest friend
Martina: step grandfather (i.e. Martina's grandmother's second husband)

9

Paul

1 at school
2 nice, funny, reliable
3 once or twice a year
4 once a year

Martina

1 when Martina was ten
2 positive, strong, strict
3 most days
4 once or twice a week

10

1 T   2 T   3 F   4 T   5 F   6 T

VOCABULARY Describing people

1

2

1 strict
2 funny
3 clever
4 confident
5 fit
6 loud
7 quiet
8 reliable

3

1 funny
2 strict
3 quiet
4 reliable
5 clever
6 fit

LISTENING

4

Jason: confident, funny
Luis: nice, speaks three languages
Kerry: clever, quiet

5

1 L   2 K   3 J   4 L   5 J   6 K

6

1 confident
2 young
3 reliable
4 loud
5 nice
6 quiet

DEVELOPING WRITING Describing a special person

7

1 and
2 but
3 and
4 but
5 but
6 and

8

1 Amalia, Laura's sister
2 in Copenhagen
3 she's a (medical) student
4 clever, confident, friendly, loud, funny
5 she makes her laugh and really understands her
6 once a month
7 go shopping, go to the cinema

9

Student's own answers.

10

Model answer:

This is a photo of me with my best friend, Flavio. He lives in Bologna. He's an engineer. Flavio's very clever and funny. He can be a bit loud sometimes, but he's reliable too. We see each other once a month. We like to go for a drink and something to eat.

VOCABULARY BUILDER QUIZ 7

1

1 *best* friend
2 *grand*mother
3 *girl*friend
4 *house*work

2

1 on   2 up   3 up   4 after

3

1 confidently
2 Luckily
3 cloudy
4 cleaner
5 reliable
6 education

4

1 set
2 trust
3 affect
4 feed
5 repair
6 make

5

1 c   2 d   3 b   4 e   5 a

UNIT 8

VOCABULARY Common activities

1

1 c   2 f   3 b   4 a   5 d   6 e

2
1 have a meeting
2 play tennis
3 go home
4 go for a walk
5 do the shopping
6 write an email

3
1 have
2 play
3 do
4 get
5 go
6 go for

GRAMMAR *going to*

4
1 'm going to
2 're going to
3 's going to
4 're going to
5 're going to be
6 's going to

5
1 I'm going to write a letter to my sister.
2 We're going to go home early because we're tired.
3 Tom's going to study for the test in his bedroom.
4 You're going to meet my new friends at the party tonight.
5 My parents are going to drive to my house.

6
1 isn't going to come
2 not going to stay
3 aren't going to have
4 aren't going to go
5 isn't going to be
6 aren't going to finish

7
1 going to be
2 're going to have
3 're going to need
4 'm going to see
5 Is (he) going to bring

LISTENING

9
go shopping in London

10
1 K   2 J   3 K   4 J   5 J   6 J

11
1 T   2 F   3 F   4 T   5 T   6 F

PRONUNCIATION *going to*

12
1 gonna
2 going to
3 gonna
4 going to
5 gonna
6 gonna

DEVELOPING CONVERSATIONS Making suggestions

14
1 What do you want to see?
2 How about Michel's Café at seven o'clock?
3 What are you doing tonight?
4 Do you want to go for a coffee first?
5 Do you want to go out somewhere?

15
a 3   b 5   c 1   d 4   e 2

VOCABULARY Life events and plans

1
1 have a baby
2 won the lottery
3 move house
4 left home
5 get married
6 stopped working
7 got divorced
8 start (my own) business

2
2 have a baby
3 get married
4 stopped working
5 won the lottery
6 moved house
7 started (his own car sales) business
8 get divorced

GRAMMAR *would like to* + verb

3
1 'd like to visit
2 'd like to learn
3 'd like to save
4 'd like to start
5 'd like to be
6 'd like to have

4
1 We wouldn't like to visit Australia.
2 I wouldn't like to learn Russian.
3 They wouldn't like to save money.
4 You wouldn't like to start your own business.
5 I wouldn't like to be rich.
6 She wouldn't like to have a dog.

5
1 like
2 'd like
3 doesn't like
4 Do you like
5 wouldn't like
6 Would you like

READING

6
1, 3 and 5

7
1 Taurus
2 Cancer
3 Leo
4 Aries
5 Gemini
6 Taurus and Leo

8
1 c   2 d   3 e   4 f   5 a   6 b

VOCABULARY For and against

1
1 crime
2 tax
3 improve
4 tourists
5 safety
6 save
7 cause
8 be nice
9 help

2

+	−
provide help	create traffic problems
provide a service	lose money
create jobs	cause problems
save money	cause crime
make people richer	make people poorer
attract tourists	lose tourists
be good for the environment	be bad for the
reduce / cut tax	environment
	increase tax
	cut jobs

3
1 tax
2 cause
3 jobs
4 make
5 tourists
6 lose
7 money

DEVELOPING WRITING Giving opinions with reasons for and against

4
1 because 2 so 3 so 4 because 5 so 6 because

5
Department store, cinema and shops

6
She's for the building.

7

FOR	AGAINST
create jobs	increase crime
provide a service	reduce parking spaces in town
make shopping easier	increase pollution
attract people to the town	increase noise
increase business for local shops	it's bad for the environment

8
Model answer:
  I think it's a bad idea because *it's going to reduce parking spaces in town*. I also think *it's going to increase pollution*, so *it's going to be bad for the environment*. Finally, I think *it's going to increase noise and crime*, so I'm against this shopping mall.

VOCABULARY BUILDER QUIZ 8

1
1 f 2 d 3 b 4 e 5 a 6 c

2
1 plan   3 date   5 pollution
2 competition   4 noise

3
1 plan   2 cut   3 run   4 blog

4
1 c 2 e 3 b 4 f 5 d 6 a

5
1 library   2 lottery   3 divorced   4 abroad

UNIT 9
GRAMMAR Present perfect

1
1 have 2 haven't 3 Have 4 has 5 hasn't 6 Has

2
1 Have you been to Prague?   4 Have you seen *Room*?
2 No, I haven't. Have you?   5 Yes, we have. Have you?
3 No, but I'd like to go.   6 No. Is it good?
     7 Yes, it's amazing.

3
1 been   3 haven't   5 went   7 see
2 have   4 go   6 seen

4
1 have   3 Has   5 haven't
2 have been   4 you ever   6 she hasn't

5
1 have been   4 haven't seen   7 has been
2 have seen   5 hasn't seen   8 has seen
3 hasn't been   6 haven't been

6
1 I **have** been to Paris more than ten times.
2 **Have you** ever been to New York?
3 Ella **has never** seen *Star Wars*.
4 When **did you go** to Poland?
5 Paul **hasn't** been to Spain.

DEVELOPING CONVERSATIONS Recommending

7
1 +   3 −   5 −   7 +   9 +
2 −   4 +   6 +   8 −

8
1 You should!   2 Don't!

9
1 You should!   4 Don't!   7 Don't!
2 Don't!   5 Don't!   8 You should!
3 You should!   6 You should!

LISTENING

11
Tick (✓) photos of St Catherine's Monastery and the Valley of the Kings.

12

	Veronica	Veronica's husband
1 Been to Egypt before	X	✓
2 Been to Luxor	✓	✓
3 Seen the Sphinx	X	X
4 Been to St Catherine's	✓	X
5 Been to the Red Sea	✓	✓

13
1 F   2 T   3 T   4 F   5 F   6 T

VOCABULARY Problems

1
1 c   3 a   5 g   7 f
2 e   4 b   6 d

2
1 his name   5 you
2 my homework   6 worst
3 car   7 idea
4 your sleep

3
2 took the wrong turn   5 missed my flight
3 hurt himself   6 felt ill
4 forgot to lock the door   7 make a mess

GRAMMAR Past participles

4
Across
1 did   3 broke   4 seen   6 stolen
8 fallen   9 fell   11 saw
Down
1 done   2 cried   4 stole   5 broken
7 made   10 lost   12 won

READING

5
1 c   2 a   3 b

6
1 a   2 c   3 b

7

1	two hours	4	£90
2	good weather	5	four hours
3	160 feet	6	a chef from *Hello Sushi* restaurant

8

1 just for special days, because it's 'a special present'
2 slow and peaceful because it's done 'quietly' and describes the balloon flight
3 above you, because you're 'looking up'
4 it's used for attaching things, and it's 'strong'
5 the person and the rope
6 strong and well; it describes the sushi

9

a 2   b 1   c 5   d 3   e 6   f 4

VOCABULARY Describing experiences

1

relaxing, stressful, annoying, boring, sad, embarrassing, exciting, scary

2

1	boring	4	relaxing	7	sad
2	embarrassing	5	scary	8	exciting
3	stressful	6	annoying		

PRONUNCIATION Joining words together

3

1 The train‿is cheaper.
2 We love‿it!
3 She arrived two weeks‿ago.
4 We slept‿in a tent.
5 It was‿a great‿experience.
6 He fell‿and broke his‿arm.

DEVELOPING WRITING Describing an experience

5

1	delicious	3	relaxing	5	beautiful
2	interesting	4	friendly		

6

1 Coldplay.
2 It was hot and sunny.
3 He / She was so happy he / she couldn't speak.

7

a 3   b 1   c 2

8 and 9

Model answer:

Have you ever seen the 'Mona Lisa'? Last month I saw it for the first time, in the Louvre museum, in Paris. I went with my girlfriend.

The Louvre was really interesting. We saw a lot of great paintings. The building is amazing, too. It was a cold day and there were a lot of people there. We waited in a long line to see the painting.

For me, it was great to see this famous painting. I wanted to see it for a long time, and I was very excited. It was a small painting, but really beautiful.

VOCABULARY BUILDER QUIZ 9

1

1	make	3	give	5	take	7	feel
2	check	4	call	6	lose		

2

1	in	3	on	5	in	7	on
2	down	4	up	6	of		

3

1	stressful	3	happen	5	check
2	sad	4	embarrassing	6	cooler

4

1 b   2 e   3 d   4 a   5 c

UNIT 10
VOCABULARY Trains and stations

1

1 d   2 f   3 b   4 c   5 a   6 e

2

1	single	4	cash	7	delay
2	return	5	platform	8	line
3	second class	6	direct		

DEVELOPING CONVERSATIONS Telling the time

4

1	thirty	3	thirty-five	5	fifteen	7	half
2	o'clock	4	quarter	6	ten	8	past

5

1	five fifteen	4	one thirty
2	eleven twenty	5	six twenty-five
3	quarter to six	6	two forty-five

PRONUNCIATION *to*

6

1 a   2 b   3 a   4 b   5 a   6 a

LISTENING

8

Conversation 1 = picture b
Conversation 2 = picture c
Conversation 3 = picture a

9

1	station	3	have to	5	isn't
2	bus	4	don't know	6	50%

10

1 c   2 e   3 d   4 a   5 f   6 b

VOCABULARY Transport

1

1 plane   2 train   3 bus   4 bike   5 taxi   6 car

2

1 taxi   2 car   3 bus   4 train   5 bike   6 delayed

3

1	park	3	pick	5	pay	7	wait
2	lock	4	run	6	book	8	stop

4

1	buses	4	get	7	catch
2	number	5	taxis	8	station
3	run all night	6	charge		

GRAMMAR *too much, too many* and *not enough*

5
1 He's driving too fast.
2 This bag isn't cheap enough for me.
3 It's too early to go.
4 This film is too long.
5 I can't buy it. I haven't got enough money.
6 You aren't walking fast enough. Hurry up!

6
countable: accidents, buses, drivers, people
uncountable: crime, pollution, traffic, water

7
1 many 3 enough 5 much
2 enough 4 many 6 much

8
1 too 3 n't enough 5 too
2 too much 4 enough 6 Too many

READING

9
The Silk Road journey is the longest.

10
1 e 2 d 3 a 4 f 5 b 6 c

11
1 4,000m 3 three 5 evening
2 Lake Titicaca 4 Romania 6 west

DEVELOPING CONVERSATIONS Where's the best place?

1
1 change money 3 shopping, cycling, dancing
2 stay, eat 4 some exercise, a haircut

2
1 stay 4 go cycling 7 get a haircut
2 change money 5 eat 8 go dancing
3 get some exercise 6 go shopping

GRAMMAR Superlatives

4

	Adjective	Superlative
short adj.	fast	the cheapest
	hot	the hottest
-y → the -iest	easy	the easiest
	dry	the driest
the most + adj	expensive	the most expensive
	interesting	the most interesting
irregular	good	the best
	bad	the worst

5
1 the hottest 4 the best
2 the driest 5 the fastest
3 the cheapest

6
1 the slowest 4 the most expensive
2 the worst 5 the wettest
3 the coldest

DEVELOPING WRITING Building a text from notes

7
1 Get off the coach at the Hilton Hotel, call Sarah and wait. She is going to pick you up from there.
2 We're not very far from the city centre. It takes under half an hour to get to Oxford Street.
3 Get the underground from Shepherds Bush.
4 Oxford Street and Regent Street are great places to go shopping.
5 And go to Soho for lunch. Try Caldo – it's does great food and there's a lovely atmosphere. There are lots of great little restaurants in Soho.

8
Student's own answers.

9
Student's own answers.

VOCABULARY BUILDER QUIZ 10

1
1 home 3 a car 5 some cash
2 well 4 the journey

2
1 *haircut* 3 *taxi* driver 5 *first* class
2 *return* ticket 4 *sea*food

3
1 lock 3 delay 5 vote
2 park 4 taste 6 charge

4
1 down 2 to 3 off 4 up

5
1 platform 3 passengers 5 journey
2 direct 4 transport

UNIT 11
VOCABULARY Restaurants

1
1 service 4 booked 7 order 10 menu
2 dessert 5 table 8 bill
3 get 6 starter 9 main
Hidden word: vegetarian

2

1	2	3	4	5	6	7	8	9	10
W	W	W	W	C	C	W	C	C	C

DEVELOPING CONVERSATIONS Ordering food and drink

3
1 Are you ready to order? W
2 Would you like any dessert? W
3 And for your main course? W
4 I'm afraid the fish has finished. W
5 I'd like the steak, please. C
6 Can I get some ice cream, please? C
7 Yes. For starters, I'll have the salad, please. C
8 OK. Then, I'll have the chicken. C

4
1–7, 2–6, 3–5, 4–8

LISTENING

6
1 a cup of tea
2 some steak
3 a glass of red wine
4 some fish
5 some water
6 a bottle of wine
7 a cup of coffee
8 coffee ice cream
9 pasta with sauce

7
Carol has: white wine, fish, some water, a cup of tea
Steve has: white wine, steak, extra vegetables, coffee ice cream

8
1 C   3 S   5 SC   7 N
2 N   4 C   6 C

9
1 b   3 f   5 d   7 e
2 c   4 a   6 g

10
1 Are you ready to order now sir?
   Yes, I'd like the steak and a salad please.
   Don't you want a starter?
   No, thanks – just a main course and a glass of red wine.
2 Can I get you anything else?
   No, thanks. Can I have the bill please?
   Of course. We usually add 10% for service.
   No problem. Can I pay by credit card?
   Yes, sir, a credit card is fine.

VOCABULARY Food

1

meat	dairy	fruit	vegetables	drinks
chicken	butter	kiwis	garlic	wine
beef	cream	bananas	carrots	water
lamb	cheese	apples	onions	beer
pork	milk	oranges	spinach	juice

2
1 g   3 d   5 a   7 b
2 c   4 f   6 e

3
1 salt   3 spices   5 beans
2 pasta   4 rice   6 seafood

4
1 milk   3 Onions   5 pork
2 beef   4 juice   6 cheese

GRAMMAR Me too, me neither and auxiliaries

5
1 me too   2 me neither   3 disagree   4 disagree

6
1 I don't   3 Me neither   5 Me too
2 Me too   4 I do

8
1 don't   3 wouldn't   5 am
2 didn't   4 can   6 have

READING

9
1 Mi Casa   2 Johnny B's

10
1 T   2 T   3 F   4 F   5 T   6 F

11

	starter	main course	dessert
Mi Casa	seafood	chicken with tomatoes and vegetables, pizza	ice cream, chocolate cake
Johnny B's	fish, salad of beans and peas	steak, eggs	–

12
1 liked   2 but   3 nice   4 friendly   5 wasn't

GRAMMAR Explaining quantity

1

Countable nouns	Uncountable nouns
apple	chocolate
biscuit	coffee
egg	fish
soft drink	fruit
sweet	meat
vegetable	sugar

2
1 a lot of, any, some   3 much
2 many   4 many, much, any

3
1 much   4 quite a lot of   7 any
2 many   5 many   8 a lot of
3 any   6 a lot of   9 some

VOCABULARY Forming negatives by adding un-

5

employed	unemployed
fair	unfair
forgettable	unforgettable
friendly	unfriendly
happy	unhappy
healthy	unhealthy
popular	unpopular
tidy	untidy
usual	unusual

6
1 unhappy   4 unemployed   7 unfair
2 popular   5 tidy   8 unforgettable
3 unhealthy   6 friendly   9 unusual

DEVELOPING WRITING An email invitation

7
1 Hi   2 Best wishes

8
1 a party
2 Saturday 10th March
3 Angela's birthday
4 It's at La Coupole on the corner of rue Dauphine and avenue Robespierre.
5 8.00pm to midnight
6 a friend

9 and 10
Model answer:

Hi Nicola
We're having a lunch on Sunday 7th July to celebrate Philippe's birthday.
It's at home from 12.00p.m. to 5.00p.m.
Bring a bottle and a friend.
Let me know if you can come.

Best wishes,
Francoise

VOCABULARY BUILDER QUIZ 11

1

1 c	2 f	3 b	4 e	5 a	6 d

2

1 hungry	3 terrible	5 unforgettable
2 unfair	4 unhealthy	

3

1 weight	3 employed	5 service
2 starter	4 combinations	

4

1 add	3 recommend	5 include
2 order	4 avoid	

5

1 pepper	2 cream	3 pork	4 nuts

UNIT 12
VOCABULARY Health problems

1

1 head	3 arm	5 back	7 leg
2 chest	4 hand	6 stomach	8 foot

2

1 sick	3 burnt	5 cut	7 cough
2 headache	4 stiff	6 broken	

3

1 OK	3 hungry	5 ill
2 hurts	4 cold	6 infection

GRAMMAR *should / shouldn't*

5
1 He should go to hospital.
2 They should take the day off.
3 You should come with us.
4 We shouldn't cancel the party.
5 She should listen to my advice.
6 You shouldn't eat too much.

6
1 You should lie down.
2 You should stop smoking.
3 You shouldn't carry those heavy bags.
4 You should get some fresh air.
5 You should put cold water on it.
6 You shouldn't go to work.

DEVELOPING CONVERSATIONS Saying no

7

1 b	2 d	3 a	4 e	5 c

8
1 You look terrible. Are you OK?
  Yes, I'm just a bit tired.
  Maybe you should lie down.
  No, really. I'm fine.
2 You've cut your hand! It looks really bad.
  Oh, it's nothing.
  Maybe you should go to the hospital.
  No, really. I'll be fine.
3 Would you like some more cake?
  No, thanks. I've had enough.
  Are you sure?
  Yes, thanks. It was delicious.
4 Would you like me to come round tonight?
  It's OK, thanks.
  But Mark's away and you're all alone in that big house.
  No, really. I'll be fine on my own.

10
1 A: Are you OK?
  B: **I've got a** headache.
  A: Maybe you **should take an** aspirin.
  B: No, **it's** nothing.
2 A: Are you OK?
  B: No, my stomach hurts and I **feel** sick
  A: Maybe you **should** lie down. Would you like some water?
  B: No, thanks. **I'll** be fine.
3 A: Ow! **I've** burnt my hand.
  B: You **should put some** cold water on it.
  A: No, it's OK. I'll **be** fine.

LISTENING

11
Jenny

12

1 headache	4 take more care of himself
2 go home	5 foot
3 chest	6 go to the hospital

13

1 On Friday	4 no
2 for more than a week	5 a chair
3 his chest, leg and arm	6 blue

VOCABULARY Feelings

1

2

1 tired	3 stressed	5 upset	7 angry
2 annoyed	4 excited	6 happy	8 relaxed

3

positive: happy, excited, relaxed
negative: upset, tired, stressed, angry, annoyed

4

| 1 | d | 3 | b | 5 | a | 7 | c |
| 2 | g | 4 | f | 6 | e |

5

| 1 | upset | 3 | stressed | 5 | annoyed | 7 | angry |
| 2 | excited | 4 | tired | 6 | happy |

READING

6

| 1 | Kim | 2 | Pritpal | 3 | Tony | 4 | Lara | 5 | Ellie |

7

| 1 | b | 2 | d | 3 | e | 4 | a | 5 | c |

8

| 1 | eleven | 3 | studies | 5 | continue |
| 2 | woman | 4 | didn't help |

9

| 1 | stop smoking | 3 | the past | 5 | the truth |
| 2 | she feels | 4 | his/the doctor. |

GRAMMAR *because*, *so* and *after*

1

| 2 | After | 4 | because | 6 | so |
| 3 | so | 5 | After | 7 | because |

VOCABULARY In the news

2

| 2 | open | 4 | kill | 6 | damage | 8 | cause |
| 3 | hit | 5 | build | 7 | protest |

3

| 2 | kills | 4 | damages | 6 | build | 8 | celebrate |
| 3 | opens | 5 | hits | 7 | protest |

DEVELOPING WRITING A letter of advice

4

1   I have fallen in love with my best friend's girlfriend.
2   About four months ago.

5

| 1 | Paragraph 3 | 2 | Paragraph 1 | 3 | Paragraph 2 |

6

He's married with a child, and he's in prison at the moment.
Paolo is thirty-two and I'm twenty-one

7

Model answer:

Dear Gabriella

You are in a difficult situation and you need to think carefully about what you're going to do.

Firstly, Paolo is in prison at the moment. What is his crime? Is it going to make life difficult for you? Is this the type of person you want to be with?

Secondly, he is married and has a child. Maybe his wife is the same age as him. Does he really want a relationship with you? How often is he going to want to see his child?

Here's my advice, Gabriella. You should think very carefully before going any further with Paolo. I don't think you should wait for him. I think you should find someone your age and enjoy your life right now.

Best wishes
Agony Aunt

VOCABULARY BUILDER QUIZ 12

1

| 1 | b | 2 | e | 3 | a | 4 | c | 5 | d |

2

| 1 | earned | 2 | joined | 3 | burnt | 4 | carried | 5 | cancelled |

3

| 1 | to | 2 | in | 3 | up | 4 | on | 5 | off |

4

| 1 | smile | 3 | warm up, warm-up | 5 | cough |
| 2 | protest | 4 | burn |

5

| 1 | c | 2 | e | 3 | b | 4 | a | 5 | d |

UNIT 13

VOCABULARY Weather

1

1	snow	4	storm	7	cloudy	10	hot
2	dry	5	ice	8	wet	11	cold
3	rain	6	windy	9	sunny	12	warm

2

1	sunny / warm	3	hot	5	cloudy
2	dry	4	wet / rain	6	storm
				7	snow / cold

3

| 1 | spring | 2 | winter | 3 | summer | 4 | Autumn |

GRAMMAR *might* and *be going to*

4

1	I'm going to meet	5	I might get
2	might have	6	I'm going to cook
3	I'm going to have	7	I'm going to see
4	might go	8	might do

5

| 1 | might | 3 | are going to | 5 | might |
| 2 | 're going to | 4 | might | 6 | 's going to |

6

1   We might have to leave early.
2   They're going to phone us when they arrive.
3   Lin isn't going to see her friends next week.
4   You might not get the job.
5   It's going to be cold and wet tomorrow.
6   It might snow tomorrow.

LISTENING

7

The weather is going to be good.

8

| 1 | c | 2 | b | 3 | d | 4 | a |

9

| 1 | T | 2 | T | 3 | T | 4 | F | 5 | F |

DEVELOPING CONVERSATIONS Short questions

10

| 1 | b | 3 | a | 5 | g | 7 | e |
| 2 | d | 4 | f | 6 | c |

11

1 Who with?   3 How?   5 Why?
2 Where?   4 How long for?   6 What for?
      7 What time?

VOCABULARY The countryside and the city

1

Across

2 in bad condition   9 rubbish   14 crime
5 horse   11 pollution   15 factory
7 crowded   12 hills

Down

1 violent gangs   6 surrounded by   13 farm
3 forest   8 fields   15 flat
4 grass   10 block of flats   16 convenient

READING

2

traffic, shopping, weather

3

1 F   2 T   3 F   4 F   5 F   6 T

4

1 C   2 S   3 C   4 S   5 C   6 S

5

1 didn't like   3 slow   5 bored
2 crowded   4 prefers   6 happy

VOCABULARY Animals

1

1 rat   3 cow   5 horse   7 pig   9 sheep
2 cat   4 dog   6 fox   8 rabbit

2

1 rat   3 sheep   5 cow
2 fox   4 dog   6 horse

GRAMMAR The present perfect to say *how long*

3

has/have, past participle

4

1 been   3 lived   5 worked
2 studied   4 known   6 had

5

1 have worked   3 have lived   5 have had
2 have known   4 have been   6 have studied

6

1 How long have you worked in your company?
2 have you known your best friend
3 long have you lived in this city?
4 How long have you been together with your partner?
5 How long have you had your mobile phone?
6 How long have you studied English?

7

Students' own answers
Eg *I've known my best friend (for) ten years.*

PRONUNCIATION

8

1 How long <u>have</u> you had your cat?
2 They <u>have</u> been together for years.

3 Has he known her for long?
4 We <u>have</u> studied English for more than ten years.
5 How long <u>has</u> she lived here?
6 Have you worked here for a long time?

DEVELOPING WRITING A description of where you live

10

City

Exciting and busy   Shops open 24/7
Lots of things to do   A lot of traffic and pollution
Crowded and noisy   A lot of problems with crime

Country

Lots of fresh air   Peaceful and quiet
You need a car to go anywhere   Boring – nothing to do
There aren't many shops   Relaxing

11

Paragraph 1: c   introduction
Paragraph 2: b   description of the place
Paragraph 3: a   summary

12 and 13

Student's own answers.

VOCABULARY BUILDER QUIZ 13

1

1 flood   3 house   5 hill
2 forest   4 animal

2

1 down   2 on   3 by   4 on   5 in

3

1 a   3 a   5 –
2 the   4 the   6 a

4

1 climb   2 smell   3 chase   4 reach

5

1 attention   3 flooding   5 photo
2 scary   4 chemicals

UNIT 14

VOCABULARY Describing films, plays and musicals

1

1 film   3 musical   5 theatre
2 play   4 concert

2

1 funny   2 scary   3 sad   4 violent

3

1 strange   3 predictable   5 brilliant
2 depressing   4 entertaining   6 terrible

DEVELOPING CONVERSATIONS *What's it like?*

4

1 b   2 e   3 d   4 a   5 f   6 c

5

1 like   3 What was
2 nice   4 the food

LISTENING

7
Aisha: exciting, funny
Julie: entertaining, strange, funny
Rashid: terrible, silly

8
1 T   2 F   3 T   4 F   5 F   6 F

9
1 A   2 J   3 R   4 A   5 J   6 R

10
Review 2 best matches the *Listening*.

GRAMMAR *will / won't* for predictions

1
1 speak   3 win   5 look after   7 live
2 find   4 work   6 be

2
1 will live to be 100   5 will speak Chinese
2 will win the World Cup   6 'll be rich one day
3 'll work abroad   7 will find life on other planets
4 will look after the environment

3
1 won't   3 will   5 will
2 will   4 won't   6 won't

4
1 will   3 won't   5 will
2 will   4 will   6 won't

5
1 I'll see you tomorrow.
2 Will they arrive before the party tonight?
3 There won't be enough money to pay for the tickets.
4 OK
5 We'll probably be a bit late.
6 Do you think you'll ever be rich?

PRONUNCIATION

6
1 a   2 b   3 a   4 a   5 b   6 a

READING

8
Sports 3   Financial news 4
National news 2   Show business 1
International news 5

9
1 two years   3 yes   5 €3 million
2 three   4 Marc Van Rijn   6 80,000
7 more than 60 years ago

10
1 Yes.   5 You accuse someone
2 No, probably not   of something bad.
3 It's a bad thing.   6 No.
4 Unhappy.

11
a 3   b 4   c 6   d 1   e 5   f 2

VOCABULARY Life and society

1

Economy	Crime	People	Climate	Healthcare
jobs	murder	friendly	warm	treatment
wages	safe	open	cold	insurance
unemployment	violence	don't talk to	dry	
		you much		

2
1 nice   3 weak   5 good
2 friendly   4 insurance   6 problem

3
1 open   3 problem   5 very good   7 wages
2 talk   4 lock   6 strong

GRAMMAR adjective + verb

4
1 d   3 g   5 b   7 f
2 c   4 a   6 e

5
1 It's difficult to find work.
2 It's easy to see a doctor when you're ill.
3 It's really nice to have a close community.
4 It's helpful to learn another language.
5 It's important not to criticise your neighbours.
6 It's good to meet someone from the same place.

6
1 It's cheap to keep your house warm.
2 It's great to have people you can talk to.
3 It's important to live in a warm climate.
4 It's interesting to learn something new.
5 It feels good to help other people.
6 It's lovely to sit in the garden on a warm day.

DEVELOPING WRITING A film review

7
The film is called *Prejudice* and the stars are Juan Santinez and Carter Jones.

8
1 c the present day   3 d A chase
2 b In San Francisco   4 c OK

9
Student's own answers.

VOCABULARY BUILDER QUIZ 14

1
1 peace   3 brilliant   5 strong
2 ending   4 unemployment

2
1 insurance   3 killing   5 acting
2 treatment   4 fighting

3
1 support   3 see   5 win
2 expect   4 play   6 injure

4
1 brilliant   3 strong   5 clear
2 open   4 depressing

5
1 d   2 a   3 c   4 b

UNIT 15

VOCABULARY Machines and technology

1

1	plug	3	vacuum cleaner	5	mobile phone
2	digital camera	4	hairdryer	6	tablet

2

2	mobile phone	4	plug	6	digital camera
3	hairdryer	5	tablet		

GRAMMAR *be thinking of + -ing*

3
1 They're thinking of buying a house.
2 I'm thinking of giving £500 to charity.
3 Sue's thinking of coming for coffee tomorrow.
4 We're thinking of seeing him in concert.
5 John's thinking of giving up smoking.
6 Are you thinking of leaving the country?

4

1	'm thinking of joining	5	are (you) thinking of taking
2	is thinking of buying	6	're thinking of selling
3	're thinking of going	7	'm thinking of writing
4	is thinking of learning		

DEVELOPING CONVERSATIONS *Do you know much about ...?*

5

cars	geography	tennis	cows	computers
tyres	countries	balls	milk	DVD
engine	oceans	net	grass	email

6
1 Do you know much about geography?
2 Do you know much about cars?
3 Do you know much about computers?
4 Do you know much about cows?
5 Do you know much about tennis?

READING

8

1	biro	4	photographic film
2	dishwasher	5	battery
3	barcode		

9
All the items in the pictures are mentioned.

10

1 c	2 f	3 e	4 a	5 d	6 b

11

1 F	2 T	3 F	4 T	5 T	6 F

VOCABULARY Computers and the internet

1

1	search	3	online	5	a search
2	a website	4	the internet	6	a link

2

1	email	4	send	7	website
2	received	5	memory stick	8	link
3	deleted	6	check	9	online

PRONUNCIATION Spelling addresses

4

1	a h j k	4	o	6	f l m n s x z
2	b c d e g p t v	5	q u w	7	r
3	i y				

5

1 c	2 a	3 b

6

1 b	2 a	3 a	4 a	5 b	6 b

7

1 w	2 h	3 e	4 h	5 e	6 w

DEVELOPING WRITING Describing an invention

8
(Last century's finest) 2

9

a 3	b 1	c 4	d 2

10 and 11
Student's own answers

12
Model answer:
I think the best invention of the 20th century is the telephone. I don't understand how it works, but I know I couldn't live without it!

People all over the world use telephones to talk to their friends and families. When you need help, you can use the telephone to call the police or hospital.

I use a telephone every day in my job. I couldn't do my job without one! I can call people in other countries and talk to them. I use my telephone a lot in my personal life, too, to call my friends and make arrangements.

In my opinion the telephone is the best invention of the 20th century because I don't know anyone who hasn't got one. It's useful and helpful. It can even save your life!

LISTENING

1
Eric asks to see a digital camera, games console, laptop and mobile phone.

2

1	£1,800	3	light	5	making calls	7	games console
2	bag	4	eight	6	£300		

3

1	this is the latest model	4	surf the Net
2	with software fully loaded	5	send text messages
3	it's Wi-Fi ready	6	state-of-the-art

4

a 1	b 4	c 6	d 2	e 5	f 3

VOCABULARY What technology does

5
2 develop your own apps
3 solve problems
4 check your heart rate
5 control everything
6 save energy
7 keep your files in one place
8 create vocabulary tests

6

Across

1 create 2 produce 5 solve 6 keep

Down

1 control 3 develop 4 check 5 save

GRAMMAR Adverbs

7

1 badly   3 well   5 late   7 quickly   9 slowly
2 early   4 hard   6 loudly 8 quietly

8

1 badly – well   4 quickly – slowly
2 early – late   5 'hard' doesn't have an opposite.
3 loudly – quietly

9

1 loudly   3 well   5 badly   7 hard   9 quickly
2 early   4 late   6 slowly 8 quietly

VOCABULARY BUILDER QUIZ 15

1

1 by   2 about   3 on   4 in

2

1 power 2 stick 3 camera 4 machine 5 cleaner

3

1 press   3 delete   5 develop
2 produce   4 save   6 drop

4

1 search 2 list 3 download 4 design 5 video

5

1 d   2 a   3 e   4 c   5 b

UNIT 16

VOCABULARY Love and marriage

1

1 partner   4 husband   7 jealous
2 wife   5 approve   8 anniversary
3 pregnant   6 wedding   9 divorced

2

1 get   3 get   5 have
2 have   4 save   6 have

3

1 get divorced   3 have a baby   5 get married
2 save money   4 have a date

4

1 out   2 on   3 in   4 up   5 up

DEVELOPING CONVERSATIONS *Did I tell you ...?*

5

1 c   2 e   3 d   4 a   5 f   6 b

6

2 has   4 saw   6 have   8 is
3 get   5 meet   7 got   9 seen

LISTENING

8

Rob and Granny

9

1 Rob – Shelley's father
2 Mum – Rob's mother
3 Shelley – Rob's daughter
4 Kevin – Shelley's old boyfriend
5 Pam – Rob's wife

10

1 good   3 work   5 on a beach
2 is   4 professor   6 a few days

11

1 get married   4 known   7 divorce
2 broke up   5 sure
3 fell in love with 6 happy

GRAMMAR Past continuous

1

1 was having   3 was staying   5 was eating
2 was listening 4 were shopping 6 were visiting

2

1 She wasn't having lunch with her family.
2 He wasn't listening to music in his bedroom.
3 I wasn't staying with friends in Jakarta.
4 They weren't shopping at the mall opposite the cinema.
5 I wasn't eating the packet of biscuits that you gave me.
6 You weren't visiting your family on the farm.

3

1 Were you talking about me?
2 Was she walking to work?
3 Were they buying some new clothes?
4 Was he calling his sister on the phone?
5 Were your parents having a nice time?
6 Was I spending too much time online?

4

1 was watching ... came   3 was leaving ... started
2 were living ... bought   4 were going ... broke

5

1 was living   5 noticed   9 had
2 was working   6 thought   10 got married
3 was sitting   7 was walking
4 came   8 looked

PRONUNCIATION Sentence stress and weak forms

6

1 W   2 W   3 S   4 W   5 W   6 S

7
1 I was <u>watching TV</u> at <u>home</u>.
2 <u>What</u> were you <u>thinking about</u>?
3 She <u>wasn't</u> <u>looking</u> for a <u>boyfriend</u>.
4 I was <u>making</u> a <u>coffee</u> in the <u>kitchen</u>.
5 They were <u>eating outside</u> under the <u>trees</u>.
6 We <u>weren't</u> playing <u>tennis</u> when you <u>saw</u> us.

READING
9
Two of the couples got married.

10
1 snake
2 to the Underworld
3 fifteen
4 over
5 Qays
6 another man

11
1 T 2 T 3 F 4 T 5 F 6 T

GRAMMAR will / won't for promises
1
1 Will you call me every day?
2 I'll tell you when I hear more news.
3 Don't worry, I won't tell anyone.
4 See you later. I won't be late.
5 I promise I won't make a mess.
6 I promise I'll pay you back tomorrow.

2
1 c 2 a 3 d 4 f 5 e 6 b

3
1 A: Bye. Take care. B: **I will**. Bye.
2 Don't worry. I won't **forget**.
3 **Will you** call me?
4 He **will** be here by five o'clock.
5 Why **won't you** help?

DEVELOPING WRITING Writing a story (with time sequencers)
4
The greatest love story
Romeo and Juliet lived in Verona. Their families were enemies. **One night**, they met at a party and fell in love. **Then** they got married. **A short time later**, Juliet's cousin killed Romeo's friend in an argument. **Then** Romeo killed Juliet's cousin. Juliet's father told her he wanted her to marry someone else. Juliet pretended to be dead but she was only sleeping. Romeo thought she was dead, so he killed himself. **A short time later**, Juliet woke up, saw Romeo dead and killed herself. **Finally**, the families of the two lovers stopped fighting and became friends.

5
Model answer:
The love story of Antony and Cleopatra
Mark Antony was a Roman General and Cleopatra was the queen of Egypt. **One day**, they met and fell in love. **A short time later**, Mark Antony returned to Rome and married Octavian's sister. **Then** Mark Antony left Octavian's sister and returned to Cleopatra. **A short time later**, Antony and Cleopatra got married. Octavian was angry and sent an army to fight them. Antony and Cleopatra lost. **Then** Antony thought Cleopatra was dead, so he killed himself. **Finally** Cleopatra killed herself after seeing Antony dead.

VOCABULARY BUILDER QUIZ 16
1
1 c 2 e 3 b 4 a 5 d

2
1 high 2 trouble 3 an anniversary

3
1 up 3 at 5 on 7 for
2 of 4 of 6 of

4
1 plant 3 trouble 5 promise
2 break 4 lift

5
1 b 2 d 3 a 4 e 5 c

CD1

TRACK	ITEM	
1	titles	
2	1.1	
3	1.2	1
4		2
5		3
6	1.3	
7	1.4	
8	2.1	
9	2.2	
10	2.3	
11	2.4	
12	3.1	
13	3.2	
14	3.3	
15	4.1	1
16		2
17		3
18	4.2	
19	4.3	
20	4.4	
21	4.5	1
22		2
23		3
24	5.1	1
25		2
26		3
27	5.2	
28	5.3	
29	5.4	
30	5.5	
31	5.6	
32	6.1	
33	6.2	1
34		2
35	6.3	1
36		2
37		3
38	7.1	
39	7.2	
40	7.3	
41	7.4	
42	8.1	
43	8.2	
44	8.3	
45	8.4	
46	8.5	

CD2

TRACK	ITEM	
1	titles	
2	9.1	
3	9.2	
4	9.3	
5	10.1	1
6		2
7		3
8	10.2	
9	10.3	1
10		2
11		3
12	10.4	
13	10.5	
14	11.1	
15	11.2	
16	11.3	
17	11.4	
18	12.1	1
19		2
20	12.2	1
21		2
22		3
23		4
24	12.3	1
25		2
26		3
27	13.1	
28	13.2	
29	13.3	
30	14.1	1
31		2
32	14.2	
33	14.3	
34	15.1	1
35		2
36		3
37		4
38		5
39	15.2	
40	15.3	
41	15.4	
42	15.5	
43	16.1	1
44		2
45		3
46	16.2	
47	16.3	